CW00740208

BORAGÓ

BORAGÓ

Rodolfo Guzmán

Photographs by Cristóbal Palma

Coming from the South

DWELLED WORDS

The June Garden (*El Jardín de Juno*) is a cognitive neuroscience research institute with which we at Mugaritz have worked for years, and they use the term *dwelled words*—for words that we use frankly, full of conscious content, in line with what we feel and think. Sincere words. In our daily life we constantly encounter empty messages, full of pat phrases, and accounts cleverly decorated with pretty terms—healthy, sustainable, traditional—that attempt to whitewash the true intentions of those using them or to appease their guilty conscience. Being aware, though, is complicated, and we must have integrity and give our lives meaning and value.

It can be difficult to pilot a project that seeks to open new opportunities beyond the comfortable topics and space of what has already been established. Building has always been more costly than destroying, in the same way that conceiving a new horizon is harder than judging. In line with this, the word *undertake*, for me and for many others, is laden with merit, not to mention heroism.

Rodolfo Guzmán opened his restaurant a decade ago, imagining the possibility beyond just doing things well. He created a new reality, unifying the concepts of *renewal* and *genuine*. Beyond the flavors and products that have represented Chile, there are other ingredients which, although they are Chilean, were discarded due to disaffection or lack of knowledge. The result of all that effort is today's Boragó, one of the best restaurants in the world, a center of creation that can boast of having been established on a great deal of passion and effort despite the indifference of many. This is no small matter, because there is no adversary more prepared to negate qualified cooking than skepticism. Even with this, the most important work done by Boragó, throughout these years, has originated outside the stove and cutting board.

Rodolfo's ideas and reflections reach the public with the desire to change reality and take on a new meaning of food. One of the underlying qualities of cooking is that it is a tool for transformation. The most obvious is that when cooking, the food's form and properties are modified, and when that food in turn is ingested, it changes us. Rodolfo and his team have continued to mark the path of change with sweetness and determination while they fill their world with dwelled words, laden with horizons and strong intentions: "We attempt to look back in order to walk forward, to connect our past with a possible future of Chilean cooking, through learning and knowledge of our territory and of our biodiversity, as well as the culture of our native peoples, the root of our origin." This book attests to Rodolfo's vision.

Andoni Luis Aduriz

HAPPILY EVER AFTER

A story that ends happily ever after is rare. Let us then honor it, as it deserves. The pitch more or less goes like this. A young promising chef puts his life on the line, fighting against heaven and earth and challenging an adverse fate. However, through a heroic self-sacrifice of bygone times, in the end, exactly when everyone has given up on him, he not only manages to communicate his uniqueness—notwithstanding the cacophony of discordant particularism and selfishness—but also becomes the flag bearer of a collective claim. Thus, the young promising chef ends up legitimizing his coronation as the spokesman of a generation on a quest for its radical liberation. And this book is the proof. The hero of this biopic is Rodolfo Guzmán (Rudy for friends) and this does not correspond to the hagiography that culinary Hollywood would love to narrate. It would be possible to find a conventional picture of Rudy dressed in his Sunday best with an arm around his wife, Alejandra, the four children in front and a Labrador at their feet. Alternatively, you could set it up. However, Guzmán is not like this at all. Behind his smile of circumstance, behind the deep brow furrows and wrinkles around the eyes, his discomfort peeps out, showing the tension that pervades him from the inside.

Rodolfo Guzmán sports a chic insecurity, the flair of instability. Warning: this is a compliment. It is impossible for him to stay still, to accept the result of a die that has been cast. Therefore, every instant is suspended between two options and there is the calm before the storm. You can read this book three times and start again from the beginning. You can spend a whole week at Boragó only then to experience again the "first-time" effect. The memory you will carry with you will not only be the discovery of the unprecedented world of flavors, Chile's quintessence, that Rudy discloses dish after dish. It will not only be the shock of a universe of indigenous, endogenous, wild ingredients and products that have been removed from the official culture (like the Mapuche Indian tribes, relegated to a limbo at the margins of urban society). Rodolfo Guzmán is the knight in shining armor, a bard of ancient splendor. What really matters though is the dramatic, spectacular, scandalous discovery that Rodolfo Guzmán's cuisine in his Boragó headquarters is nourished by a more concrete universality, which has never severed its umbilical cord with the recent past of European cuisine.

There is the path of a broader Latin American movement, with its famous brigadier generals: Gastón Acurio, Alex Atala, Manuela Buffara, Virgilio Martínez, and Enrique Olvera. Each of them is at the root of an introspective journey, from Peru to Mexico passing through the forerunner Brazil, in search of the land of their origins crossing recondite districts—from the Amazon jungle to the steep Andean highlands, from the tropical coast to the most deserted Mexican backcountry. These chefs return from their trips laden with tantric experiences and new challenges. Fish and plant produce that had never been documented is now on geographical maps. The ingredient, the thrill of its exciting discovery, is never an end, just a mere starting point.

Rodolfo Guzmán is an explorer, part ethnologist and part harvest and handmade goods shaman. He never overlooks anything in nature—bitter herbs, shrub pests, or languorous berries that melt in your mouth or roots, flowers, algae that are longer than lianas and fleshy like an abalone crossed with marine artichoke hearts. He wastes nothing. In every one of his dishes, one detects the generosity of his offer, a tribute to nature's legacy that is his essential source of inspiration. One also tastes culture through his discoveries. Guzmán almost never speaks in the first person singular. Instead, he speaks in the name of an anthology of all of us together. He speaks on behalf of a wider group, with the dream of an attainable community with whom he can share passions and ideals, a better world without separations or social and food hierarchies. This would be a world where words and deeds would no longer be remote (such as during Pinochet's dark years) or concealed by official historiography (the utopias of the Allende era). A world that is without emphasis but with a relentless pace, slightly wobbly but still forward moving, all following the rhythm of a ternary tempo with jazz inflections.

What sets Guzmán apart from the chefs of his generation is not only his innate capacity for abstraction, part of his apprenticeship at Mugaritz; what makes him different is his cult of the contemptuous instant, of the incomplete focused on the last minute. If he were an image, he would not be an omniscient and omnipotent demiurge, a deus ex machina who sits atop his pass, the control tower of a menu theorized at the table. If anything, he reminds us of the pulsating inspiration of the original Pierre Gagnaire. The whole team involved in rectifying a variant of the *jus de tête des crustacés* while in full service, Gagnaire would be on his knees with a chinois between his legs in a race against time. The electrified staff would be waiting for the last essential retouching, with the feverishness of being in a triple somersault without a safety net.

Is Guzmán an old-style chef? A reckless improviser? Those who have never seen him running through the woods and up the coast, those who have never seen him risk everything to capture the perfect note, the hue of the definitive meaning, are far from having understood the uniqueness of the young chef. His smoked mushrooms cooked at a very low temperature on an outdoor brazier, an increasingly concentrated broth of mutant algae to simulate the imperfectible dashi, his nalca—a kind of Chilean rhubarb transformed into a tsunami of umami. Guzmán's cuisine is a natural one, writhing in a pantheism of unusual and bluffing flavors, but always fleeing from the frigidity of a find, from the recurring temptation of simple assembly. There is the rush of serving as the corollary of a long-term process. His cuisine is not afraid of change. It is cooked with ingredients that are agreed upon, interrogated, sublimated, in a composition of temperatures and textures that are not inclined to the compromise of literalness.

René Redzepi at Noma shifted the debate level to the plane of "reinvention of nature," by bringing into the spotlight fish and vegetable produce that had been ignored by Scandinavian cuisine for centuries. This was a palette of flavors that Guzmán would define as endemic—the danger of a too literal interpretation has reared its head in kitchens across the world. However, in this way, Guzmán trusts instinct and is wary of all upstream thought. Few cuisines are able to synthesize and completely transform their food products. He respects the intrinsic qualities, history, and origins of the ingredients, while bringing produce to unreached cooked and processed heights, often oxygenated by a perpetual anxiety of recreation. Thanks to Rodolfo Guzmán, the new Chilean cuisine connects the missing dots and reboots linking the submerged history, the battle of the present and the future on the horizon. It is no longer the era of raw foods as a backdrop, where the ingredient is treated as an archaeological find. Although he is Chilean, Guzmán, perhaps unconsciously, embodies the old Chinese saying: The future is never in front of you; it is already present and manifests itself from behind you. We could call this a Copernican revolution.

Guzmán's homeland shelters him from the insane fads of our times in the food business. Out of sight but at the heart of the current debate on tomorrow's cuisine, one must seek Guzmán among the concrete mythologies that fuel the Chilean imaginary. As he prepares to move his restaurant from his old Santiago location to an unusual place on the high plains above the capital, he marks a decade since the beginning of the collective adventure of Boragó. It will follow the tradition of agricultural collective work and indigenous communities who, once or twice a year, in tune with the seasons, move their wooden houses on small wheels drawn by sheep and horses, with the participation of the local population (as is done on the island of Chiloé). This notion of nomadism, change, and collectivity fits the work of this Chilean chef like a glove.

Now that the mental work in progress and the slow construction of a new identity is able to emerge fully from the pages of this book, it is easier to understand the anxiety and urgency of the Chilean chef. He wants to leave his isolation, to descend from the solitary high peaks of creation, and to dialogue where the community bonds can be renewed. It is not a coincidence that the Minga tradition of community gave its name to The Minga Project, a study for a proposed international symposium, which in 2016 evolved into the Ngelemen symposium. There, chefs including Desramaults Kobe, Magnus Nilsson, and Jock Zonfrillo—with intellectuals, craftsmen, scientists, ethnologists, botanists, artists, and journalists—freely debated and jointly developed a project to position Chile as an international gastronomical hub. Universality and regional difference created a Promethean task for a chef who is not even forty years old, who is isolated from decision-making centers, and whose sparse availability is also the keystone of his essentiality.

In his part of the world, Rodolfo Guzmán's cuisine is the amazing exception in a universe that conforms too much to the rules that elsewhere have more and more force. His voice is unique, positive, and dissident, not risking its purity for the sake of commercial compromise. We are no longer isolated voices. More and more people believe that the Boragó 2.0—to be inaugurated in 2017, nestled at the foot of the mountains and a stone's throw from the center of the capital—will be the transmitter of new signs of life. It will express a profound cultural renovation that goes well beyond the narrow limits of a kitchen, and be an entity able to speak a language that knows no borders. It will embody the dream of a culinary Esperanto, where everyone—both diners and the Boragó team—can tap into concrete fragments of experiences and reflections and embrace them, once reviewed and adapted in the light of one's own experience and needs. This is exactly what this Chilean chef has always done.

Warning: Boragó's wings are quivering. And the Guzmán tornado is brewing. Wherever you are, enjoy the ride.

Andrea Petrini

INTRODUCTION

When I was growing up, although my family didn't have much money, we had a true sense of home. My parents worked together and spent many hours at their jobs every day. I remember my mother telling me that they were working so hard in order to make things better for us. That's when I realized I had to be a good kid. I am the eldest of three brothers, so I was used to being alone before my brothers were born. As I grew up and had to also start thinking about my brothers, I began to understand and become more aware of our family situation—for example, how hard my mother also worked at home, and how much she valued the quality of food for her kids. I am still trying to figure out how she had so much energy during the weekends, when she prepared all her amazing dishes. She was an extraordinary cook and everyone in my family—including my father, her biggest fan—loved the food she prepared, especially the desserts. I think her talent came from her mother, my grandmother.

My mother taught me to be grateful for everything in life, but especially for the food on our table. She taught me to eat everything without complaint because work had gone into creating every meal; and that there is no such thing as inedible food—only food you decide not to eat. I used to be a picky eater, but something my mother said clicked and now I eat everything. I love food in all its permutations, but I had to learn how to appreciate the taste as well as the meaning of a meal.

Like it was yesterday, I can remember the mouthwatering feeling my brothers and I had while waiting for my mother's desserts. She taught us cake-making techniques, such as adding juices from seasonal fruits and using ingredients that were rare for a home pantry. When my extended family would get together on weekends, food would become even more important. My uncles and my mother would all bring dishes of food and sharing the meal was a highly anticipated event, especially for the kids. While everything was prepared over Chilean *espino* charcoal—widely used in Chile—one of my uncles, who was highly skilled at preparing both steak and vegetables, was often discussing his theories about how to correctly treat the slow-roasting steak on the grill. The *asado*, the art of barbequeuing in Chile, is almost a religion.

My father was one of the most creative people I've ever met, but he was penniless when he started his printing business. With hard work he found financial success. I remember helping him at the print shop when I was a kid. Once, after I had spent weekend after weekend with him at work, he noticed that I was sulking and he caught me saying, "Why can't I have this and that just like my friends?" He told me, "There's a big difference between you and your friends. If you want something in life, I'm not going to just give it to you, you have to fight for it and work for it. When you grow up, you will be able to do anything you want, but you will need to work hard to get it." I didn't understand what he was talking about until I was much older: That keeping busy and working hard can bring you success and happiness. You just have to keep toiling away tirelessly to make what you want happen.

SUMMERS IN THE COUNTRYSIDE BY THE COWS

I spent many summers with my grandmother in the countryside where, less than one hour's drive from Santiago, I was transported to a magical place where food was real and traceable. I remember drinking fresh milk each morning, still warm from the cow; collecting pure mountain water in a huge can hanging from the roof; and having chickens running around while I helped my grandmother collect the eggs. For breakfast, my grandmother would serve me *pajarito* yogurt—which was one of the foods I hated as a child. *Pajarito* yogurt (what we widely call kefir) is strong, acidic, and fermented and an important Chilean tradition. My grandma used to persuade me to eat it by sweetening it with wild fruit jelly. I would lie to her and say that I loved it, but really, thanks to my sweet tooth, it was just an excuse to eat loads of her homemade jelly, which I think she knew all along.

Every year on my grandmother's birthday, two things always happened: a lamb was sacrificed and then slowly cooked *al palo*, over the embers, for around six hours. The following day, the leftovers would be cooked with cognac and broth, and served to the whole family. Unfortunately for me, I didn't like either the roasted lamb or the leftovers, as I thought the flavors of both were too strong. Nowadays, these very flavors are critically important to me as a chef, I suppose because they remind me of my childhood summer memories. In our day-to-day lives we don't realize how lucky we are to have taste memory. As a chef, I feel you can make these memories as influential and meaningful in your cooking as you want.

ON MY WAY TO BECOMING . . .

I didn't plan to end up in a cooking school or work in a restaurant kitchen when I was growing up, but one of my best friends suggested giving it a try. I was a bit lost, like most kids, and my friend said he could really see me at cooking school. The more I thought about it, the more it felt like a natural and comfortable choice, and everything started to fall into the right place. I realized later that working in a kitchen felt natural to me because food was so important in my family when I was growing up. This makes me truly believe that cooks are born cooks; they become professionals when they realize they are passionate about food. In my case, this wasn't any different.

When I first started working in a restaurant, I began as a *stagiaire*—a restaurant intern—before being promoted to *chef de partie* of various stations. Thanks to my passion for all things sweet, I had the opportunity to run the pastry station, and it turned out I felt more comfortable running the dessert station than any other.

However, as soon as I started working in a Santiago restaurant, I felt disappointed and frustrated with my situation because it seemed that everyone working in the kitchen would rather be doing any other job in the world, as if it was only circumstantial that they ended up as kitchen staff in a restaurant. It felt as if no one in those kitchens shared my passion for cooking. I was also unhappy to see how condescending the chefs were to the staff, and how they held themselves apart from the actual work. So I started hating going to work every morning, feeling lost and thinking I had made an awful choice and shouldn't have become involved in a profession like this—that maybe I should have dedicated my time to something that wasn't what I loved most.

Meanwhile, I discovered magazines and books about wonderful Michelin-starred restaurants in Europe, where everything seemed magical and amazing. I read about their incredible approaches to food that seemed to work perfectly and looked like nothing I had ever seen before. At that time in Chile, our own food culture wasn't considered important at all. The most popular and celebrated restaurants were those whose owners traveled to Europe, Asia, or North America, and brought restaurant concepts back to Chile to copy.

I realized I wanted to become a part of the world I saw in these magazines and books. Then one day at the restaurant where I was working, I heard a cook talking about the gastronomic happenings in Spain, especially in the Basque country. It sounded completely different to what I was used to in Chile, and it sounded exciting enough for me to want to find a *stage* or a cook position in Europe, where I could learn and immerse myself in their high culinary levels. Without a firm job offer in hand, I went to Spain and knocked on doors to see what would happen.

Between 2003 and 2004, I worked in three restaurants and fully immersed myself in this new culinary world. To be inside those kitchens and interact with many people from all over the world was a revolution for my mind. I felt so lucky—to be able to treat food with deep care and respect while cooking with the best ingredients I had ever seen. I wanted to learn and experience more and more. It was around then that I started to realize my country's serious potential for gastronomy, and that no one had seen it in that way yet. I began to dream that at some point in my life I was going to have the chance to open my own restaurant. Once that thought crossed my mind, it was all I could think about.

GEOGRAPHIES

LESS IS MORE

I opened Boragó in 2006 after I found a small, run-down bar with the potential for thirty-eight covers in the Vitacura district of Santiago. I had wanted to open my own restaurant for many years, so I was eager to get started, but I had no partners and little money. At the time I thought that because I had worked at some of the best restaurants in Europe, opening a restaurant on my own would be a guaranteed success. I had a lot of experience in running kitchens as both *sous chef* and *chef de cuisine*, so I felt confident I could make it succeed and I thought I had all the details sorted out in my mind.

I knew that I wanted to establish a kitchen team dedicated to cooking with ingredients rooted in the Chilean landscape and culture. Until that point, no one had paid attention to Chilean ingredients and cuisine. Traveling through the country, I had begun to learn a lot about our food heritage, and I wanted to share that with my team. I envisioned us using that experience as a starting point, then pushing forward, working with mainly endemic ingredients that the old Chileans—Mapuches—had been using for thousands of years, reconnecting Chilean people with their culinary heritage. I felt anxious to begin a serious learning process.

I was (and still am) convinced that a good restaurant has to understand its society, territory, geography, origin, seasons, and traditions in order to produce outstanding food. I had met chefs in restaurants in Europe with amazing knowledge about the use of rare produce. The situation in Chile was totally different. I wanted Boragó to be the kind of restaurant that was constantly learning and generating knowledge about how to produce great food. But to do this, I knew the journey to find our own cooking path was going to be long.

People weren't going out to dine very often in Santiago, yet compared to other Latin American countries, we had one of the most diverse endemic pantries in the world. I realized that this was a huge opportunity. All the restaurants in Santiago were working with frozen seafood and meat—not a single restaurant was making use of indigenous ingredients, such as mushrooms, wild fruits, seaweeds, halophytes (succulents that grow near the coast), or plants, and I could not understand why. In the south and north, these were everday ingredients, but not in Santiago. I decided that in the following ten years we were going to promote our food culture and set up an infrastructure to enable us to use our country's natural resources, like they were doing in restaurants across Europe, Japan, and North America—and I was not going to give up. As Chilean chefs, we weren't rooted to our land or culture. The transition to a greater awareness and attachment wasn't going to be easy. But I was young and naive and thought I could change the world.

Very few restaurants in Chile knew how to cook seafood well, so most of the time it was overcooked and flavorless. Even though our country has a huge variety of aquatic species, restaurant menus and markets offered a limited selection of fish and shellfish, which was often imported, led by what was in demand with consumers. I thought, *Surely the best fish for us to serve has to be fish straight out of the water, rather than the most expensive stuff imported from Japan. Our coastline must be full of species that we have never eaten in Chile, but should!* My dream was to serve local seafood that was uncommon in restaurants, yet plentiful in the sea. I imagined all the amazing flavor combinations we could create.

I could not believe that all the ingredients I saw during my travels could be growing in our country, but it was almost impossible to source them for our restaurant in Santiago because they were not in demand in the restaurant industry. I kept asking myself: When did we stop meeting the people who grow and harvest our food? What do we know about carrots, asparagus, onions, beets, cilantro, or any other produce we buy? Vegetables take a long time to grow, but we are no longer connected to that process. When we first opened the restaurant, I was obsessed with meeting the people who harvested our ingredients, from the land and the sea. I wanted to work out the best way to bring the ingredients to the restaurant from locations across Chile, as well as grow them ourselves according to our needs.

I decided we would build a network of people foraging, growing, and harvesting the food out of the ground for us, just like the Mapuches did thousands of years ago. The Mapuches say, "When someone is cooking, somebody else is harvesting from the ground, and no one is more important than the other." This way of thought represents a chain of collaboration, connecting everything around you and understanding it as a whole.

However, I did not know that running a restaurant required so much more than just creating great food. From a business point of view, it quickly became a big nightmare, as my vision turned out to be a complicated way of operating a restaurant. We came across problems I had never seen anywhere else I had worked.

Chile is a long country with around 2,600 miles (4,200 kilometers) of coastline, where the logistics of transportation from one region to another can be a problem. No other restaurant in Chile had tried bringing ingredients

all the way from Patagonia, the Atacama Desert, Chiloé, or Araucanía, or even tried to work directly with fishermen to source local seafood. Moreover, finding a way to store and pack the ingredients we wanted to cook with was also a huge challenge, especially as we were using some ingredients that no restaurant had ever served and no one was able to tell to us how to store and prepare them appropriately. We had to find our own way to get the quality ingredients we wanted, and then figure out the logistics of transportation.

I also didn't realize that storage would be a problem. Having so many ingredients proved to be very difficult, because we didn't have enough customers eating at the restaurant to keep up with the amount of ingredients I wanted to use. However, I didn't want to accept this fact, I just wanted to do it. Everyone I knew—businessmen, colleagues, local food critics, and my family—said I was out of my mind by focusing on stocking the restaurant with so many ingredients that would be wasted rather than taking care of the business. My bank account was in the red, and the gastronomic Chilean press did not look favorably on my vision.

In 2006 and 2007, when I first started to serve these new ingredients at Boragó, luxury ingredients were being imported; whatever came from within Chile was considered to be of lesser quality. When diners from Santiago asked about the country of origin of the ingredients we were serving, we would explain that the ingredients were locally grown, and they couldn't believe it. We were championing a new Chilean cuisine and ideas never before explored.

Since the time Spaniards settled in the Chilean territory five hundred years ago, we've been trying to emulate everything European. In the early 1990s the same happened with North American culture. We never tried to just be Chileans and we never bothered to develop that feeling of national pride . . . until recently.

At least 80 percent of native Chileans have Mapuche blood in them, so we could say that we are the perfect example of mestizos—those who have mixed blood with indigenous peoples. Adopting the practices of other cultures, especially through food, was a way of not recognizing our roots, and I wanted to change that at the restaurant.

I asked myself why, for example, imported white truffles should cost more than four thousand dollars, whereas white strawberries from Purèn should cost less than twenty dollars per kilo. After all, nature didn't put the prices on things—we did—and both ingredients were equally amazing. For me, the added value in white strawberries from Purèn was that they are an endemic ingredient.

At the beginning of 2007 we were only serving two imported ingredients: black truffles and foie gras from a great small producer. Both were extremely expensive and we served them to justify the quality of our food. But after thinking about it for a while, I decided no ingredient from outside the country was going to be used in our restaurant, and I got rid of them.

A few weeks after that, we started to travel throughout the country to meet people we could work with and learn from. We mostly met Mapuches and other local foragers and small producers. We would ask them to gather wild fruits, mushrooms, halophytes, seaweed, stems, and roots, among many other foods that grow only in short windows of time and in some of the most remote places.

Fortunately for us, most of the people whom we asked for help accepted. It was a challenge because it was so important to me that the ingredients were as fresh as if the restaurant was located near where they grew. At the beginning, delivery needed much improvement, since we had to figure out the best containers for transport and storage, whether it was for a unique wild fruit from Patagonia or a flower in the Andes that bloomed for only three to four weeks a year. Soon we were able to manage the delivery from many locations in Chile—places like the Atacama Desert, which has no humidity; or Araucanía; or Patagonia, where Tehuelches—Mapuches from Patagonia—developed their culture.

As the number of people we worked with increased rapidly, our food slowly started to be composed of these unique domestic ingredients. It also came with a learning process, of which we weren't entirely conscious. Year after year, the process where the ingredients started to appear was slowly turning into a ritual for us, wherein we knew that the next year, for a short window of time, certain ingredients would be there again. We also knew that it was worth the wait, not only because of their different and unique flavors, but also because of the connection they represented. Meanwhile, we were always meeting more people who could provide different ingredients.

Most of the foragers were afraid of not being able to deliver year-round, and we wanted to be conscious of what was happening with the foragers and the natural cycle of their product. As months and years went by, we built relationships with more foragers. And with each season we worked out what other fresh produce they could supply for us.

However, at the same time, the nightly service felt like a roller coaster: the restaurant was fairly empty, yet we were constantly and quickly learning, by cooking with ingredients never before served in restaurants in Santiago.

Quisco parasites

I had enough money to run Boragó for only three months. During that period our family, friends, and acquaintances came to the restaurant, but otherwise we were empty, and I went into heavy debt. It was an uncertain and lonely time, and I thought we would have to close the restaurant for good. Not many people knew we were open, and pretty much the only way to be successful was to receive good press.

One day, I wasn't feeling well and arrived to the restaurant later than usual. My maître d' handed me the phone with a prestigious airline magazine on the line, telling me they had nominated Boragó as one of the best restaurants in Latin America, and that we would appear in the magazine on all the flights arriving in Santiago from different destinations. I thought this was some kind of joke and said very bad words to the guy over the phone. But after calming down and listening to him, I realized it was true. Almost overnight, we went from being nearly empty to fully booked. We were still losing money, mainly because I had yet to learn how to run a real business, but I felt confident running a kitchen—and that was it.

Right around then, I met my wife, Alejandra, who at that time was running her own architectural firm. Within three months of seeing one another we decided to get married. She told me she would close her office to work in the restaurant, so I could focus more on the cooking. I told her she was insane and was worried that working in such close proximity was going to ruin our relationship. But Alejandra was convinced that we had to build this as a family project and she absolutely believed in what I was doing. I was dealing with the smartest and bravest woman I had ever met.

THE CRASH OF THE WAVE

The sudden success following the publication of the airline magazine article produced contradictory reactions from the local culinary press, which continued to insist that what we served was fodder for cows. The local gastronomic scene wanted to see Italian, French, Spanish, and Asian restaurants with foreigners as head chefs—not Chilean restaurants with native ingredients, far less led by Chilean chefs. With the exception of the airline magazine article, I was not getting far with the press, as there was no interest in trying Chilean food with seasonal endemic ingredients; it was considered both boorish and cheap. High-end food was something that came from outside the country.

Eventually the local press began to take notice of us, but with headlines like "There's No Way We Can Call This Food" or "These Guys Are Cutting Plants That Taste Awful, Go Somewhere Else!" (The awful-tasting plants they were referencing were the very same the Mapuches had been using for thousands of years.) Some journalists gave us a maximum of six months before we would shut down, and when those six months were up and we had managed to survive, they just added another year or two.

To improve our relationship with the local food press, and explain to them what we were trying to accomplish, I invited them to dine at the restaurant. But after eating there, they said what we were doing at Boragó was an insult to tradition. At twenty-eight years old, high-tempered, and blunt, I told them to go to hell, and that the next time they they planned to eat at the restaurant, they would have to pay their bill. None of them returned, and it soured the situation even more.

This was frustrating not only for me but for my team. Considering that it is a remote country even within Latin America, it was a struggle to get visitors to even come to Chile. Social media was nacent at the time, and other than the printed press, there was no way to tell food and travel enthusiasts about our vision. After that quick wave of international attention from the airline magazine, reservations started to slow down again.

In 2008, the massive economic crisis shook the markets in Chile, and the business really started to struggle. To cover the operating costs and stay afloat, we started a catering business on the side, but the income was barely enough to survive and I had almost no money. It was a dark and lonely time, but still, I was doing everything I could to keep the restaurant alive. In time, the economy got better and we started to cover our debts and once again pay employees' salaries through the catering income.

The catering side of the business grew, but as it wasn't what I wanted to do, I grew increasingly unhappy and conflicted. I convinced myself that I had gotten lost, since my deepest passion was to open a uniquely Chilean restaurant, but I had ended up just surviving. I felt I was just doing a job—people were happy with it, but it wasn't the food I wanted to make. I thought that something was wrong with me. I could not spend the time I wanted on creating new recipes. I was lost, alone, and I thought I had sold my soul. Many nights we only had about two guests, and sometimes there were none.

AFTER THE NIGHTMARE, ANOTHER ONE

In 2009, after three years of running Boragó, I viewed a large house for sale that had once been a restaurant. It was amazing but also much bigger than our existing restaurant, with a big infrastructure to match, especially considering we were only about five people working in the kitchen. When I first saw the house, I wanted to move the restaurant there, but financially it seemed unattainable. So I searched for a business partner, so we could afford to remodel, but the feedback was that it would be better to leave Chile and establish the restaurant in Europe, Asia, or the United States. After a lot of searching, I failed to find a partner. I also failed to secure a loan. However, after a government support program showed investment interest in me, a bank finally agreed to give me a loan. I never received the government support in the end, but I had the loan. Aside from a small amount of money in my savings account, that was all I had.

When the bank told me my loan was approved and therefore I could invest in the new house for Boragó, I was supposed to be happy, but I had mixed feelings. I did not know how to deal with the finances of such a big undertaking. That was when Alejandra decided to work with me at the restaurant. In this way I could spend my time in the kitchen, and she would take care of the business side.

In the following years, even though I had Alejandra by my side all the time, we had to face a situation that was worsening every day, because my debts increased with every passing year. It was the opposite of a healthy enterprise, in which everything that happens within it affects the project positively: everything that was happening just increased the daily problems, including the relationships among our team. The dining room staff wasn't receiving enough compensation and some staff members were following goals that were different from the original project, both in the kitchen and in the dining room. We didn't have the time or resources for it to work in a better way.

Each summer since we had opened, Santiago would be a city without inhabitants. Since it is so close to the coast, mountains, and countryside, the people of Santiago had no reason to stay in the city. By 2011, I had been trying to sell the restaurant for two years without success.

Then suddenly, at the end of 2011, we were told by a European restaurant guidebook publisher that we would be featured in their next publication, along with many restaurants that had three Michelin stars. They said that from the moment it was published, people from countries all over the world would know about us and what our work was about. When the review was published, the effect was immediate.

In the first days of January 2012, the restaurant had enough bookings to allow us to pay the bills. Our losses ended and our debts were no longer increasing. We had a stable demand throughout that year, when Andrea Petrini, a very important journalist I had never met, came to visit us. It seemed incredible that he came from France just to visit our restaurant out of curiosity. Along with this important milestone, we turned five years old, and Andoni Luis Aduriz, with the team of Mugaritz, agreed to come and cook with us to celebrate the anniversary. From that moment on, we started receiving countless foreign visitors who wrote about food, and we even captured the attention of some European magazines. There was a noticeable change in the growth of our restaurant.

In 2013, the Latin American version of the World's 50 Best Restaurants awards—Latin America's 50 Best Restaurants—was created and we were told that we were on the list. It was surprising that we appeared in a high position in the ranking when the restaurant was practically unknown not only in Chile but also internationally. I still remember the day before the list was published: there were no more than ten people seated in the restaurant. The next day our booking system was full from mid-September up to mid-October. This transformation was completely savage. From that moment on, the economy of the restaurant abruptly changed and, knowing the dining room was going to be full every day, I could dedicate myself exclusively to the creative part.

ORDERING, SORTING, AND VISUALIZING

On a daily basis and as years go by, our operation has turned more complex, so being organized is critical to achieve what we do; otherwise it would be impossible. This has translated into the practice that absolutely everything must be organized and planned ahead of time. Usually organizing seems to be something obvious and simple. However, organizing our restaurant required a great collective endeavor.

As time passed, we met more and more people who were able to send us ingredients that grew during short periods of time—even for just one week a year—which we call "pre-seasons." As a result, we started planning our calendar, and that helped us prepare to cook with these very specific ingredients during the year. Diego ("Gordo" to the family) has an essential job: he coordinates everything, from the moment an ingredient departs from the most remote places to its arrival at the door of our restaurant. Even though our suppliers live so far away, we consider them a very special part of our team. Unfortunately, they are not present in our dining room every day, but they are as indispensable to our job in the kitchen, since without them, we wouldn't be able to cook these special dishes.

Carola

Red changles

As these ingredients reach our facilities, absolutely everything must pass through a tagging system we created called OSV, which stands for "ordering, sorting, and visualizing." This is particularly important for ingredients that are freshly harvested. We do not preserve anything and we only use things in season. To have all this so nicely organized, OSV must function in the freezing chambers, in the different sections of the kitchen, and in the service itself, so we can organize the *mise en place* and the timing. Eventually OSV expanded into the process of creating dishes too. Since we have so many changing ingredients over the year, it helps us organize our ideas and menus so everything is well-scheduled, and we can match ideas with ingredients and processes of cooking.

FROZEN CHICKEN

I believe as cooks we can experience two major revolutions in our minds. The first is when we start cooking, progressing from knowing almost nothing to cooking practically anything—a vegetable, a plant, animals, or even bread. This noticeably changes our way of understanding food and the possibilities.

I also experienced a second, more powerful revolution that transformed how I see this profession: it was when I became a parent. I started to question and try to understand things that wouldn't have crossed my mind in the past and that resulted in meaningful discoveries.

For example, we tend to think of frozen chicken the way we think of a chocolate bar: it comes in a package, and on a normal day you unwrap it, thaw it, and cook it for your loved ones. That would be enough for them to enjoy it. But the moment you ask them to pick out the chicken at the farm, slaughter and pluck it in front them, and cook it in the same manner you usually do, your loved ones, especially if they're children, might avoid eating chicken for some months or even the rest of their lives.

I try to always remain aware of the fact that everything we cook has, at one point, been alive. If we learn to understand where our food comes from, we become more involved with our environment and we improve as cooks. After all, the goal of serving someone food is to make them happy. We can have a great disconnect from the food we eat—where it grows, and how it's harvested or slaughtered. From the time when we are children, we should know where our food comes from and how it arrives at our tables.

WORDS ON CHILE

WITH SOME GASTRONOMIC PERSPECTIVE

Chile is the southernmost country of the continent and geographically very different from the rest of South America. The world's longest continental mountain range, the Andes, towering above at 23,000 feet (7,000 meters), stretches along the eastern border of the entire country from north to south, and the cold waters of the Pacific Ocean are on the western side. In the middle part of the country, even in the summer, when the temperature can be as hot as 82°F (28°C) near the shore, you can jump into the sea where it is only 50°F (10°C). This climate makes seafood and plants look and taste very intense.

To the north of the country lies the Atacama Desert, the driest desert in the world. It is also the birthplace of spectacular native people that used unique ingredients unknown elsewhere—even within the rest of Chile. You can find these ingredients between 8,000 and 16,000 feet (2,500 and 5,000 meters) above sea level.

Toward the center lies Araucanía, where the biggest concentration of Mapuche population lives surrounded by the Nahuelbuta coastal mountain range, densely packed with Chilean araucarias, the tree of life. Chiloé, Juan Fernández, and Easter Islands are rich sources of indigenous ingredients used by natives, and are also the places where this unique culture lives.

All along the country, the peaks of the Andes are fully covered in snow almost year-round. There are also many lakes and glaciers around them, especially towards the south. Big green valleys are located in different areas of Patagonia, including its northern region, where there is a jungle like the Amazon forest but drier and colder. During the Ice Age, when more parts of the Earth were frozen, this place was warm, rich in preserved biodiversity. This forest is called the Valdivian rain forest.

The southern part of the country has a huge concentration of glaciers; lush, green forests; and immense steppes, with a vastness punctuated only by native shrubs. At the very bottom of the country is the southernmost, largest, and second-least-populated region of Chile, the region of Magallanes and Chilean Antarctica. No other place lies farther to the south across the whole planet. Here the summer is very short and most of the year the region is covered with snow.

Over 2,900 miles (4,700 kilometers) of the Pacific coast are affected by the Humboldt Current, which brings the cold waters of Antarctica to the entire Chilean coastline. Perhaps this means a big effort for sea creatures to migrate from one place to another, but for me, cold salty water translates into a lot of intense and beautiful flavors. Life near the rocks on the coast of most isolated places in Chile remains mostly undiscovered and is full of new possibilities. Most of our aboriginal people developed their lives around the rocks; these rocks are covered in thousands of different succulent plants that are growing in salty enviroments and seaweed, mushrooms, stems, roots, seeds, wild fruit, and many other species.

THE CULTURE ON TOP OF THIS LAND

We have organized and classified this landscape from a gastronomic and cultural point of view mainly to understand our possibilities in terms of cooking. However, knowledge of the territory is not all: for thousands of years, Mapuches relied on their own cooking methods, which were embedded in their worldview. None of us seemed to truly pay attention to this before, and that is something we want to make deeply ours.

The Mapuche is one of the oldest cultures in South America, and its people have spent almost 13,000 years on this land. In a way, by ignoring their culture, we are ignoring our roots. Like many cultures dating back thousands of years, the Mapuches developed their lives around seasonal indigenous ingredients, which are not only delicious but also were used for medical purposes.

Unlike other indigenous populations of South America, most of whom practiced agriculture, the Mapuches were foragers capable of constructing a wide network across the land to share knowledge, ingredients, and food through a barter system. Their polytheistic religious practices allowed them to develop their culture on the basis of the land they inhabited, while respecting living beings around them in a collaborative way. Using only what they had access to, the Mapuches were able to understand and develop a vast knowledge based on food, cooking methods, and even food preservation.

LOOKING BACK TO MOVE FORWARD

I believe that a new or evolved cuisine is a subjective thing to talk about or classify. I like to think that cooking is constantly moving back and forth in time and so requires no classification.

The food we serve at Boragó involves many things, such as the understanding of seasonality in a geographically diverse country. That may sound simple but may be one of the most challenging ways of working in a kitchen. Take a minute to consider the perplexing number of ingredients that only exist in small amounts in highly specific locations for a brief period of time.

We had to look back in order to move forward. This is the very reason it is hard for us to describe the food we serve at our restaurant: because it involves the past and the present, as well as knowledge that probably comes from our journeys through all the cultures around the world.

The fact that some of the foods we cook are based on strong traditions doesn't mean they cannot evolve. On the contrary, what we eat should be evolving continuously as we acquire more knowledge over time. Therefore, at the restaurant it is essential for us to constantly challenge what we do and how we do it.

Rock spinach

Chaguals

ONCE UPON A TIME

THERE WAS A TRIP TO THE ATACAMA DESERT

The first time I went to the Atacama Desert, I couldn't believe my eyes: a place so dry that any life there is considered to be a true miracle of nature, considering the zero percent humidity. The days are very hot, and the nights are cold all year long, but especially in the winter. When you walk there, in a high desert mostly surrounded by mountains, the sensation of immensity is powerful. When I first learned of the communities that developed their culture in such extreme living conditions, such as the Atacameño culture, it made me think about food from a point of view completely different than the one I had before my trip. At between 8,000 and 16,000 feet (2,500 and 5,000 meters) above sea level, even my body felt different from when I am in the city.

In the winter, snow falls on the highest mountains in the Andes. When you look around the desert you don't see much, only small bushes that at first glance all seem the same, until you get close and then realize how different they are from each other. And the taste of their leaves, fruits, stems, or roots is mind-blowing. Everything becomes even more interesting when you meet some of the Atacameño people, who can tell us about how their families lived using these ingredients, as well as the properties of each, and even the ways in which they were prepared and cooked.

Visiting the desert helped me better understand how seasonal cycles work there—and elsewhere. In the Atacama Desert, the behavior of ingredients—and the flavors that form as a result of such extreme conditions—is completely different than in any other ecosystem.

Practically everything I saw around me was edible, with flavors so different to what I'd tasted before, I didn't even have a taste memory as a reference point. Affected by winds and extreme hot-to-cold temperatures in a time lapse of less than twenty-four hours, most of the plants and fruits look like familiar plants or bushes, but they have completely different flavors. I felt like a kid in a candy store.

Being in the Atacama Desert was like being a painter who had painted only with ten colors and was suddenly shown three hundred more. My mind was racing—it was too much information—and I am still, to this day, attempting to process it.

As I walked toward the mountains, I stopped to try each plant, which upon close inspection all looked and tasted different. Immediately I knew it was going to be the beginning of something new and different for us. I felt that all Chilean chefs should have the opportunity to visit and know this place that has developed such a deep culture around these plants—a culture from which most Chileans, including myself, are completely disconnected. Not only was this an opportunity to expand the possibilities of our kitchen, it was also a chance for significant economic development for the plant-gathering communities in this area. Places such as these are so rare and unique in the world these days that it is important to do everything we can to protect their survival and establish a responsible and sustainable collaboration practice. Fortunately, the Atacameños are the only ones who can work this land because they have the knowledge to do it, and that is comforting.

My mind was at high speed; it was as if I had discovered a whole new planet! I felt that the most important thing for us as a team during that trip was to make contact with the people who would become important to us, with whom we would begin to build a trust-based relationship over the years, and today they are essential to the work we do at Boragó.

Desert seasons are completely different than those in other regions around the world, since it's dry and hot throughout the year—even in the winter—despite the great variations in temperature between day and night. This also makes the plant cycle completely different. For the greater part of the year these plants are all available, and each plant has its own cycle when it flowers and gives fruit. The sole exception is a phenomenon called the Flowering Desert. When it occurs, plants that have been in long periods of dormancy and have not been seen in years appear in the desert. It is common for several types of wild onion to appear after the rainfalls. The Flowering Desert, however, occurs specifically in late September. Obviously the amount of rain influences the plants. This phenomenon may occur years in a row or not occur at all for several years.

COPAO

The copao is a wild fruit that grows from the north-central region of Chile to Atacama and comes from a plant in the Cactaceae family that can grow up to 20 feet (6 meters) tall. It is one of the most ancient species, existing since the last glacial period (110,000 years ago). Its fruit appears in the summer, from the middle of January to the end of March, and its texture and size vary from the beginning to the end of the season. We have noticed that the ones that grow close to Atacama reach a noticeably larger size, their texture becomes more robust, and their flavor is a little sweeter. The ones that grow in Coquimbo, especially at the beginning of the season, are sticky and acidic. During the summer, this ingredient is at its peak.

Rica rica

This fruit also has valuable nutritional and medicinal properties, such as a high content of potassium and vitamin C.

TOLA

The vast majority of the plants from the Atacama Desert are bitter tasting, and tola is no exception. But unlike other plants, tola has a very tolerable bitterness, an intense aroma, and a particular sweetness in its outer resin, which protects the foliage from insects. It grows at 13,000 to 14,700 feet (4,000 to 4,500 meters) above sea level.

TOLILLA

The tolilla is a plant similar to tola, but more aromatic than other plants of the Atacama Desert. It has a delicate flavor and light bitterness and its taste and texture make it perfect to cook when it is fresh. It grows at 13,000 to 14,700 feet (4,000 to 4,500 meters) above sea level.

RICA RICA

Rica rica is probably the most delicious ingredient of the desert. It is deep green, a size almost between a bush and a small tree, and grows at an altitude of 11,500 feet (3,500 meters). When rica rica flowers, it becomes even more aromatic. We always use these flowers when we have the chance—they have a mild mint scent, even stronger than the plant itself. At the restaurant we also grind the leaves, turning them into fluorescent green dust with an aroma that is out of this world.

MUÑA MUÑA

This small aromatic and slightly bitter plant grows near rica rica. In addition to its medicinal properties, it works well in infusions. One of the methods we have learned to maintain the aroma of desert plants—such as muña muña—and remove their bitterness, is based on the way in which the Japanese handle tea. First, the leaves are steamed, then dehydrated, and finally the infusion process is done in three-minute bursts. This allows us to maintain all their qualities while removing the bitterness.

COPA COPA

Copa copa is an exceedingly bitter plant that grows at an altitude of 11,500 feet (3,500 meters). It has one of the most interesting scents. When the leaves are ground and stirred into milk, the color turns intensely blue, the bitterness disappears, and a beautiful aroma emerges. Because of how well it works with dairy, it is a plant that is exceptionally suited for ice cream.

ROSE OF THE YEAR

The rose of the year is a wild rose that can be found only after rainfall, when the Flowering Desert occurs. It has an intense aroma and flavor that we have not seen in other plants. We use the plant to make infusions, ice creams, and broths, or simply use the whole petals, which are edible.

WILD ONION

With the arrival of the Flowering Desert, wild onions also begin to appear. These are big and succulent flowers; some have a mild flavor and others are intense. Once the flowers are cut, the bulbs can be used just like an onion. Wild onion bulbs were found in the Atacama mummies' clothing dating back thousands of years, giving evidence that they were being used by the Atacameños.

CACHIYUYO

Cachiyuyo is a bush with an algae-like texture that grows in the Atacama Desert at 8,000 feet (2,500 meters). Its high salinity allows it to ferment on its own once it is removed from its natural environment. When taken anywhere else in Chile, its moisture increases over time. Consequently, its salty flavor increases and transforms into something astonishing. It is commonly used in the restaurant in desserts or salads or just the leaf in its natural state.

CHAÑAR

The chañar, a beautiful tree, grows at 8,000 feet (2,500 meters). Similar to a walnut, the exterior part of the fruit has a sweet resin, giving it a natural candy-like texture. For the Atacameños it was a very important source of energy due to its high sugar content. We prepare the *arrope* of chañar—a syrup made with the natural sugar of the fruit—in big barrels directly over an open flame. It results in a really sweet syrup with light touches of chocolate.

CHILEAN CAROB

The Chilean carob in this area is similar to chañar and grows at the same altitude. We also prepare a Chilean carob syrup, just like chañar, but the flavor is completely different. It's more floral, similar to honey, instead of the *arrope* of chañar that has chocolate notes.

CUME CUME

This is a member of the Cactaceae family that produces a very aromatic tiny fruit, sweet and sour and in some cases a little astringent. The season is quite long and, as with every other plant in the Atacama desert, it has served as a reliable food source for the Atacameños for hundreds of years.

ANCHOVIES

Anchovies are an undervalued small fish with incomparable flavor. In Chile they were never considered for human consumption, and due to their small size and fast reproduction, anchovies have been used to produce fishmeal to feed other species. Using Chilean sardines or anchovies is often more atractive to us at the restaurant than using more expensive or larger species, although they require very gentle treatment during their cleaning and cooking. We use them mainly in fermentation processes and for garum (a fermented fish sauce).

A FEW WORDS ON SANTIAGO

THE PLACE WHERE BORAGÓ IS LOCATED

Santiago is located in the center of Chile. During the year, the weather is mild, making it quite a nice place to live. Founded in a deep valley that is surrounded by the high mountains of the Andes, like a big natural hole, it is also a city where you can get a true sense of the passing of the seasons. From within the city, everywhere you look you see mountains in the distance. In the winter, it takes about forty-five minutes to reach the ski centers—this is a big reason why many people travel to Santiago from all over the world, especially at the end of autumn and into the winter. In the summer, you can get to the beach within an hour.

Summer in central Chile is a dry time, and it is also a great season to grow fruit and vegetables. In the fall, leaves start to fall from the trees and you can smell the earthy aromas from the plants around the city. You can feel the mushroom season coming especially around the outskirts of Santiago, or at the *precordillera*—what we call the foothills of the Andes mountains—that divide the city into different sections. In the winter, the mountains are covered in snow from top to bottom, but it doesn't snow much in the city itself. The air becomes extremely dry. When the freezing mornings are coming to an end and spring is around the corner, you can see and smell it everywhere you go. Walking down the street is like entering a perfume store.

There is a window of time between winter and spring that lasts for about three weeks. We call this the "pre-spring phenomenon," during which different plants, trees, and bushes start to come into bloom. At the restaurant it took us several years to become conscious of this. In modern societies we tend to miss the small changes in our surroundings and have stopped paying attention to them. I am convinced that if we became more aware of them, we would eat and live better, for we would acquire a stronger sense of our environment.

Regardless, during the past ten years we've learned so much from places around Santiago as well as from the *precordillera*, which has given us an insanely deep pool of ingredients to cook with. Santiago is also completely surrounded by native trees, plants, and wild fruits during different periods of time that occur throughout the year. To observe, for me, is a simple activity—it means spending time looking at the things around you, and can be used as a time of deep reflection. Most of the food we serve at the restaurant mirrors this observation process. These days we are highly conscious about every little thing that it is happening around us, and we feel great about this achievement. We are treating these events like thousands of small windows that stay open during a short time each year. We feel they are open for us to grab . . . and then we make choices. With those choices, we learn and cook every day.

QUISCO PARASITE

The quisco, similar to the copao cactus, is a member of the Cactaceae family that grows on the mountains and the pre-mountain range of central Chile. It grows more easily above 4,000 feet (1,200 meters) in the pre-mountainous range of the Santiago valley toward the north side of the city. The most interesting thing about the quisco is a phenomenon that occurs in the pre-spring, when it is infected by a parasite called *quintral* that grows in some of the quiscos. This plant produces a truly unique fruit that looks like a little pink grape with a meaty texture. It is slightly sticky, with a pleasant aroma similar to lychee fruit. Unfortunately, it only appears during a three-week window and regrettably, no one yet knows how to harvest it on a large scale, so we have to forage it ourselves. But the effort is completely worth it, because the fruit is absolutely delicious! The quintral of the quisco has to be served as soon as it is cut from the cactae, as it won't last longer than four days in good conditions. We don't preserve it, as it would lose the soul and the uniqueness of its flavor.

CHILEAN PALM TREE COCONUT

The Chilean palm tree coconut is indigenous to the central coast of Chile. By the end of the summer and just before the beginning of fall, during a window of approximately three weeks, a yellow fruit that looks and tastes a lot like a small mango appears. Once it falls on the ground and a few days pass, the external layers fall off and the coconut appears. These coconuts are very small and evenly sized, about ¾ of an inch (2 centimeters) in diameter, and their flavor is similar to conventional coconuts. At the end of fall, the coconuts are firm and less milky than during mid-season.

SEA URCHIN

Chilean sea urchins have unparallelled texture, size, and flavor, which greatly varies depending on their size. When they are big, between 2 to 3 inches (5 to 8 centimeters), their flavor is floral and you can really taste the sea in them. When they're even bigger, at 6 to 8 inches (15 to 20 centimeters), they're equally floral but acquire strong meat-like notes, almost like a foie gras. The place where they are extracted also impacts the flavor and texture. The sea urchin we appreciate the most at the restaurant comes

Sea carrots

Ulte

Sea urchin

from central Chile, mainly from a place called Quintay. The sea urchins from northern Chile are usually less floral, but they have spectacular umami properties. In the south, they turn sweeter, because many rivers flow into the sea from the mountains and that affects the salinity of the ocean there. Depending on where they come from, we use and treat sea urchins in different ways.

Often, when we serve a course with sea urchins in the tasting menu, we are able to use only one tongue or *lengua*—how we call it in Chile—because of their size! When serving them raw, they are treated in only one way. We call it "drying the sea urchins" because their texture is almost as if they dried up on the outside and kept all the moisture on the inside. When tasting them this way, it almost feels as if they explode inside your mouth, much the way a raw egg yolk does. This is something very simple that I learned from fishermen, then we adapted and improved it until we obtained a better texture and sensation when biting down on one. We open sea urchins just a couple hours before serving. Then they're cleaned and strained, and we preserve the "tongues" with their interior water at 36°F (2°C). We place them on a stainless steel plate with a lot of space between the "tongues." Just before being served, they are placed in a large mesh strainer and submerged in their own cold water for 1 minute so they shrink.

KOLOF

Kolof, or *cochayuyo*, as it is commonly known, is one of the most well-known algae in Chile, with a unique honeycomb interior and a deep brown color on the outside. Unfortunately, kolof has a bad reputation because it is often prepared the wrong way. It can be found in any market in Chile in its most common form: dehydrated. We have found many ways to use its entire length. Considering the different types of climate along the length of the country, kolof can be used year-round because it reproduces quickly. Kolof is usually harvested lying fresh on the shore.

CHOCOLATE MUSHROOMS

This is the only mushroom that can be foraged in Santiago, and with good reason: it grows on sycamore maple, poplars, and willows 10 feet (3 meters) above the ground. Chocolate mushrooms have a firm, almost meatlike texture. They grow close to the mountains. The first time we tried them was thanks to Giuliana, a friend and mycologist, who showed us a tool she had made: a long rod with a knife at the end. Two people are needed to gather them: one person cuts with the tool while the other stands under the tree and catches them as they fall. Throughout the year, the mushrooms' characteristics change a lot. In early winter, they smell like yeast, but at the end of the season, around August, more like chocolate. The foraging of these mushrooms has become a sort of ritual at the restaurant.

KIRINKA

We started using kirinka in 2007. It is a tree that grows on all the hills of central Chile up to an altitude of 5,000 feet (1,500 meters). Its pods are full of hard seeds—so hard that it's possible to lose a tooth trying to chew them. Once we discovered that if we roasted the seeds, we could obtain a flavor similar to coffee, we began using them in many preparations including desserts, meat, and stocks. We thought we had discovered something important in terms of flavor until we visited a Mapuche community. They said without a hint of irony, "Oh, kirinka, we've been using it for the last two thousand years, it's very recent . . ." Currently we use kirinka instead of coffee at the restaurant and we brew it in an espresso machine. The ideal harvest time is right after summer and at the beginning of fall with the first rain. This is when the tree drops the pods.

PENCA

Penca is a wild artichoke that appears from pre-spring to the end of spring in central Chile, and in some cases until the beginning of summer when there are nearby streams. Penca grows close to kirinkas and is hard to cut because of its big thorns. It boasts a spectacular artichoke flavor, an aroma that is slightly more astringent than its farmed cousins, a crunch slightly similar to celery, and a faint bitterness, which we remove by immersing it in brine with 1 percent salt.

WILD RADISH

Wild radish is similar to horseradish but much lighter in taste and less spicy. We often forage it at the coast, close to the rocks. We have also tried planting its root in the fields and it adapts perfectly well. At the beginning of its season, we use the stem and leaves—with their celery-like texture they contain mostly water. Later in the season, we also use the flowers as a condiment and the young pods for their smooth texture and spicy flavor.

LOCO

Locos (*Concholepas concholepas*), as they are known in Chile, are one of the most beloved sea creatures in the

Kolof

Kolof root

Sea strawberries

country. They are a carnivore type of mollusk, with a diet consisting partially of mussels and other small mollusks. The diet results in differences in texture and taste—locos are known for their intense flavor. Because of their firm, rubbery texture, they must be pounded to soften them before they are cooked. Traditionally, locos are boiled in water and served with mayonnaise and beet (beetroot) salad or with lettuce dressed with lemon. The longer locos are boiled, the more tender they become—they can be as tender as a boiled potato. The flip side of prolonged cooking is the lack of flavor, so ideally, we find a sweet spot where the locos don't lose all their flavor and their texture is just soft enough.

While locos can also be eaten raw, their tough texture makes them hard to chew. To get around this, we use Chilean papayas, which contains an enzyme called *papain* that softens the meat. Visitors to Chile have a hard time understanding why Chileans are so crazy about locos and why we love their slightly rubbery texture so much. It's just one of those things that doesn't have an explanation—I think they are spectacular and I refuse to hide my love for them.

FIG WOOD

The fig tree is one that, in addition to its fruit, provides many possibilities. For example, the branches are good for smoking food. We use fig wood to smoke different types of meat; it imparts a flavor as sweet as the figs themselves.

SEA CARROTS

Sea carrot is an algae shaped like a carrot, and if you bite into it right after picking it out of the ocean, its crunch will remind you of a carrot as well. Sea carrots are hollow and retain seawater. In some cases, when they are found on the shore in the morning when they're fresh, that liquid has turned into a thick "dashi" with an umami flavor. We have found several uses for this algae, not only freshly cut because of its texture, but also for infusions and stocks, for example.

CONGER EEL

Chilean conger eel (*Genypterus chilensis*) is highly appreciated in Chile. There are many traditional preparations where it is mainly served as a soup. The flesh has an intense sea flavor, but the most extraordinary aspect is its firm, collagen-rich texture.

SEA STRAWBERRIES

Sea strawberries, also known as rock strawberries, are astonishing! They belong to a large plant family, succulents, some of which I have seen abroad, but not all of them are edible. They do not need soil and can grow directly on rocks. The fruit, which is the only edible part of the plant, is ripe in February, toward the end of the summer. The plant and its fruit behave like a strawberry, and the fruit tastes and smells like strawberries, but with a hint of saltiness. When sea strawberries are harvested, they give off a strong scent of strawberry and are juicy and soft. By the end of the summer a few berries are still available to harvest, and when you eat them it seems like the berries have become caramelized on the inside.

PACO CRAB

The meat of this type of crab has an unbelievable high quality of flavor and texture. We like them even more than the southern king crab. They are delightful when raw, especially because of their sweetness and juicy legs. We also use their gonads and brains to make emulsions. The way we like to use them is to remove the shell of the pincers and then poach them in seawater for 40 seconds.

PICOROCO

Picorocos are delicate. The meat of this crustacean is as elegant as that of a Patagonia king crab or maybe a Juan Fernández lobster. These creatures are seasonal and most commonly found from spring to the end of summer. They are traditionally cooked whole in stocks, in addition to being used in *curanto*, a traditional preparation from the south of Chile. If picorocos are incorrectly handled or overcooked (which happens often), they give off an aroma like ammonia and their delicate meat loses many of its more subtle properties.

Traditionally, picorocos are never used raw, but we discovered that they are spectacular uncooked. We started serving them this way several years ago to highlight the sweet and umami sensation they produce. It is important to clean them well and separate their organs, which are really strong, from their flesh. One of the most important things we do when selecting them is to smell the vents: if they do not give off any scent, we will serve them raw. At first sight, the way picorocos energetically snap their claws might lead us to think they are high quality. But that's not always the case and they can produce a really nasty taste if they're not in good condition. Furthermore, it can be difficult to use them efficiently since the shell is big and the inner meat behind each pincer is not plentiful. To make better use of them, we prepare garum with the

Picorocos

Chocolate mushrooms

Pine mushrooms

inner portions—the finished product is even more floral than garum made with anchovies. When slightly steamed, both the texture and the flavor of picorocos are unbelievable. The same happens when they are slightly cooked over embers.

BEACH SWISS CHARD

Beach Swiss chard grows directly on the sand all along the central coast of Chile. It looks like a regular chard, but since they are halophytes, they are meaty and saline at the same time. This plant's season lasts for approximately five months, from pre-spring to the final months of the summer.

CHOCHA

Chochas have a texture that is both resistant and soft at once. These mollusks resemble a high-quality clam that tastes like umami-charged sea. They are very different from other sea creatures we have tasted; they are more like Chilean razorclams and locos.

JIBIA

This giant squid would never be served at a good restaurant in Santiago because in Chile it is viewed as vulgar and too cheap. Actually, it *is* cheap, but it is incredibly tasty. Because it is so thick, you can ripen it as if it were a piece of beef, and you can size the cut based on your needs. Jibia can grow up to 10 feet (3 meters) long. Due to their size and large number, they have become a plague and are feared sea predators. Cooking them in large amounts is helpful for other sea species, and that is exactly what we do!

ROCK PARSLEY

Rock parsley has a strong hint of salt but also a thick and crunchy texture, in addition to a slight scent of mandarin orange.

ROCK CLOVER

In the restaurant we call this unique halophyte "rock clover" because it grows on rocks, although its real name is *Oxalis carnosa*. In comparison with the well-known clover, this one is more succulent (it can be more than 1 millimeter thick). It is salty and acid at the same time, so it can be cooked in a variety of ways while still preserving its salinity and acidity in a perfect manner. Rock clover is an important plant in our kitchen, and we have used it for several years in a variety of dishes. Some years the season has been very long; sometimes it has lasted five months, which is about average. Rock clover is normally dormant by the beginning of the summer, but it starts to grow and thicken again by pre-spring.

SEA STAR

Only the flower of the sea star can be eaten; the stem is not edible. The flower smells like honey, tastes like an onion, and is salty. It is a phenomenal ingredient. Sea stars grow directly on the rocks, and when you are walking among them, the honey aroma is intense. When eaten, they are crunchy and vegetal. Sea stars are one of the ingredients that we avoid touching with our fingers when serving, because all the aroma and flavor can adhere to the fingers, robbing the flower of an important part of its character. The sea star season lasts four weeks along the central coast. Some years, it has extended to five or six weeks.

Rock parsley

Rock clovers

THE COUNTRYSIDE

During the years before the restaurant's rise in popularity in 2013, we had had access to truly unique ingredients and had developed logistics with gathering communities and small producers throughout Chile that worked well—but on the basis of a very small demand. This was also true of the ingredients we harvested ourselves, according to the season in the forests, on the coast, and even in the mountains around Santiago. With the increased volume, we were not certain that we would be able to continue to use the same ingredients. Nor were there any restaurants in Chile that used those ingredients. It could have been useful if they and we were trying to help each other.

We began to contact all the people who sent us ingredients, looking at the possibility of obtaining significant amounts for what appeared to be a new stage for Boragó. And we decided to look for a farmer with whom we could begin to plant and grow our own vegetables in our own way, based on our specific needs.

RENATO APPEARS

In one of the organic farmer's markets where Alejandra and I bought vegetables on Saturdays for our children, I had the opportunity to meet a man named Renato. He said, "These vegetables are from my fields! It's all done biodynamically, but I don't have a certificate," and I quickly asked him if he would be willing to produce all of our vegetables. The following Monday I visited him and he explained that he rented his farm in order to provide people with something different and meaningful, putting to one side several economic aspects, which many farmers would never do. He appeared to have strong beliefs regarding food, as well as a passion for harvesting vegetables. I thought he was a bit ahead of the times. It was clear that we could do important things together.

With time, we began to work together and produce many vegetables for the restaurant. Until then, we knew absolutely nothing about agriculture, but we began to learn new ways of organizing the fields in relation to the restaurant, taking into account that anything we wanted to do required a lot of planning and time. Certainly one of these ways was to be able to plant real wild vegetables, some of which had never been grown in fields.

The results of this collaborative work with Renato were without a doubt very satisfactory. We eventually grew an enormous number of plants, including some halophytes, which we had to go to the coast to collect. We also began to use vegetables that would often be thrown away in the countryside in order to give them a different treatment in the kitchen. We tried to have a complete vision of everything we planted, using the flowers, stalks, and roots.

These days all the milk we use is also milked in the countryside, which allows us to obtain the high quality we need for our preparations. Renato comes to the restaurant twice a week, but we also go to the countryside at least once a month, to see what is going on and to discuss the new things we can do. This allows us to be connected with the final result.

A DAY WALKING IN THE COUNTRYSIDE

Several years ago I had a little obsession about being able to understand how a good-quality cheese is prepared. I was told that a Swiss man, a skilled cheese maker, was coming to the south of Chile to work on a new project and that he could teach me. I finally managed to immerse myself in the world of cheese, and to understand what this artisanal artform really consists of. I had the opportunity to make Camembert cheese and the process seemed incredible.

But one day, walking in the countryside with Renato and part of my team, I said, "I know! We could find a way to produce proteolysis inside a vegetable," which initially seemed like a far-fetched idea. Basically this meant expanding the flavor of a vegetable while producing the texture inherent to the aging of cheese. Despite the fact that it took us a long time to reproduce the specific conditions and achieve the result we were looking for, we managed to create in vegetables a texture similar to a Camembert cheese. But the truth is that what most intrigued us was the possibility of achieving a different flavor, which could help us to cook in a different way. In time we were even able to start improving the flavor of the various vegetables, in the same way one does with cheese. Obviously this way of treating the flavor of a vegetable meant we had to plan the food we would offer at the restaurant some time in advance. Of course it also opened an important window for anyone who is lactose-intolerant, because now they could enjoy this "cheese-vegetable."

PARTRIDGE EGGS

These eggs are an ideal size for our tasting menu: they weigh only 30 grams (1 ounce) and are the size of quail eggs. Compared to chicken eggs, their most striking feature is the creamy texture of the yolk when both cooked or raw.

COUNTRYSIDE GREEN TOMATO

At the restaurant, we use tomatoes only during the summer season, since that is when the best ones with the most unique flavor are available. Fortunately, we have planted plenty of Limache tomatoes, a type with a lot of umami, in the countryside. We have them for the summer season, but there are years when the temperature drops rapidly at the end of summer and the tomatoes cannot continue to ripen. We simply use these unripe green tomatoes in different sauces, broths, or salads, to name a few of their uses, and the result can be just as amazing as with ripe tomatoes.

A MAGICAL PLACE CALLED ARAUCANÍA

For those who haven't visited it, Araucanía is an unimaginable place. This is the region where the Mapuche people developed their fascinating culture over thousands of years. From east to west, Araucanía is characterized by its coastal plains, the coastal mountain range, the intermediate depression, and the Andes mountain range. There are three large rivers: the Toltén, Imperial, and Bío-Bío. In addition, the area is home to a number of lakes, as well as two of the most active volcanos of Latin America: Llaima and Villarrica. The sights seem to be taken straight from a fairy tale.

In this part of Chile there are an enormous number of endemic plants, thanks to the richness of the soil. A large portion of them are used as both food and medicine. A variety of shrubs, plants, lichen, moss, and giant ferns grow abundantly in the humid climate. Even though jungle-like forests are characteristic of the area, there are places with drier conditions that are protected by the Nahuelbuta mountain range, which acts as a climate screen and allows the existence of the rain forest.

COAST PINE MUSHROOM

Two species of mushroom grow in all the pine forests along the central coast of Chile and they are frequently confused: *Suillus luteus* and *Boletus granulatus*. Both are traditionally dried and smoked over native wood. In the beginning we used them in limited ways, but in recent years we have started innovating with them and they have become important to the restaurant. They grow at an immense rate in the fall; in the forests it looks like the soil has exploded with mushrooms! Sometimes we are able to pick up to 220 pounds (100 kilos) at once. When exposed to fire, their texture is fascinating: they become jelly-like inside in spite of the outside being roasted. They also change a lot over time: When young, they are firm and small. When they grow larger, they acquire a stronger flavor, and their texture starts to resemble that of a marshmallow, then their color turns yellow. Both mushrooms are truly delicious if used and stored correctly. Their season can be long and there have even been years when we gathered them through the winter until spring.

WITCH POTATO

This is one of Chiloé's four hundred varieties of native potatoes, with a flavor that is bitter and slightly sweet at the same time. The witch potato cooks fairly quickly because of its moist flesh. When cooked, the potato acquires an intense violet color and has a nice firm texture.

MICHUÑE POTATO

This is another Chiloé potato larger than the witch potato with a purple color. When cooked, it is drier and acquires a nutty flavor.

BLACK LUGA

There are several types of algae in Chile. All of them have a delicate texture, even when used raw. Black luga, in particular, is one of our most popular algae during its season, which is long, due to its availability from central Chile south to Patagonia. This species stands out for its texture after scalding, which is reminiscent of al dente pasta. The scalding time varies depending on its age: If it is in the reproductive stage, it must barely touch the boiling water and then cool down in an ice bath, otherwise it becomes jelly-like and unpalatable. (We heat it briefly just before serving.) To identify if black luga is in the reproductive stage, we look for small dots and a rough texture, which is pleasant when eaten. When it is not in the reproductive stage, it is necessary to cook it in boiling water for approximately 2 minutes at the most; if you pass that time it becomes rubbery. It is still important to place it in an ice bath to stop the cooking.

ROCK SPINACH

There are two types of rock spinach on the central coast of Chile. Both are halophytes, and therefore they have a high concentration of saline when compared to a conventional plant. One type is meatier and has a soft flavor. The other is much more acidic and exceedingly crunchy.

BLUE MAPUCHE CHICKEN EGGS

This is a unique breed of chicken, which is evident when we see the roosters: they do not have a tail, and this is also the case with the hens. In addition to this odd appearance, the hens lay blue eggs that have a much higher amino acid concentration than those of the more commonly found countryside chickens.

SEA CHICORY

This sea algae is highly valued at the restaurant because of its texture and perfume. We use it fresh as a salad but, because the season is short, we also smoke it, preserve it, and use it to infuse cold and hot stocks to give them a marine scent. We also use both the fresh and smoked algae to prepare dashi, which results in a delicate floral flavor. The smoked algae can be used to make sea merkén.

Witch potatoes

Male arrayanes

Chupones

Nalca

PIURE

Piure is one of the most peculiar sea creatures I have ever seen. It lives inside what looks like a stone but is completely soft. This "stone" is easy to cut with a knife. Piures range from 2 to 3 inches (5 to 8 centimeters) in diameter. They are a bright orange color and resemble a mass of organs inside the "rock." Their skin is also thick and has an intense iodine flavor, which makes many people in Chile unwilling to eat them. However, they can be very floral. We started removing the interior part that contains the most concentrated amount of iodine, and discovered that when using only the skin, it has a subtle citric taste. The season is quite long, stopping only during the winter.

CHILOÉ'S GIANT GARLIC

Chiloé's giant garlic is large in size but softer and less intense than other types of garlic. We use it a lot in fermentation. Its flowers, which grow during the spring, have a sweet similarity to garlic but are softer in flavor, so they can be used as the perfect seasoning.

ULMO HONEY

Ulmo is a very aromatic tree. Bees that visit it produce the best honey we have ever tasted at the restaurant. We also use ulmo honey and beeswax to age different types of meat, especially Patagonian guanaco meat, which acquires a floral, honey, and buttery taste when aged in this manner.

MALE ARRAYÁN

The male arrayán is a fruit that starts appearing during the pre-fall, a brief period at the end of the summer. It is a vivid purple color has a rather large seed that makes it difficult to work with and does not yield much flesh. We often dehydrate male arrayán because it acquires an interesting texture that undergoes light caramelization while maintaining its bitterness. On other occasions we use it raw to add a touch of bitterness, as if it were a seasoning.

FEMALE ARRAYÁN

Female arrayán shows up by the middle of fall. After its flowers bloom, the fruit starts to appear. It is normally ripe by the end of the fall, and can even last into the beginning of winter as long as there is no intense rainfall, which tends to ruin the season. We use them in several ways when they are unripe because they are astringent and add layers of flavor to our preparations. Sometimes we also preserve them using a traditional Japanese preservation technique called *umeboshi*. We even dehydrate them to handle them as a dry seasoning because in this ripening phase they are aromatic. We use the ripe fruit fresh because they are juicy and tender. Their seeds are big but soft and often used in some preparations. We also make a fermented paste with female arrayán that is similar to miso.

QUEULE

Quele is a unique fruit with a flavor that is different than any other. It has a strong floral scent and is astringent and acid. The size is almost the same as an apricot. It is not eaten fresh because its flavor is too intense; it is always cooked. It grows in small quantities in Araucanía during the beginning of fall.

WILD BLACKBERRIES

Wild blackberries grow in all types of environments, and in the countryside we plant them as a hedge. The season begins in the middle of the summer, and by the end of January or the beginning of February they turn very sweet. We think that this fruit has two phases: Right before they are ripe and turn black, they reach a good size and are acid and solid, and their color is completely red. That is our favorite time of the year to harvest them. The ripe black ones, harvested by the end of February, gently explode inside your mouth.

PEWÉN

The pewén, or araucaria pine nut, is from an indigenous tree of Araucanía. Its pine nuts have been the sacred food of the Mapuche people for thousands of years. The Mapuche used this fruit as the base of their diet not by coincidence but because of its high nutritional value, in addition to having a nice strong aroma and a unique flavor. The pewén nut is succulent and generally 1½ to 2¾ inches (4 to 7 centimeters) long. To this day, the communities that live in the area depend on gathering it. They use it to make pine nut flour and for many other purposes.

CHUPÓN

This wild fruit grows in large amounts during the fall. The plant is similar to aloe vera but it can become enormous. Chupones grow close to the heart of the plant and on the base. They are shaped like large thorns and are sweet, with big seeds that are easy to eat. If preserved, chupones start to ferment in a pleasant way after a few days and their aroma becomes even stronger. Going out to gather them is like stepping into a candy store. Because of this,

Murtillas

Pewenes

there is no child in southern Chile who does not know about chupones. They grow abundantly in Araucanía and northern Patagonia.

MURTILLA

Murtilla, as Chileans call the different species in the Myrtaceae family, are a wild fruit with an intense and unique flavor. Every single one tastes different. We used to think there was only one type of murtilla, but there are actually more than sixty-two. They are resistant to cold and strong wind. They start to appear by the end of the fall. We value them a lot at Boragó. Their flavor is somewhere between an apple and a rose.

White murtilla is the least common variety. It grows on the hillsides close to the beach in Valdivia and is the most popular because it is so aromatic. Mr. Pascual, one of the people who makes our food possible by foraging the best ingredients in his region for us, introduced us to this species, which is hard to identify. Sometimes they are fleshier than common murtilla, as well as sweeter.

Black murtilla is sweet but also acid. Its skin is more robust than other varieties and it is a dark red-purple color. During their season in April we are able to acquire a large volume of these.

MELÍ

The melí is probably one of the oldest trees in the Valdivian jungle. Many there are more than six hundred years old. You would not imagine that the thick and fibrous leaves could be edible. However, when you take a bite, they have an intense but gentle taste and they give off a strong and sweet aroma. Melí grows only during the fall and only in small amounts; it is very sensitive to rain because the fruit is located on the tips of the tree's branches. This also means that it is the perfect food for birds, so it isn't easy to gather. It is large and meaty for a berry, and its seeds are big, so they are usually removed before the fruit is used. Its intensity allows us to use it in elaborations, extracts, and other methods of preservation. Having this fruit available every season is a true luxury.

LUMA

Luma is a special tree. Its wood has been used for thousands of year to smoke food and to prepare preserves through different methods, both excellent ways to preserve food. It is a solid and aromatic wood due to its high content of essential oils. By the end of the spring, it produces a fruit that has a scent similar to their tree leaves; it is a shiny, meaty berry with small seeds. Like melí, luma's flavor is like nothing else. It grows abundantly in the Valdivian jungle.

LOYO

Members of the Boletus family, loyos are the most appreciated mushrooms at the restaurant. We start to become very excited when their season starts to appear because of the romantic relationship that we, as Chileans, have with the mushroom season. Bright yellow, loyos have a smooth and meaty texture; the bigger they are, the more delicate their texture becomes, yet the more intense their flavor becomes. Found in pre-fall and sometimes into late fall, the season for the loyos is unpredictable and can be as short as three weeks to as long as a month and a half, it depends on the amount of rain that falls after their bloom so that they don't absorb too much water. Mr. Pascual, our forager in the south of Chile, is the person responsible for supplying this treasure to Boragó year after year.

CÓGUIL

The cóguil fruit grows on the tree called coguilero. It is rare, grows only in a specific place in the Los Ríos area, and appears at the start of fall. It contains several large seeds, has a strong aroma, and is a little sticky. In spite of cóguil being one of the more recent additions to our kitchen, we have found sensational uses for its skin.

CHILEAN HAZELNUT

This hazelnut is different than traditional hazelnuts. It has excellent medicinal properties. When the fruit is freshly picked from the tree, its flavor is lightly bitter and astringent and the texture is similar to the fresh horseradish. Traditionally the Mapuche people have roasted hazelnuts, and they still do so to this day. Roasting removes all the acidity and bitterness. What stands out to us the most is that when these hazelnuts are boiled, they acquire the consistency almost of a tuber and become very floral.

LUCHE

Luche is one of the four most popular algae that used to be gathered by the *lafquenches* (the Mapuche name for people who live on the coast of the Araucanía). They compact it and then smoke it in tepú, lenga, and tepa wood, which have a special aroma when used for smoking. You can still find luche in markets around Chile prepared the artisanal way (although it is not always prepared properly). When luche is pressed, fermentation occurs inside, thanks to the seawater. After this they are suspended over light smoke for months.

Loyos

White strawberries

Chilean hazelnuts

The season starts with spring. At the restaurant, we gather it on our own, and we have managed to improve the fermentation process. That greatly increases the flavor and gives it a texture similar to black garlic.

WHITE STRAWBERRY

White strawberries are one of the ingredients that Chileans eagerly anticipate. They have a significant emotional value, similar to white truffles for cooks in Italy. Unfortunately, the season lasts only two to three weeks at the start of the summer. They are endemic to an area called Purén, and can also be found at the base of the Nahuelbuta Mountains. Their meat is completely white, their aroma and flavor incomparable to the common strawberry, and they don't last for very long after they are cut. They only grow in the wild, so they are foraged for us by local communities. It is said that they are the original strawberries, which were taken to Europe centuries ago and modified over time to become today's familiar red strawberry.

CHANGLE

Changle is a delicious mushroom that appears toward the end of fall in an area stretching from the region of Bío-Bío (VIII region) to the region of Aysén (XI region). Its fragility demands good kitchen skills to prepare it. We have four species, all of them different in terms of texture and water content. They look very similar to corals. During the last couple years, we have learned how to use them well by curing them, making escabeche, and grilling them, among other cooking techniques.

CHILEAN MOREL

There are two main types of morels in Chile, and five further variations. The first type, *Morchella esculenta*, exists in other parts of the world. The Chilean cone morel (*Morchella conica*) exists only in Chile. It has an intense flavor and a sturdy texture resistant to high cooking temperatures above 140°F (60°C). It is commonly dehydrated and exported abroad. At the restaurant we use it only when it is freshly cut during the season, which starts with the arrival of spring. There are also three other types of Chilean morels, which are variations of the main two above. They are usually mislabeled because people don't know how to distinguish them. To us, however, their differences are important because they affect the cooking and flavor. People who know about mushrooms call them "false Chilean morels," but the truth is that they are *Morchella elata*, another species of the *morchellaceae* family.

Both the caps and stems of *elatas* have a smooth texture, which means they are not resistant to high temperatures like the other morels. They mostly look the same but are thinner and the cap grows directly from the stem. The flavor is lighter and they don't have the characteristic yeast scent of the *Morchella conica*. They are also greatly affected by humidity, absorbing large amounts of water, which alters their texture. Regardless, their intense flavor is sensational.

NALCA

Nalcas are incredible plants. They grow mainly on the hillsides close to the sea from Araucanía to northern Patagonia. All parts of the plant are used. The leaf is used to cover the pit where the *curanto*, a traditional preparation from Chiloé, is cooking; it acts as a pressure cooker, retaining the smoke from the native wood as well as the steam from the different seafood, potatoes, and meat.

When the plant is young, its tender, sweet root is useful, as it was for the native people. The root must be cut at a precise moment to retain its delicate flavor. A few days late, when they are taller than 3 feet (1 meter), they become too fibrous. When the stem is cut, it looks like rhubarb, especially because of the intense red color once the skin is removed. However, the flavor is completely different; it is not even close. Nalca is both astringent and acid. It is generally eaten with lemon and salt. Unfortunately, its season is short—only a month to a month and a half.

SHOE MUSSEL

We call them shoe mussels (*choro zapato* in Spanish) because they grow to be about the size of a shoe. Their texture is spectacularly creamy, especially when served raw. They're equally delicious when cooked. There is a big difference between males and females: The males are like any other orange mussel. The females, however, are completely black and taste a lot like iodine, which is why we treat them with a completely different method. The only way to tell them apart is by opening them. The first time I tried them was in the Fluvial Market in Valdivia, a spectacular city that is the capital of the Los Lagos region and the starting point of Patagonia from north to south. This is not a big market, but harvesting communities of the area sell their ingredients there all year round, and one of their products is the shoe mussel. When you arrive at the market stall, the seller opens one in front of you and pours lemon juice into it. The first time I tried one was impressive: it felt like an oyster injection straight to the mouth.

Digüeñe

PATAGONIA NOW!

What impacted me the most the first time I went to Patagonia was the silence. It was immense, like nothing I'd ever experienced before. Patagonia is an amazing place. It has short summers and long, cold winters, in addition to strong winds at certain times of the year. It is also highly diverse in terms of ecosystems, thanks to the submersion of the Andes mountains that creates a whole ecosystem for sea species. In the cold sea off the coast of Patagonia, there are so many species that have unexpectedly intense flavors, such as the southern king crab, one of the most delicious species in the world. It is a large sea critter and it makes us happy to have it in the restaurant.

The Andes stretch across Chile from its most boreal point down to Cape Horn. In general, vegetation in Patagonia is affected by strong winds, which causes a larger presence of bushes rather than trees. Fortunately for us, it is full of wild fruit, in addition to a number of aromatic plants and wild herbs that were the food of aboriginal people for thousands of years. One of these is *llao llao*, or *pan de indio*, a parasitic mushroom that grows on mirre and coihue, common trees of the area. This mushroom was used as a medicine and was one of the main food sources of the Kawesqar and Tehuelche peoples. The mushrooms were also dried and used as miniature bags for transporting seeds and making fire. Its texture is unique and it has a light sweetness and texture.

PUYA

Puyas are wild plants that grow on the hillsides along the coast, from the central region of the country to the northern part of Patagonia. The edible part is the root, which has a delicate and elegant texture. It had never been domesticated or planted in a field before, but we managed to grow it and obtained excellent results by planting it one year and harvesting it the next. The roots can keep growing for a long time—between six to eight years. Puya has a relatively long season: it lasts for almost six months.

DIGÜEÑE

This mushroom goes by many names, depending on the area. There is a great digüeñe-gathering tradition from central Chile down to southern Patagonia. There are five species, some of them distinct due to their size, but all of them have a mild flavor. When you break them in half with your hands, they don't look like any other mushroom. They are bright orange, like a mandarin, and their texture is sturdy but a little sticky. They are commonly used in salty preparations. However, when split, it is clear that they can work well in desserts. Most of the time we use them that way—maybe because the inside reminds me of mandarins. They are also good at absorbing any flavor, like sponges, which makes them versatile.

PEJERREY

Pejerrey isn't considered an expensive fish. It has always been cheap to the point that people prefer not to use it much. Its meat is white, delicate, and has a unique flavor. This species changes a lot in terms of flavor depending on its location, as it is found in both fresh and salt water.

PATAGONIA WILD APPLES

Chauras are the true wild apples of Patagonia, not only because of their texture, which is practically the same as an apple. The fruit can withstand very low temperatures perfectly while hanging on the branches. While chauras belong to two different families that range widely in colors and sizes, they all have a mild flavor and a crunchy texture. Their skin is thick and the interior is sturdy but easy to bite into. Three types that we value highly are described below. There are foraging communities that pick them season after season exclusively for the restaurant. Many of them grow in remote places where almost no one lives and the harvest seasons are short.

Black Wild Apples

These are a little smaller than other wild apples. At the start of the season they are crunchy and have the flavor of a red apple, including the same sweetness. At the end of the season, almost by the end of the winter, they acquire a more truffle-like flavor.

Pink Wild Apples

Pink wild apples have an acidic and floral flavor and are the most aromatic of all. They can grow to be about three times the size of the other apples by the end of the season. They are our favorites.

White Wild Apples

There are two types of white wild apples that belong to different botanical families, grow during different seasons, and differ in size and flavor. The first one is ripe in the fall and is the softest of all. It grows in small quantities in northern Patagonia. The second is a little larger and its texture a little sturdier. It grows on the coast and in some cases, in the sand close to glaciers.

Pink wild apples

ELABORATIONS AND DESCRIPTIVE PROCESSES

ELABORATIONS AND DESCRIPTIVE PROCESSES

I have always thought, or wanted to believe, that knowledge can take us far, even when we speak of the evolution of a culture, and I think that in my own country we have not had the chance to generate knowledge as a basis for our society. I don't know if this is because we are a country that is too young or because of our focus on economic development, which does not allow us to stop and try to understand how important this knowledge could be for a country like ours. It is unquestionable that societies in the present day develop at an uncontrollable speed, which probably doesn't leave us much space to reflect on a subject like this.

Throughout history, Chile has exported products without processing them too much, for example, copper: We have become experts at exporting raw copper, so why should we want to build our knowledge beyond what is needed to extract the raw material? In the end, knowledge takes a long time to develop and is undoubtedly expensive to pursue. For this same reason, we rely on other countries for this knowledge, and we then buy it, even if it deals with resources—even those related to food—that exist only in Chile.

Since we began the restaurant, I have felt that there is a great opportunity to generate knowledge and learning, not only from the gastronomic point of view with ingredients that are truly unique, but also in terms of developing sustainable supply chains, creating benefits for many. This would start a virtuous circle, along with beginning to appreciate our own culture, which is doubtless the most important thing in a country. Culture is capable of evolving and becoming more meaningful.

In Chile, the Atacameño people did not have any type of cultural exchange with the Mapuche people, much less in a gastronomic sense. Without a doubt, there is a great opportunity for this in the present day, since cultural interaction can happen easily, and is something that Boragó has done within its own walls, which lately has even expanded outside the restaurant.

Knowledge is a tool that describes the history of human beings and is so versatile that it can be applied in any culture. Due to my work I have been lucky enough to be able to travel to several countries, where it has been possible for me to study preparations that have taught us new paths and new ideas—often ancestral preparations that could in many cases be adapted to Chilean ingredients. When we experiment, initially we don't know what will happen, but we are often surprised, and even create variations or ideas with cooking methods that we have not seen in any culture, or at least that we have not heard of.

After ten years as a team, we realized that up until now we have been simply learning, accepting that maybe our learning process has been much longer than that of a conventional restaurant, which may sound favorable or unfavorable, depending on your point of view. For us this is a fact, and I believe that it is good to know who you are and what you have lived through, because this allows you to evolve and learn faster. Always remaining quiet allows you to listen better, above all when you want to become a professional learner, which is maybe what has unintentionally happened to us.

We reached a turning point for our kitchen and for the restaurant in general in 2016, because for the first time, we believed that we were really beginning to cook. We had finally acquired a thorough knowledge about the territory and our culture, obtained a significant depth of understanding regarding the seasonal cycles of central Chile where we are located; and at the same time we managed to capture those small seasonals windows as they open and close throughout the year. We also know what grows from the mountain range to the coast, and from north to south. We have learned at what time to harvest and how to do so, as well as the difference in an ingredient at the beginning, middle, and end of its season, even if that season is only one month long; although it might not seem so at first glance, the differences are astonishing, which allows us to achieve absolutely different results when using them in a kitchen like ours. We have also found out, or in other cases discovered, the properties of the ingredients: how they should be cooked, the advantages of eating them raw if necessary, and who ate them traditionally. A few years back we thought this was all the same, but in time we realized that they are three completely different properties. In the upcoming years, we will surely continue to learn and go into more depth regarding these approaches to the ingredients. But for the time being, we can say we have learned to expand the flavors of the ingredients that we use in a way that we had never imagined we could. In Chile there is no other record of this type of experimentation with endemic ingredients like these.

The same is true of the cooking methods, or simply processes, that have enabled us to achieve unusual and different results. Many of them do not pertain to our culture but can certainly complement it well, opening new areas for dealing with particular ingredients to achieve better and more subtle flavors.

"Point 0" is what we called the start of 2016, since it reminds us of when we just started ten years earlier. We know the way we cook will change a lot in the coming years,

Version 1: The Hunt of the Deer
→ 266

Version 2: The Hunt of the Deer (dessert version) → 267

simply because we have learned to expand the flavors of the preparations through the ingredients we use, most of which are found in wild settings, as well as how we prepare and cook them. We have applied much of this knowledge acquired through the years to traditional cooking methods or preparations of the Mapuche people, and some even to methods that we have always used, with excellent results.

For many of what we call "new" flavors, we must wait a long while to know how they evolve through time, even though they are made with ingredients that we have been using for ten years. We believe that these ways of thinking about an ingredient or a preparation can come from anywhere in the world, and in many cases can enrich, expand, and at the same time complement or even improve some that are familiar.

There is no doubt that our trip to Asia, and especially to Japan, has greatly affected the way we cook today. We cannot deny its influence. The way that we look at the ingredients, treat them, and care for them has turned us toward a different approach to food, which we didn't have before that journey.

GARUM

The first chef I heard speaking about garum in depth, many years ago, was Andrés Madrigal, whom to this day I greatly admire and consider to be a chef very much ahead of his time—or in this case very behind! Garum is probably one of the oldest preparations of all times. It has its origins with the ancient Romans, who achieved a preparation full of umami through the fermentation of anchovies and their offal.

That original garum was prepared with whole anchovies, in which the enzymes of the interiors and the protein of the fish were required to achieve a proper fermentation, a complex process. As a restaurant we do not want to replicate this preparation, but we do always seek the quality of umami in our food. This leads to many questions: Is it possible to shorten the fermentation period and still achieve significant results in terms of flavor? Is it possible to make a 100-percent-vegetable garum? (And when we speak of vegetable, I lean toward seaweed without a doubt. In Chile we have over 750 species and many of them have unique tastes and properties.) The same question occurs with wild fruits: Is it possible to make a garum with these alone? Or even with mushrooms?

OUR GARUM AND HOW WE MAKE IT

When we prepare our garums, we know it takes a year or more for them to become truly interesting. The most efficient and interesting preparation, and the one with which we are the most comfortable, is using anchovy offal as the base. We process the fish along with their interiors, but always removing the heads, until we have a fairly rustic paste, adding salt in a proportion of 20 percent, in respect to the weight of the paste. It is important to mix it well and spread out the salt so it can be in even contact with all of the mixture. This makes correct fermentation possible within a range of 59°F to 82°F (15°C to 28°C), avoiding the development of undesired bacteria during the process. The mixture must be stored with pressure applied to it, which helps the salt to be in absolute contact with each bit of the garum. We begin to stir it every week, and in many cases that has helped accelerate the fermentation process. The minimum suggested time is six months: the desired floral notes begin to appear at the third month, but they are accentuated even more from the sixth month onward. We then strain it overnight through a fine cloth to achieve a fine and shiny liquid.

We have carried out this process with Chilean sardines, Chilean silverside, and various shellfish, all with different results.

PIURE

The piure, a strange-looking sea creature, has an unappealingly strong flavor. Its skin, however, resembles citrus and we have used it successfully as a preparation, wrapping it in a puree made of mandarin zest and hazelnut-infused butter. The floral aroma of that preparation led us to prepare a garum with piure. We prepare it by crushing the piure completely; its guts make up practically 70 percent of the total weight, and we use this to obtain an excellent fermentation. We add 20 percent salt, mixing it well to ensure that the salt is well distributed throughout the mix. We store it between 59°F and 82°F (15°C and 28°C) wrapped in a cheesecloth (muslin) so it can ferment properly for six months, with excellent results. The part that takes us a long time is the filtering process: we strain it through a fine cloth with weight over it for about twelve hours, sometimes more, until a fine and shiny liquid is achieved.

WILD FRUITS

There is an astonishing amount of edible wild fruit in Chile. The largest concentration is found in the central region of the country through Araucanía, North Patagonia, South Patagonia, and down to Tierra del Fuego. It is almost incomprehensible that such a spectrum of flavors can exist in the middle of nowhere and in vastly different ecosystems; some grow on bushes, trees, or ground-covering plants, just to name a few; many grow during the winter, even under layers of snow, and enjoy very short summers. They have different textures due to their shape and size. Some of them grow during brief seasonal periods and some during longer ones. It is also worth mentioning that there are also wild fruits that grow in the Andes and that some were recently discovered in the Atacama Desert. During recent years we have asked ourselves why not make a miso made of wild fruit, as well as garum completely prepared with wild fruit. We have found a way to use these fruits in both preparations. That has helped us expand their possibilities by not just preparing and serving them in a traditional way.

To make a garum with wild fruit, we combine the fruit with pajarito yogurt whey and papaya scraps. Papaya contains papain, a rich enzyme, and together with the whey and the wild fruit it allows a fermentation process that is similar to traditional garum within six months.

Quail's Nest with Autumn Mushrooms → 229

Rockfish, Sea Lettuce, and Violet Garum → 233

Pâté Berlín → 227

Leaves are pleaced on different volumes as wind would!

Murra miso and olive oil emulsion.

First Prune leaves of Spring in the city

on umeboshi salmuera

- Brushed on Murra miso

Jibia: smoke on tepú and plancha (Caramelized)
- Chilean mandarin skin (unripe)
- 1 leave of roe

CUTTING WILD MUSHROOMS

AGING MUSHROOMS AT 11,500 FEET

Pine mushrooms (both *Suillus luteus* and *Suillus granulatus*) have a fairly long season along the central coast of Chile, thanks to the abundance of pine forests, even in the rocky areas. There is a great tradition of mushroom gathering throughout Chile. The Mapuche people use them not only as food but also as medicine, and gather and barter with them in their communities. Traditionally the gatherers take the skin off the caps, cut and remove the stems, smoke the mushrooms over native wood, and then dehydrate them in the sun. When the mushrooms are rehydrated, they take on a soft and meaty texture along with the smoked flavor.

I had the opportunity to meet some people who live in the mountains and to learn about their life in the Andes, as well as about the way they eat. That gave me an idea! At the end of the summer, before the start of the mushroom-gathering season in the woods along the coast, we could hang the mushrooms at an altitude of 11,500 feet (3,500 meters) and leave them there for the winter, at a temperature between 0°F and 10°F (–12°C and –18°C) with practically zero humidity and exposed to cold winds. I thought that these conditions might create a unique flavor. The idea was to keep them in the open air as if they were clothes hung out to dry until the end of the winter, and finally to slice them as if they were high-quality ham.

MUSHROOM GARUM

In the case of preparing garum with mushrooms, we simply crush them with 22 percent salt in respect to the weight of the mushroom paste. Because the enzymatic activity is lower than that of fish offal, we use pajarito yogurt whey in a proportion of 5 percent to the total weight of the paste. We store it between 59°F and 82°F (15°C and 28°C), with a weight on top of the mixture, covered with a cheesecloth (muslin) so that it can breathe and ferment properly. We stir it every two weeks. The storage period is no less than eight months to achieve excellent results; any less than that and the strained liquid is very aqueous and lacking in complexity. We prepare this mushroom garum in two ways, with and without koji, and both results are truly delicious and different in flavor to each other, since the one with koji remains very floral and the one without koji tastes very earthy.

We use loyos (*Boletus loyo*) often in preparations at the restaurant, and we make use of the trimmings to prepare mushroom garums. The other species that we use is the pine mushroom (*Suillus luteus* and *Suillus granulatus*), which we gather in large amounts to cover the demand in the restaurant.

DEHYDRATED AND SMOKED

Fall and spring are the seasons when the greatest number of mushrooms appear throughout all the regions of Chile. In the central region, just an hour away from the restaurant, mushrooms grow in massive numbers in coastal forests located on top of cliffs. We have foraged up to 220 pounds (100 kilos) of the mushrooms by ourselves, and we treat them the same way we treat many algae: through dehydration and smoking. We store and use them over the rest of the year as essential ingredients in many broths, infusions, and other types of preparations.

ICE CREAM: REPLACING SUGAR WITH UMAMI

Ice cream has been an obsession at Boragó: we are always searching for the perfect texture and an interesting flavor. Interesting flavors, though, do not always include sugar. We try to steer clear of sugar anyway, which is why umami seems to be an excellent alternative. During the year, we make ice creams based on different types of mushrooms and we are able to reduce the sugar content almost to zero thanks to the mushrooms' starch content. This gives us not only a satisfying flavor but also a pleasant texture.

In the restaurant, everything on the menu is created in accordance with our kitchen equipment. When a guest orders ice cream, the spinning begins exactly when the dinner service starts. Absolutely everything, even the containers, is planned with this procedure in mind for one simple reason: I am an ice-cream lover and believe there is nothing more delicious than ice cream fresh out of the machine. It is worth mentioning that our ice-cream recipes are not created for the Pacojet, but rather for the ice-cream machine; otherwise they wouldn't work correctly. The machine we use is a simple cylinder with cooling blades and a capacity of 5 quarts (5 liters). This means that the pasteurization process with all types of milk is fully handcrafted.

Even when we use other flavors, to strengthen the pleasant sensation of ice cream we add mushroom extract in small proportions, as well as algae, which in many cases are deodorized and serve as natural thickeners. The mixture of these two elements allows us to create ice cream with a smooth texture that is solid, but melts quickly in the mouth. However, our ice creams do not store well.

HANGING OVER THE EMBERS

In April 2016, our summer ended abruptly and the weather immediately turned cold. There was a lot of rainfall and the mountains surrounding Santiago were quickly

Mushrooms aging at 11,500 feet (3500m) in the Andes

covered in snow. After a few days, the forests in central Chile turned from dry to intensely green and the mushrooms began growing really fast. We gathered so many mushrooms that we couldn't carry them all. We had to think of ways to use the tremendous amount we had gathered, especially since it seemed that the season would be long. We started studying to see if any other cultures suspended mushrooms over hot embers to roast them. We didn't find any, so we created our own hanging rack, similar to a baby's crib mobile, from which we hung mushrooms over low embers for hours. While they were roasting, we moisturized them with mushroom mojo. After four to five hours, depending on the size of the mushroom, they developed a soft and firm texture. The flavor became concentrated but you could also taste the embers. We burn only kirinka wood in this process, which we continue to follow. Once we remove the mushrooms from the embers, we slice them with a sharp knife and use them in different preparations.

ALGAE-COVERED VERSION

Because these mushrooms grow on cliffs close to the sea, they are affected by the salt air. I thought that we could achieve a similar effect with aged algae, so we wrapped the mushrooms in algae and smoked them on a rack over low embers for four to five hours. Every hour, we moistened them on all sides with mushroom mojo. When sliced, the texture of these mushrooms is very smooth and the flavor is permeated by the sea. We generally use this in other rock plant–based preparations.

Mushrooms hanging over the embers

Mushroom wrapped in aged algae hanging over the embers

Chupe of Quintay Mushrooms Left Hanging in the Mountain Until the End of Winter → 241

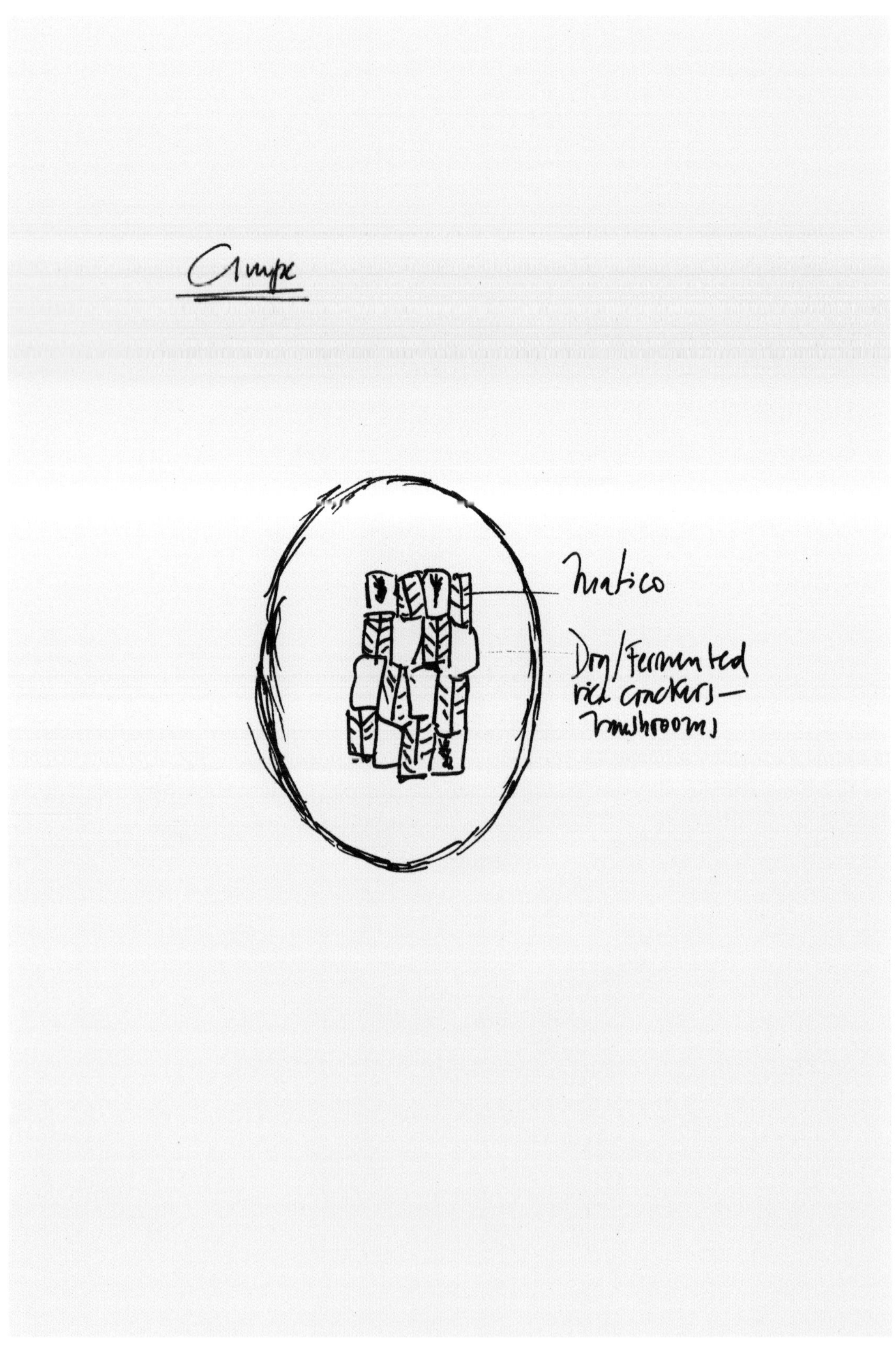

End of Autumn Quintay Mushrooms Chupe → 236

Pine Mushrooms Wrapped in Sea Lettuce → 240

Mushrooms from Early Autumn → 252

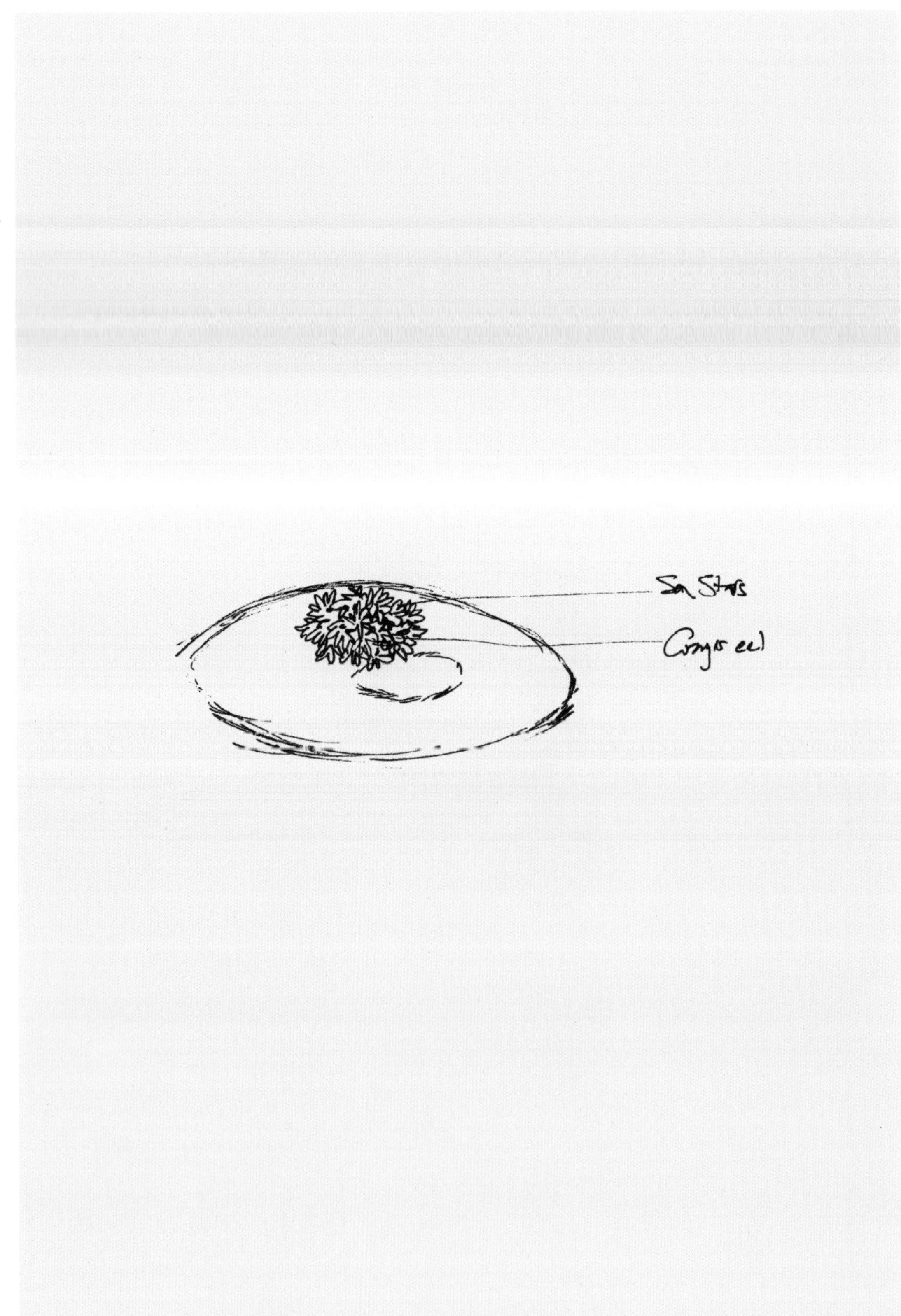

Caramelized Pink Cusk-Eel and Sea Stars → 237

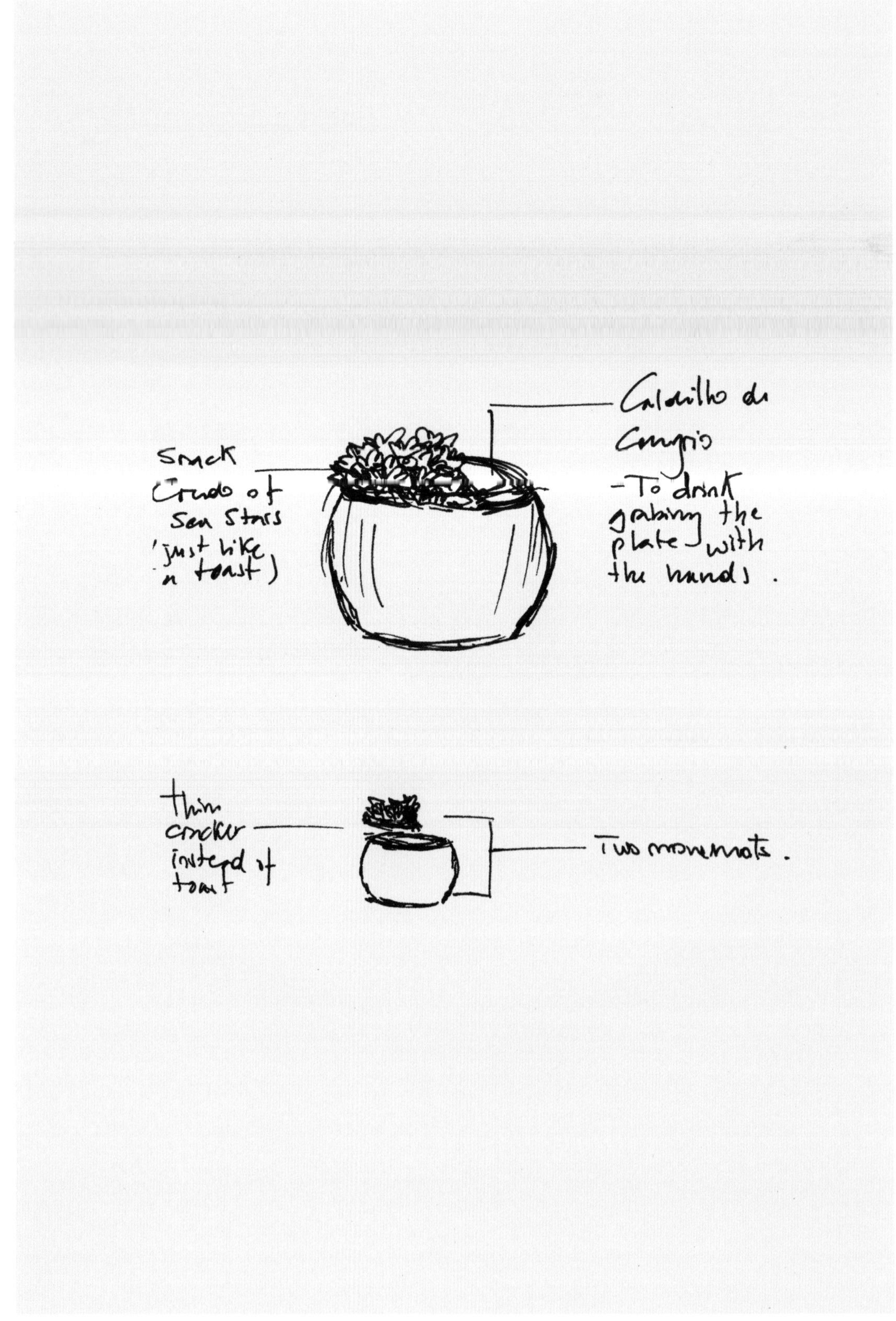

Version 2: Flowers Crudo and Cold Fermented Conger-Eel Caldillo → 238

Version 1: Flowers Crudo and Cold Conger-Eel Caldillo → 237

Sea Urchins from Quintay with Black Luga, Chagual, and Vegetable Milk → 240

PAJARITO

FERMENTATION, THEREFORE ANAEROBIC OR NOT ANAEROBIC?

Pajarito yogurt, or kefir, as it is most known worldwide, translates as "little bird" yogurt. It is an important tradition in Chile despite the fact that it comes from the Middle East. Pajarito yogurt is prepared in the countryside everywhere, and without a doubt represents one of the most rustic flavors of our culture. Normally it is mixed with wild spring or summer fruit jams. It would be practically impossible to buy since the tradition is to give it as a gift to another person or family—which makes sense since pajarito reproduces quickly, enabling it to ferment in ever increasing quantities (helpful in a restaurant but troublesome at home). The texture of pajarito yogurt is viscous, due to the fermentation, but also thin. It has an acid taste and an almost fizzy quality, as if it were a sparkling wine.

We have used pajarito yogurt since the restaurant started, but we did not get good results easily in the beginning. Fortunately, over the years we have come to understand how the combination of bacteria and yeast like to be treated, and to the extent that we managed to humor them and make them feel comfortable, we began to achieve good results. Pajarito is a mix of pathogen bacteria (*Lactobacillus acidophilus*) with yeast (*Kluyveromyces marxianus*), transforming it into a natural and beneficial food. The bacteria need milk's lactose to feed on and to produce the yogurt; they are fairly resistant to temperature, and can ferment milk in different environments without problems. They reproduce at a great speed, and the higher the quantity of pajaritos, the faster the fermentation. There are certain variations in the final result, depending on how the fermentation process is done. Different results can be achieved when they are left to stand in milk, principally different intensities of taste, and this varies with the number of days of fermentation. After one day, the yogurt has a mild taste with little consistency; after two days, a little more consistency, an acid taste, and the yogurt does not yet separate from the whey; on the third day the flavor is even more intense and the yogurt begins to separate naturally from the whey; now the yogurt can be carefully removed from the surface, leaving the whey in the bottom. Then the yogurt has to be passed through a sieve, stirring with a spoon until the entire mix has been squeezed through. The result will be a yogurt that is slightly liquid but thick at the same time.

Naturally, temperature affects the speed of fermentation as well. The temperatures that we maintain fluctuate between 68°F and no higher than 95°F (20°C and 35°C). It is always recommended to use a plastic sieve since pajarito reacts to metal; aluminum mesh is especially to be avoided. The types of milk used, of course, affect the final result. We have experimented with milk from various animals, some popular in Chile such as donkeys, Chilota sheep, goats, and of course cows, having different results with all the milks

It is important to always bear in mind that the ideal way to ferment yogurt with pajarito is to avoid moving it at all, so that it can generate exopolysaccharide links; these are achieved only when at absolute rest. At the same time pH plays an important role in achieving thickness, taking into account that this is much more acidic than conventional yogurt. We have tried raising the pH to 4.6 with excellent results. In order to obtain an outstanding result, the yogurt must be strained after fermentation. There are also two important results to keep in mind after fermenting in an hermetic way, or just covering the container on top with a cheesecloth (muslin), which enhances the yogurt with less acidic flavor. Once they have been used several times it is always recommended to wash the pajaritos and remove the milk residue, because they can reduce the life and quality of the pajarito yogurt.

Pajaritos can be kept at 30°F (4°C) for fourteen days with no problems.

Greek yogurt, with its smooth, creamy texture, and full-bodied taste, has always seemed exceptional to us. We have managed to imitate its texture, filtering pajarito yogurt through a cheesecloth for five hours at 30°F (4°C). After the straining, we remove the yogurt and beat it manually for approximately one minute to oxygenate and mix it well, until a single consistency is achieved. (Yogurts with different intensities of fermentation can be achieved by utilizing this process, whether or not exopolysaccharide links have formed.) What is interesting is that the creamy consistency and smooth taste of Greek yogurt can be achieved with only one day of standing.

One of the fascinating characteristics of pajaritos is that they can be dehydrated. They must be left at room temperature until they are crystallized and completely dry. This process often takes from three to five days, depending on the humidity of the enviroment and the circulating air. Then they can be kept frozen or dry for up to three months.

It was important for us to be able to understand how pajarito yogurt works, since it gave us the possibility to create other preparations that we have not seen elsewhere, and it also helped us to expand the flavors that we are used to.

Pajarito as a condiment

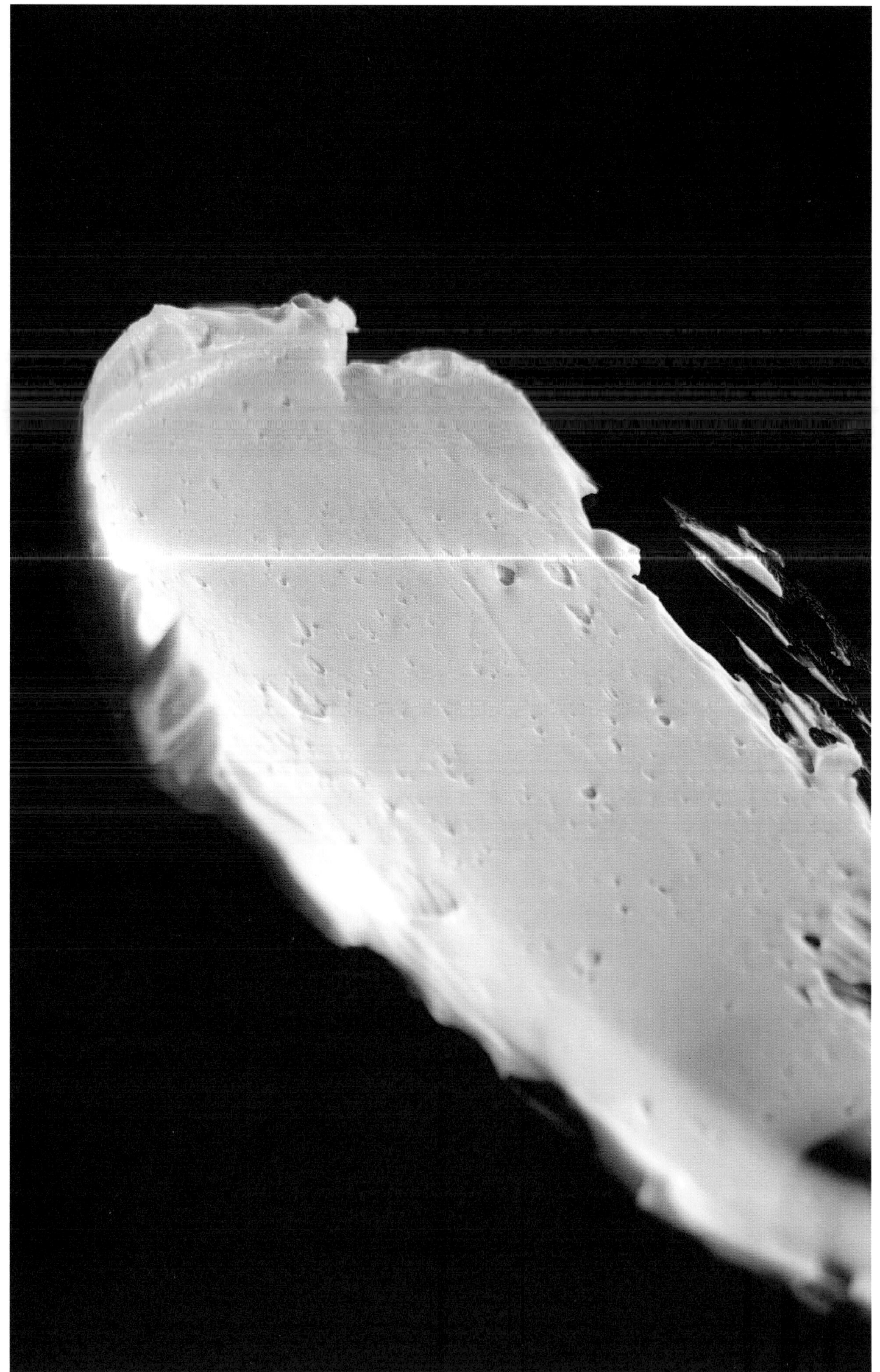

Filtered pajarito yogurt

OTHER POSSIBILITIES

FOOLING THE PAJARITO YOGURT

We spent a lot of time thinking about other things we could do with pajaritos, but the fact that they need lactose to feed and thus be able to produce yogurt was limiting. In the kitchen, we often prepare vegetable milks with different seeds or nuts, and these work exceptionally well for us, not only in desserts but also with wild plants, halophytes or meats, and fish. Some years ago, we tried to find a way to fool the pajaritos, making them believe they were standing in milk when they were not, in order to be able to produce 100-percent-vegetable pajarito yogurt. The way that has worked best for us so far has been to measure the quantity of lactose that the pajaritos consume at certain temperatures. We then managed to give them the quantity of lactose—including almond milk and sunflower milk, among others—necessary for them to ferment. We were able to obtain high-quality lactose, taken from organic milk. What occurred was a much slower fermentation process, although the result is certainly good, above all with nut milks: the yogurt is acid, but with a spectacular vegetable taste. It can even be strained the same way we strain regular pajarito yogurt, achieving the same creaminess as Greek yogurt.

PAJARITO CREAM

In some of my trips to France, I had the opportunity to taste high-quality crème fraîche, and I thought it was delicious. We attempted to achieve something similar with pajaritos. Initially we fermented at room temperature during the summer with a proportion of 20 percent pajarito yogurt with respect to the cream: the result was good. But better still, and most surprising, is what we have called pajarito cream, where the combination of the umami flavor, acidity, and texture is exceptional. We make it by using the same 20 percent of pajarito yogurt, but we process 1 quart (1 liter) in a yogurt maker that does not go beyond 95°F (35°C) for seven hours. The result is truly amazing, with a spectacular quantity of umami. It is important to bear in mind that a high-quality and hopefully artisanal cream should be used for this preparation in order to achieve complex and floral flavors.

WHEY FROM PAJARITO YOGURT
AND HOW WE USE IT YEARS LATER

One of the reasons why we did not use pajarito yogurt whey for several years was the fact that the aroma is not very appetizing. But when we began to strain the yogurt in order to achieve the texture of Greek yogurt, we obviously had a significant quantity of whey for which we had to find a use. Often necessity is the mother of creativity—and this case was no exception. This whey is rich in proteins, so it is something that one would want to drink every day for its benefits. We noticed that the viscosity—that is, the thickness and how elastic this liquid could appear—varied a lot according to the temperature. We began to cold-infuse the whey for several days with different tree leaves and achieved some unique floral flavors, such as with avocado leaves, fig leaves, eucalyptus leaves, and different seaweeds, among others.

AS DRY SEASONING

At one point we had a large production of pajaritos, since if conditions are favorable they reproduce quickly, and we reached a point where we did not know what to do with them; so we began to use them as an acid seasoning. The result was excellent, like a complex wine whose flavor was capable of evolving over a short time. Exactly the same thing could happen in a preparation: the changes started to appear after a day. We dehydrate the pajaritos at 113°F (45°C) until they are crunchy.

In recipes we have mixed the dried pajaritos with vegetables, and the texture and taste surprise us, since the pajaritos pop in the mouth as if they were caviar. Along the same lines, we use them in infusions with wild plants as digestives.

Rose-of-the-Year Cuchuflí → 222

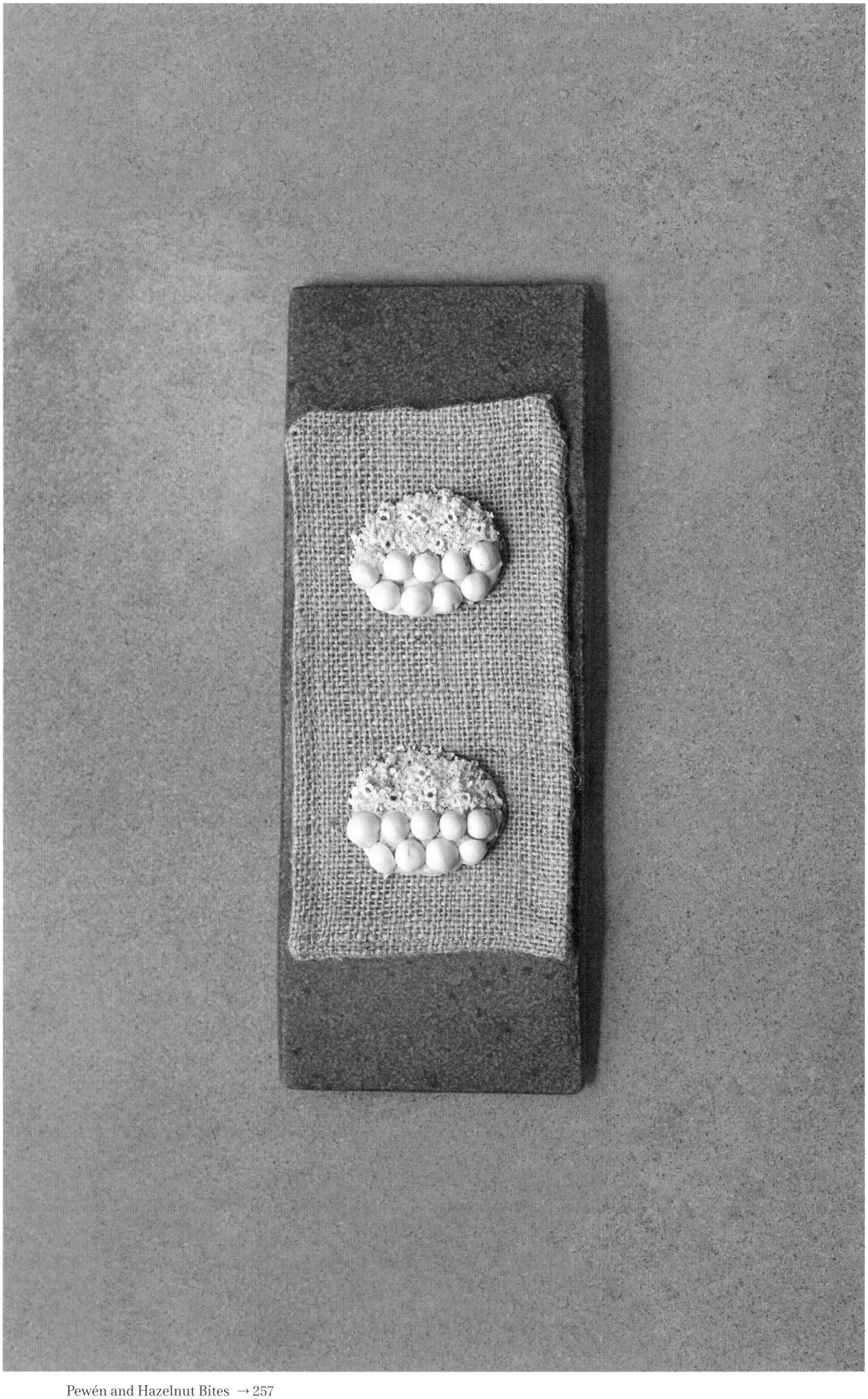

Pewén and Hazelnut Bites → 257

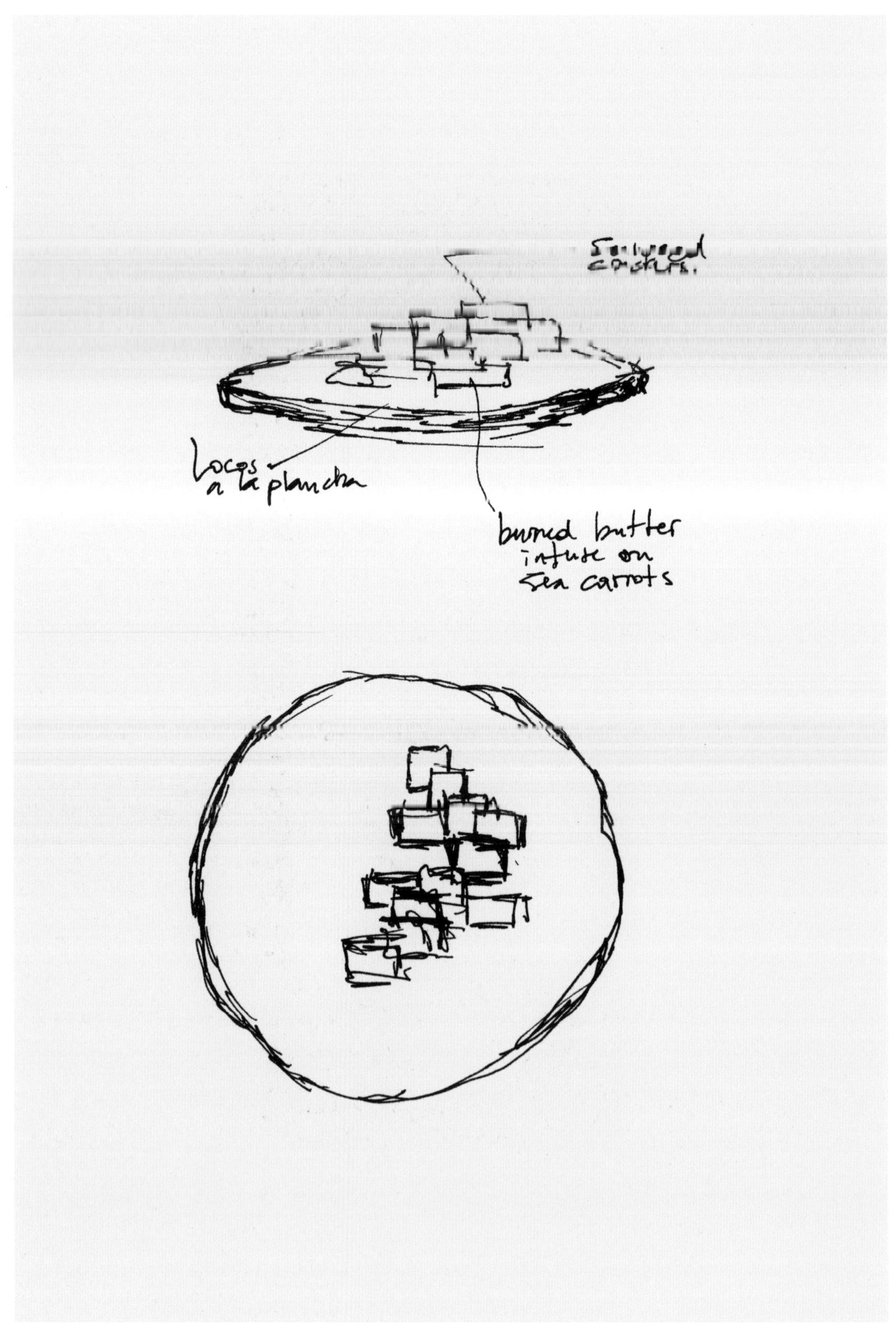

Slightly Caramelized Locos from Antofagasta with Kolof and Sea Carrots → 239

LAMB ROASTED ON THE CROSS

AS THEY DO IT IN PATAGONIA . . . AND OUR OWN WAY

Patagonian lamb has a strong flavor, even in comparison with other lamb around the world. This is principally due to the nature of the pasture in that area. The meat of animals that are raised close to the coast of Patagonia, called coastal lambs, has a pronounced saline taste, different from those that are raised in land.

Roasting a lamb on a metal cross is an important tradition in Patagonia; it originated with the gauchos, the local shepherds. While it may seem a simple, even primitive, way of cooking, it requires great skill to achieve an excellent result. The lamb for this technique usually weighs 29 to 31 pounds (13 to 14 kilos) and the procedure consists of tying the lamb's legs to a metal rack in the form of a cross with its head down. Then a fire is built with native wood, usually tepa, tepú, or luma—these woods contain essential oils with a singular aroma, which begins to come out when the fire is started and gives the animal a particular smoked flavor. The rack holding the lamb is positioned perpendicular to the embers at approximately 90 degrees. As the burning wood turns to embers, the lamb is slowly moved closer to the fire in order to obtain a good caramelization of the skin, leaving the meat juicy inside. During the cooking, the lamb is turned over in order to roast all four sides. At the end of the cooking process, just before cutting it up, the lamb is positioned very close to the embers. This process takes approximately eight hours.

A L'INVERSE FOR A BETTER SERVICE

The traditional method of cooking lamb isn't easily adapted to the serving requirements of a restaurant like ours. Above all, and taking into account that there is no turning back, it is important to calculate the speed with which we cook the animal; otherwise it could be over- or undercooked. We decided to get 20-pound (9-kilo) Patagonian lambs; this is not a typical size, but it is the perfect size for us and allows us to control the fire according to the dinner service and its dynamics. The fat of an animal of this weight is different than that of a larger one; proportionally there is less of it, and it doesn't have the strong flavor of a bigger lamb.

We have developed our own way of roasting lamb on a metal cross, which we call "à l'inverse." It is based on our needs, considering how the kitchen works and the time when people are scheduled arrive in the dining room. The name we give it reflects the fact that it is the opposite of the traditional method: We position the lamb with its neck up on the rack, and we start roasting it practically on top of the embers. Then we gradually move it away until we reach the 90-degree angle at the end, cooking it on only one side and keeping it completely raw on the back until the very end. Just before meal service, we turn it over 180 degrees and expose it to an aggressive fire, which we decrease gradually towards the end of the meal service. The final result is extremely juicy, and on the skin side it is completely caramelized.

It is important to tie the lamb firmly to the cross, placing the neck toward the upper part of it. We do this on a cutting board with the animal's ribs upward, and we break the soft tissue of the legs to tie them as close as possible to the cross, so they are practically parallel to the cross. We then make small transverse cuts in the muscles between the shoulders and the neck on each side, which loosen them enough to be able to press firmly on both shoulders and tie the upper part as evenly as possible. When we do this, we press the shoulders down until we hear the ribs separate. This does not mean that the ribs have broken; they should remain intact. We also remove some excess fat from the legs. We use wire to tie each limb as far away from the other as possible, tightening it as much as possible. This produces a completely even caramelization, and at the same time ensures that the lamb will not loosen. We tie the neck and three consecutive points in the spine, ensuring its firmness during cooking, as with the arms and legs.

The lamb roasts for approximately 10 uninterrupted hours. We cut the meat directly onto the plate. Each customer receives a different cut of the lamb, depending on the time they arrived at the restaurant.

USING CHILEAN ESPINO EMBERS

The preparation for roasting lamb over the embers begins with making our sauce, or mojo as we call it. This prevents it from dehydrating during the prolonged cooking, as well as providing it with flavor and a light seasoning.

We apply the sauce throughout the cooking time, especially on the ribs, legs and the raw back. We have the amazing luck that there are many wild pepper trees and mandarin orange trees in the area around the restaurant. So we prepare a bunch of leaves from both trees to use to apply the sauce, providing an incredible aroma to the lamb as it gets glazed with the sauce during the cooking.

For the fire, we always use Chilean espino, a tree with an incredible aroma and embers that emit excellent heat. At the start, the embers must be completely red hot. Then we spread out a thin bed of burned-down espino embers, which are capable of radiating heat evenly over the entire animal.

The cross we use is made of iron and has grooves that allow it to be adjusted to several different cooking positions. The first position is very close to the embers. At the beginning, and above all during the first two hours, it is important to keep the animal hydrated, which we do by hitting it with the bunch of leaves dipped in the sauce. (At the beginning of autumn there is not much wind where we cook, but at the end of autumn there is a fair amount, and the outdoor temperature remains around 50°F to 55°F [10°C to 12°C]. Our roasting technique means that during cooking, the lamb's back remains raw. To prevent the wind from dehydrating it, we melt the fat that we removed initially and brush it over the back during the roasting process.) Approximately every three hours, we move the cross farther away from the embers until the 90-degree position is reached, constantly feeding the embers, but always with the idea of a gentle and even heat. When we do it this way, the cooking is centered from the hips to the neck, since at this point the legs are caramelized only on the front and are raw on the back.

CUTTING UP THE ANIMAL DURING SERVICE

The service at the restaurant begins at 7:00 p.m., and this is the precise time when we must have red-hot embers ready to be added to the other embers, in order to create an aggressive heat. At this moment we turn over the rack, rotating it completely, and we expose the raw part to the intense heat of the embers at a 90-degree angle. The legs at this point require another two hours of cooking, since they are thick and bad conductors of heat, due to the large amount of meat on them. Despite the fact that they are already caramelized, the timing coincides perfectly with the timing of the meal service, since the legs will be the last parts of the animal to be served. We cut the animal in clean symmetric cuts, treating it almost exactly the same as fish. We even use a long, thin classic Japanese filleting knife, which allows us to cut deeply and precisely into the caramelized skin.

The first part that is ready is the ribs, which do not have much meat since they are from a small animal, but they do have caramelized skin with a good flavor and crunchiness. We distribute them as the base of each portion, and we then cut the back, removing the steaks, then the upper legs and shoulders. Before we reach the bottom legs we cut the neck, which does not have much meat but produces a high-quality cut with tender meat.

SOME INTERESTING VARIATIONS

We are currently attempting some interesting variations regarding flavor, such as maturing the lamb in beeswax. We have also tried wrapping the lamb in various types of algae, achieving a significant concentration of amino acids, which besides giving it marine and saline notes, produces a spectacular flavor. We do this by first hanging the lamb for three days wrapped in seaweed. We then use the same technique to roast it over the embers, all the while wrapped in algae, with the difference being that because the animal now contains less moisture, it requires only eight hours of cooking.

Mojo

Hydrating the lamb with mojo

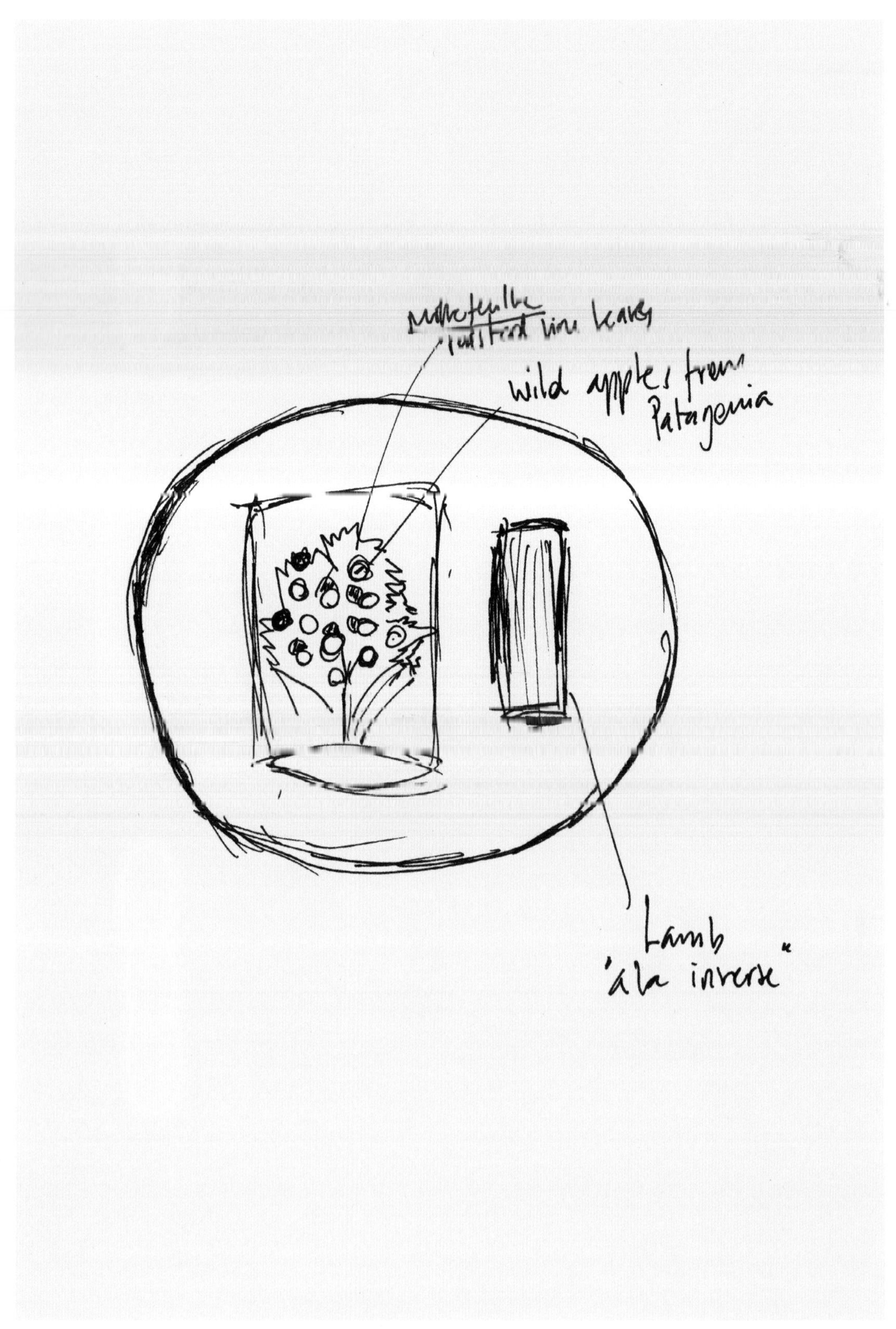

Mille-feuille of Vine Leaves, Wild Apples, and Magellan Lamb Cooked à l'Inverse → 269

Piures and Mandarin Skin Bonbons → 251

MAN DOES NOT LIVE ON BLACK GARLIC ALONE

PERHAPS ON BLACK VEGETABLES

THE PROCESS FOR BLACK GARLIC

Today black garlic has become popular in restaurants around the world, not only because of the texture and flavor that can be obtained through fermentation, but also because of the dramatic appearance. So we started to do it ourselves with Chiloé garlic that is bigger, more floral, and less intense than common garlic. We created a good black garlic, but at the same time we asked ourselves what would happen if we found a way to obtain a similar result with other vegetables.

OTHER BLACK VEGETABLES

So we started to experiment with other vegetables, such as carrots, beets (beetroots), Jerusalem artichokes, and quince, among others—some even develop a meat or chocolate aroma. To achieve this, we use plastic wrap (clingfilm) to wrap the vegetable along with a small amount of seawater, and then wrap that in aluminum foil. We store it for three months at 130°F (55°C) to let it ferment. It is important to let it cool before using it.

This can be done with any vegetable. Without a doubt, this preparation helps us expand the possibilities in terms of flavors—they possess a staggering complexity that we hadn't imagined before.

Black Flower →248

PLANTS OF THE ATACAMA DESERT
AND HOW TO TREAT THEM

HOW TO GET RID OF THE BITTERNESS

The edible wild plants of the Atacama Desert have gastronomic properties that have opened a new window into dishes, preparations, and elaborations. From the first time we tried these plants, we noticed that they possess certain indescribable aromas that often have the complexity of a perfume. However, they all share one feature: they are very bitter. This is probably because of the extreme conditions in which they grow—this is an ecosystem with zero percent humidity and extreme temperature variations from dusk until dawn. Using bitter flavors in food is fantastic, but at a certain point it becomes a limitation. We started putting effort into getting rid of the bitterness while preserving the aroma and, in many cases, the texture too. During one of my trips to Japan I learned about a brilliant way to treat tea leaves that eliminates the bitterness. We started doing something similar here, and it works perfectly with nearly all the plants of the Atacama Desert.

We take the plants and steam them at 140°F (60°C) for one hour, then dehydrate them for 48 hours at the same temperature. Then, when we are using them to cook, we finally infuse them for one minute, whether it is to use the infusion to infuse another ingredient or to make soups or infusions of the plant by itself. This way, we can obtain the unique aroma of these plants while avoiding the bitterness completely.

COLORS AND SOME RESULTS IN CERTAIN TYPES OF MILK

We have noticed that certain plants contain substances that, when mixed with different types of milk, like donkey, goat, or sheep's milk, can alter its structure and color; for example there is the case of goat's milk and copa copa, which turns the milk blue and gives it an exceptional bittersweet flavor.

Parfait of Bitter Plants → 224

Rica Rica Cold Cream, Cachiyuyo, and Cucumber Salad → 223

Llama Crudo → 221

OUR OWN MERKÉN

MERKÉN ELABORATION PROCESS

Merkén is a preservation process and a seasoning that has been used by the Mapuche people for thousands of years. It has a spectacular flavor, which is spicy, salty, and smoked. It is said that the main ingredient of Chilean cuisine is smoke, and the process for making merkén may explain that. The Mapuche communities use a similar process with many other different ingredients. The process itself is related to the *rukas*—the traditional Mapuche huts, where a fire of native woods would burn in the center. These fireplaces were natural and necessary heaters in the south of Chile, with its cold, long winters, short summers, and abundant rain. It's this kind of fireplace that allows for the *thapi* (pimento or red bell peppers) to be suspended for six months in a cloud of smoke. The result is an intense smoking process that ends up drying the pulp of the pepper completely, almost as if it were jerky. This is then mashed with stones, alongside an array of various seeds and aromatic herbs, until it forms a powder of smoky flavor with intense aromas of native woods—that's merkén. The firewoods used in the process are those usually found in the forests of the region, especially tepú, lenga, tepa, and luma.

Another version of Merkén exists, with a similar process; the difference being that the entire thapi pepper is boiled for about 40 minutes until it's soft, in a ratio of 1 quart (1 liter) of water for every 5 peppers. They are then drained and mashed coarsely until it becomes a dry paste, which is then preserved. During the preservation process, a light fermentation will occur, producing a slightly fizzy sensation in the mouth. The paste that is mashed by hand produces a better fermentation.

DIFFERENT KINDS OF MERKÉN

In the Chilean tradition, only one kind of merkén exists. At the restaurant, we always wondered why we couldn't just make merkén out of anything, so as to end up with twenty or thirty kinds of merkén. So that's what we started to do. I mean seaweed, mushrooms, wild stems like nalca, wild berries, halophytes, herbs, fish, meat, wood, and so on. We achieved excellent results, which work as a base on top of which to increase the flavor of many preparations—as is the case with sea flavors, woodland flavors, and many others.

Shoe Mussels from Valdivia with Rock Green Sauce → 258

UTILIZING KOMBUCHA

Kombucha is a delicious and fermented healthy drink. The ways we use it at Boragó are many: some are for fizzy refreshments and for others we treat the bacteria as if it were meat, since its texture is similar to a squid. When we decided to use it in this way, we had to start reproducing the culture rapidly, which takes up a lot of space. But this also allowed us to understand the most efficient way to do it. In order to produce kombucha, we needed a starter; the mother is an infusion of rose of the year at 10 percent sugar. From here, two ways of reproducing it exist: the first consists of mixing 50 percent kombucha that has already been fermented with 50 percent of a new base and then adding 10 percent of the overall liquid weight in sugar. By combining both liquids and adding the sugar, a new mother will begin to grow. While this process is somewhat slower, it's nonetheless the most efficient when it comes to producing the largest volumen of kombucha mother. The second way, and probably the fastest, is to wait on a batch with a mature mother, which, in the span of about a week—most probably every three days, depending on room temperature—will start shedding peels of kombucha mother. These husks are what we then remove and place in a different container—also at 10 percent sugar—so it may again reproduce and grow quickly. In our case, we have to plan several months ahead before serving this preparation.

ATACAMA DESERT PLANTS

Kombucha works exceptionally well with all plants from the Atacama Desert, becoming very flowery. This is particularly so with rose of the year, which is a phenomenon that appears when the desert sprouts due to spring rain. The rose of the year harvest happens once a year over a small window of time in a very specific geography. Through our relationship with Paty, one of our foragers from the north of Chile, we are able to source a sustainable amount of it, revitalizing an ingredient that no one else had been using.

Ice Brûlée of Plants → 224

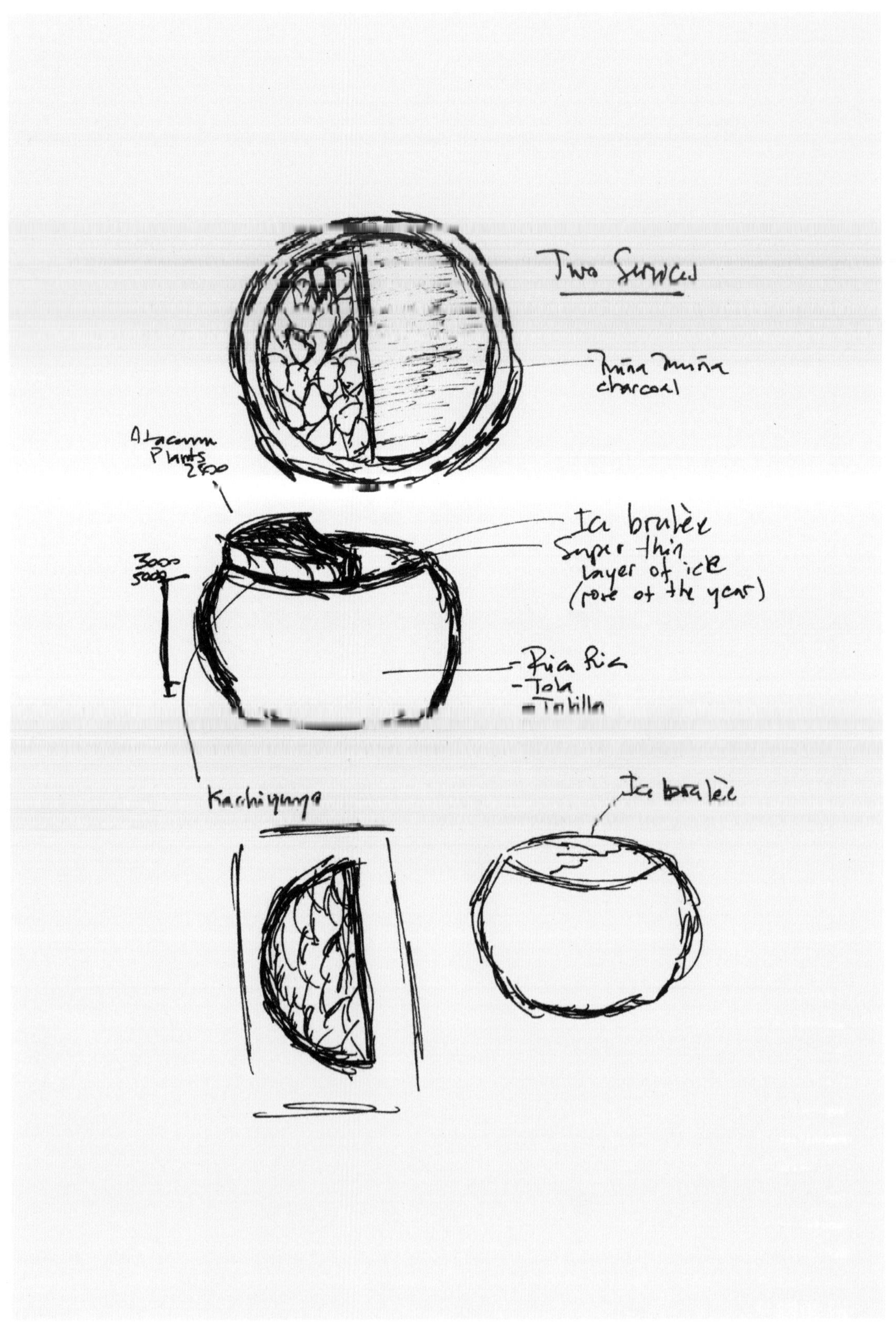

Ice Brûlée of Plants and Rose-of-the-Year Ice Cream Sandwich → 224

CHEESE VEGETABLES

Vegetables carry a wide array of possibilities, and you can always opt to use organic or biodynamic vegetables. In Chile's case, we're talking about a country where life has become much more expensive, particularly during the past few years. So choosing well is not necessarily about the more expensive choice—I'm talking about organic markets, where you have the chance to meet the farmers and agriculturists who work their land in the most natural possible way. At Boragó, we are lucky enough to be able to grow our own vegetables, and to choose and organize them according to our needs. To envision the taste of cheese in a vegetable as a result of natural fermentation might seem too complex, or pretentious—but the truth is that the result is simple enough to achieve, and it provides an almost molten texture that is also very aromatic. Finding a way to treat vegetables like true cheese changed the way we cooked, while at the same time broadened our tastes. What at first looked impossible became something quite simple.

PROTEOLYSIS IN CARROTS

We figured we would begin with the most difficult vegetable, so that the rest would seem simple. Thus, we started with the carrot.

At first we couldn't achieve consistent results—especially once we factored in the restaurant's service, where volumes are relevant. We reached proteolysis—when proteins break down into smaller polypeptides or amino acids—in carrots in three weeks, after which we managed to achieve consistency by controlling absolutely every variable, and so reduced the time to one and a half days. With this process, the inside of a carrot becomes almost as floral and meltingly soft as a Camembert. The main concern is managing to control the process before inoculation, as well as the fermentation process and then the storage. For this, it's necessary to scald each piece of carrot for 40 seconds and then leave it to cool to room temperature. Then it will be time to infect it with *Penicillium candidum*. Fermentation takes place between 54°F and 56°F (11°C and 12°C) at 13 percent humidity—never warmer. If the temperature should ever fall below that, the fermentation process will be considerably slower.

INFUSIONS OF CHEESE VEGETABLES

We also use cheese vegetables to fortify stocks and broths through a twenty-four-hour cold infusion at 39°F (4°C). They can be used as viscous but intensely flavored vegetable liquids. We determined their use depending on their thickness while cold.

Cheese Carrot Chilenito and Sea Strawberries → 227

Chilean Espino Coulant → 249

UMEBOSHI

The first time I was in Brazil, I was fascinated by the way they treated figs, because something that seems so essential to us in Chile was practically impossible there: to gather a ripe fig from a tree. In Brazil, because of the extreme heat they experience during summer, they explained to me that as soon as a fig ripens, it falls from the tree and rots on the ground. Therefore the tradition is to harvest them green and cook them completely unripe in sugary water to create a sort of green fig syrup. This preparation caught my attention.

Umeboshi is a Japanese preparation that we have always found delicious. Traditionally it's prepared with unripe plums. It's not just the aroma of umeboshi that's so unique, but also its texture, which reminds me of *mote con huesillo*—a typical Chilean dessert. In the restaurant, we prepare it with an endless variety of different fruits, and we do so in two ways: one takes fifty days, the other six months. The first is much more sour, but with a soft texture, while the second is much more floral. The only fruits we don't ever use are plums, since throughout the year we find other unripe fruits in places we probably won't visit again for a long time, so we make the best of them.

For instance, we take figs and prepare them in two ways. The first one involves fermentation inside a jar, using 3⅓ pounds (1.5 kilos) of fruit and 30 percent sea salt—alternating fruit and salt until the jar is filled. We then apply pressure to the surface and seal it. We let it rest for twenty days, and in that time you can see how the liquid is drained from the fruit, to the point that the fruit is almost covered with its own brine. Once twenty days have passed, we remove the fruit and allow it to dry in the sun for two days, after which we return it to the jar, cover in brine again, and let it rest for thirty more days before it is ready to be used. This is a more traditional way of making umeboshi, except we do it with figs instead of plums.

The second method is simple but gives a different result. This one takes six months and the umeboshi becomes much more floral, with a firmer texture and, in the case of the figs, much less rugged skinned. It entails packing the figs in completely green fig leaves with 8 percent salt proportionate to the weight of the fruit. It's important that the salt is uniformly spread over the figs. The figs are vacuum-packed; if for any reason the package loses some of its pressure during storage, it must be vacuum-packaged again. The longer the fermenting stage, the stronger the aroma. No less than six months is my recommendation. The result of this method reminds me of that unripe fig preparation from Brazil, but without the sweetness.

Valdivian Salad with Cenizo, Queule, and Chilean Alive Huepos → 264

RESCOLDO

Rescoldo is an ancient cooking method that has been used by the Mapuche people for thousands of years. Its origin lies in the cold weather and wind typical of the area where most of the communities are located. The climate made it more effective to cook on the ground. Rescoldo cooking consists of using completely consumed native wood embers set on sand. Normally the cooking takes place the day after the embers are prepared. The more embers there are, the better the results, because the main feature of this method is that whatever is cooked undergoes nixtamalization—cooking in an alkaline environment, in this case in the embers. One of the more traditional preparations is rescoldo flatbread, a bread that is rustic and dry. Rescoldo cooking is also used for potatoes and results in a smoky and intense potato flavor. This method is widely used in Chiloé, where there are over four hundred species of potatoes. Witch potato is probably the one that gives the best results through ash-based cooking, due to its dark and intense violet color, astringent flavor, strong aroma, and low water content.

VEGETABLES

Rescoldo is capable of producing a flavor and aroma that few other cooking methods we know about can do. The embers must always be prepared at least five hours before starting to cook. This method works well with potatoes and other non-starchy vegetables, and it results in a texture similar in both cases because the pH of the vegetables is modified during cooking through nixtamalization. This produces a charred outer layer on the vegetable and a smooth inner texture like a fine puree. The way we do it at the restaurant always consists of piling up the embers used during the day and leaving the vegetables or potatoes inside the ashes until the following day; the embers maintain a constant moderate temperature. Many times the ash-cooked vegetables are basted in either animal fat, algae, vinegar, or a flower extract emulsion, depending on the season, and are glazed with their own juices or other liquid afterward. This makes them look similar to meat and offers a good option for vegetarians and people with food allergies. We also sometimes simply thinly slice the vegetables and use them as part of another preparation, and they can be mashed to make a puree.

BEAUTIFUL FISH UNDER THE ASHES

In some cases, and especially when cooking with short-season species like those from pre-spring—when some ingredients appear for only three weeks—the smooth flavor and delicate texture of these vegetables can be overshadowed by very intense flavors. During this time of year we tend to use fish as a condiment and not a central element, in terms of both volume and flavor.

People might think that achieving a delicate texture in rescoldo fish is impossible, but it isn't, at least not for us. We make a sort of ash stove with hot rescoldo, a little hotter than what we normally use for vegetables or potatoes. I know it sounds subjective to say "a little hotter," but this is a traditional process that is impossible to quantify and precision depends solely on practice. I am talking about hot rescoldo with burning embers mixed with cooler embers from the previous day, to elevate the internal temperature of the rescoldo.

We spread a thick layer of sea salt and 2 percent sugar in a metal pan, add the fish, and cover the pan completely. We then submerge the pan in the ashes and let it cook for eight hours, steaming the fish slowly. The result is perfect; it has a light ember aroma, and the fish has become delicate and acquired a smooth flavor. It is worth keeping in mind that when serving it, the fish can break. We use this type of cooking only once a year, to pair with ingredients that have light flavors, such as pre-spring wildflowers.

TRU-TRUM

This preparation is of Mapuche origin and consists mainly of raw mashed potatoes, which are wrapped around a native wood cylinder. The bigger the diameter, the more difficult the cooking process becomes, requiring a higher dexterity and control of the rescoldo. The raw potato dough must be crushed evenly around the cylinder by hand so that the roasting will be even. At the same time it is important that the temperature of the ashes stays the same during the cooking; otherwise two different textures will result. The uneven cooking makes it harder to handle when removing the tru-trum, and the result is lower to the one obtained with proper use of the temperature in the rescoldo. To get a proper rescoldo, the proportions of embers from the previous day and burning embers must be the same. A large amount of embers is not required during the cooking; you don't want the exterior to burn. As it roasts, it is important to turn it slowly and continuously over a period of at least five hours. To remove the tru-trum, we slice it vertically with a knife over the cylinder and pick it up slowly with our hands. It can be done in sections. During the dinner service, there is no way back and the temperature must be constant. Because of this it is important to calculate the moment when the tru-trum will be served, because it has to be warm from the heat of the embers. If the type of wood used gives off essential oils, it can heighten the tru-trum 's complexity of the flavors.

Rescoldo cooking with carrots and beets

Witch Potato Baked in a Long Rescoldo → 255

Pre-Spring Wild Vegetables Wilted on Burnt Butter and Steamed Rollizo Fish → 246

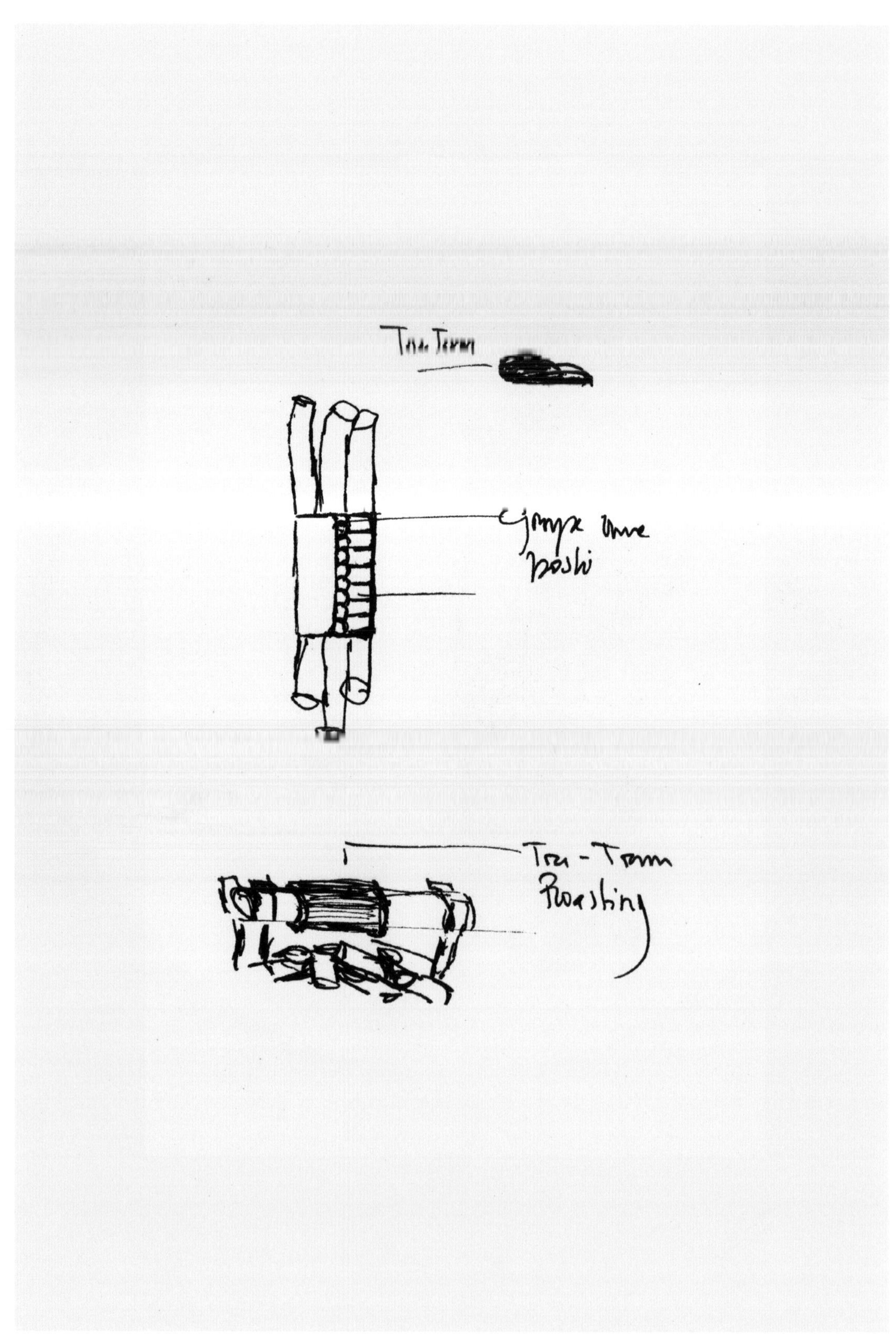

Tru-trum and Chochas → 224

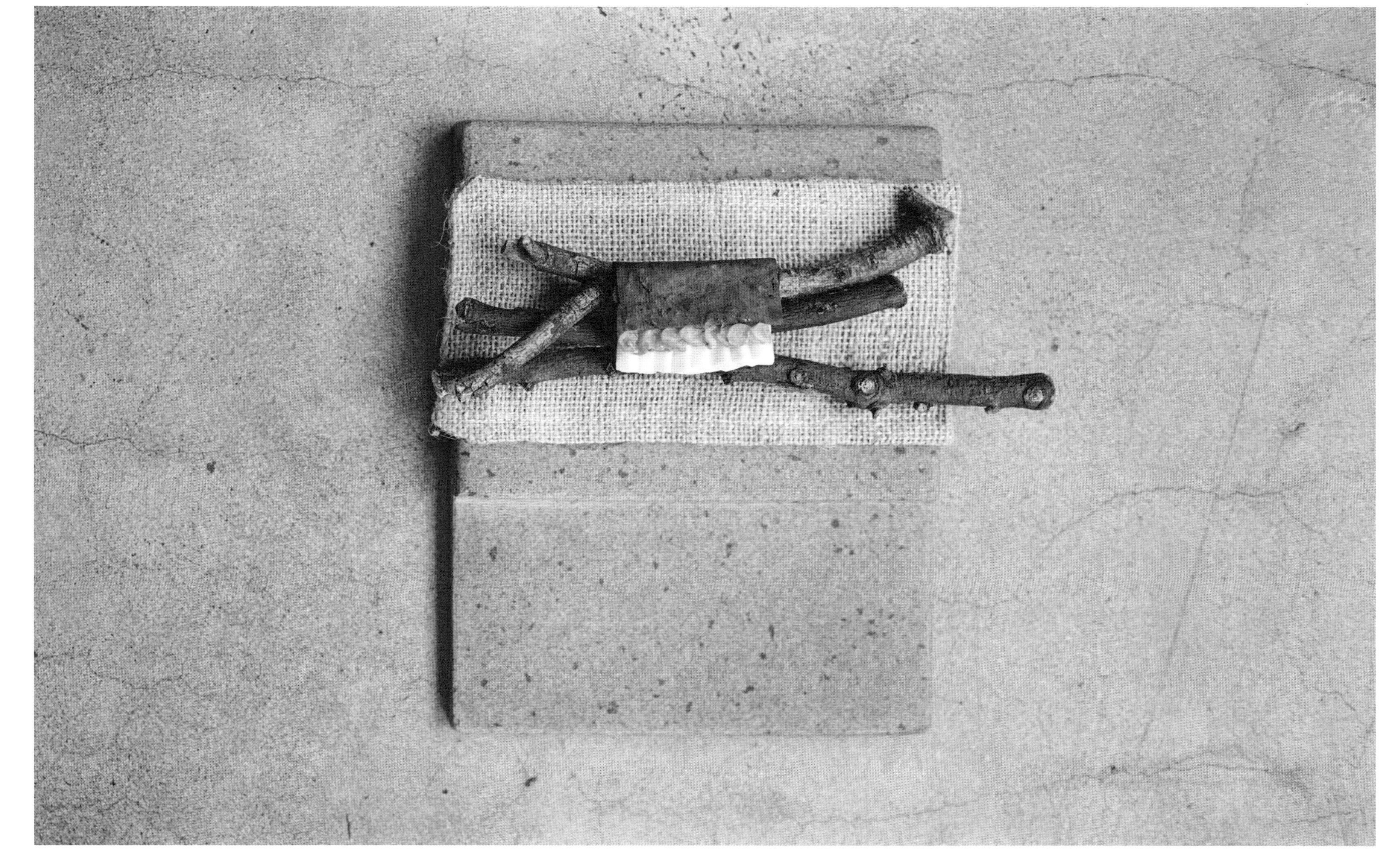

ROCK PLANTS

Rock plant is the name we give to halophytes, and they are one of the most important ingredients for us at the restaurant. They are plants that, in many cases, grow directly on rocks without the need of soil and for us they represent the transition from sea to land. In some ways, rock plants are like algae—they can survive in high levels of salinity—in other ways, they are like plants, full of chlorophyll but with a thick texture, so I see them as a transition between sea and air. Many of them can contain up to 38 percent protein. Why am I mentioning the importance they have for our day-to-day cooking? Simple: In Chile, the coast is 2,600 miles (4,200 km) long from north to south, and the sea is very cold here. Due to the geography, there is a tremendous number of rock plant species that are delicious and highly nutritious, and at same time have features that are praised in our kitchen, such as crunchiness, interior salinity, and pleasant aromas.

In the past, we believed that rock plants were delicious but thought they could only be served grilled or raw. However, a couple years ago we started discovering ways to cook them that allowed us to expand their texture and flavors in different preparations. Many of the species are highly seasonal, but many others grow during a long period of the year. Unfortunately, none of them are currently used in Chile, despite the fact that native peoples used them in the past. However, we want to use all of them according to their seasons. For now there is no one who can harvest them the way we want, so we have to do it ourselves. I am sure that in a few years there will be someone who can do this for us in a precise manner and include all the existing types. Through the restaurant, we are promoting the creation of the first natural halophyte farm in Chile.

BLANCHED

Raw halophytes have an incredible texture and intense flavor on their own. Considering that these plants are so thick, crunchy, and juicy, when they are scalded they acquire another texture—smooth, soft, and almost meaty. We often scald them in animal fat, fat emulsions with fish collagen, burnt butter, or kolof root reduction. All of these options are used for hot salads.

RAW AND GLAZED

In some cases we need to prepare courses that are very fresh, and the texture of raw halophytes is spectacular for this. In these instances what works best for our preparations is a lemon and olive oil emulsion. We also use some herbal oils—some are citric—algae, or roasted algae sediments, which we use to glaze the halophytes with a brush.

WITHERED

The texture of withered halophytes, sometimes including the stems, is completely different than when they are raw. They become quite similar to algae, becoming a translucent green. This effect can be achieved on a grill or by grilling on charcoal. In both cases it is important to hydrate them during the process because they are exposed to an extreme temperature on only one side. Otherwise, they will just become dehydrated. In many cases we use mojos, just as we do with our roasted lamb, to prevent dehydration. This way we obtain the crispy or grilled aroma but not the dehydration. Some halophytes that are thicker can even be cooked in rescoldo. In that case, we remove them from the ashes, clean them well, and then deep fry them in oil at around 86°F (30°C).

Version 2: Creamy Rock Plants with Mushrooms from the Same Place → 231

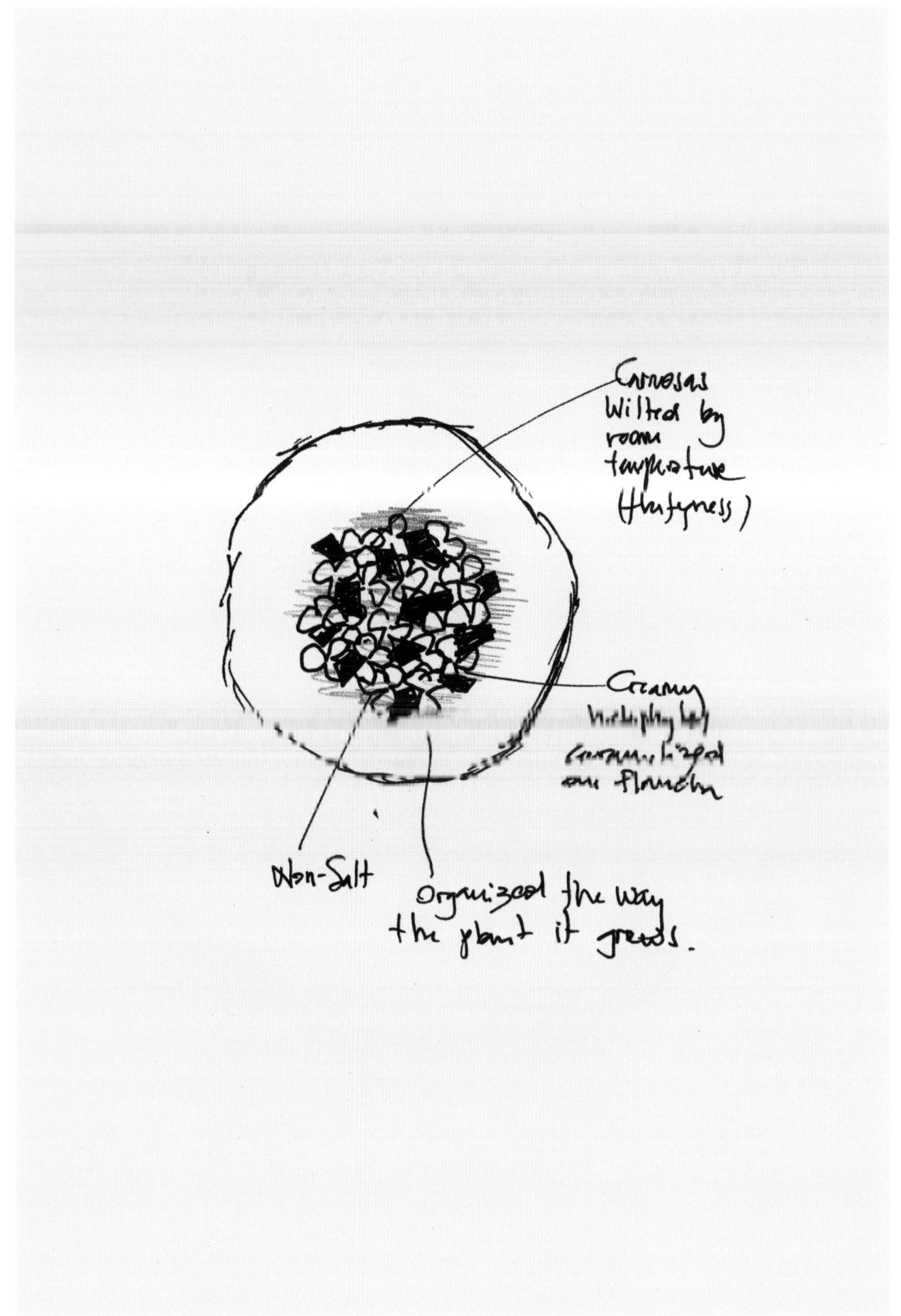

Version 1: Creamy Rock Clovers and Other Plants from Isla Negra → 230

STEAMING

Steaming is one of the techniques that requires the most skill in the kitchen. We use it for fish, vegetables, and other kinds of seafood. We use a simple tool that we adore: a bamboo steamer.

Whenever we steam sea creatures or fish, we let them age first; we believe that this defines the flavors better because there is a vast concentration of amino acids in the fish's flesh. In some cases, to concentrate the sea flavors even more, we use slightly dry sea algae to wrap the seafood in order to allow the low-temperature convection to oven-age them. Then, after two or three days of aging (the exact amount of time depends on the seafood), we steam them.

Steaming is a method we particularly appreciate when cooking aged jibia. Jibia is an underappreciated sea creature in Chile. Chileans tend to say it is vulgar and cheap. Actually, it is really cheap and I still can't understand why: its qualities are amazing from any perspective. Jibia is a giant squid that can be up to 10 feet (3 meters) long and is a natural predator along our coast—a hint that we should eat it. We cut it up in layers of approximately 12 × 1½ inches (30 × 4 cm) and let it age between two and three days; then we steam it. This leaves us completely satisfied because it creates a texture that is similar to a very tender steak.

Steamed Loyos → 256

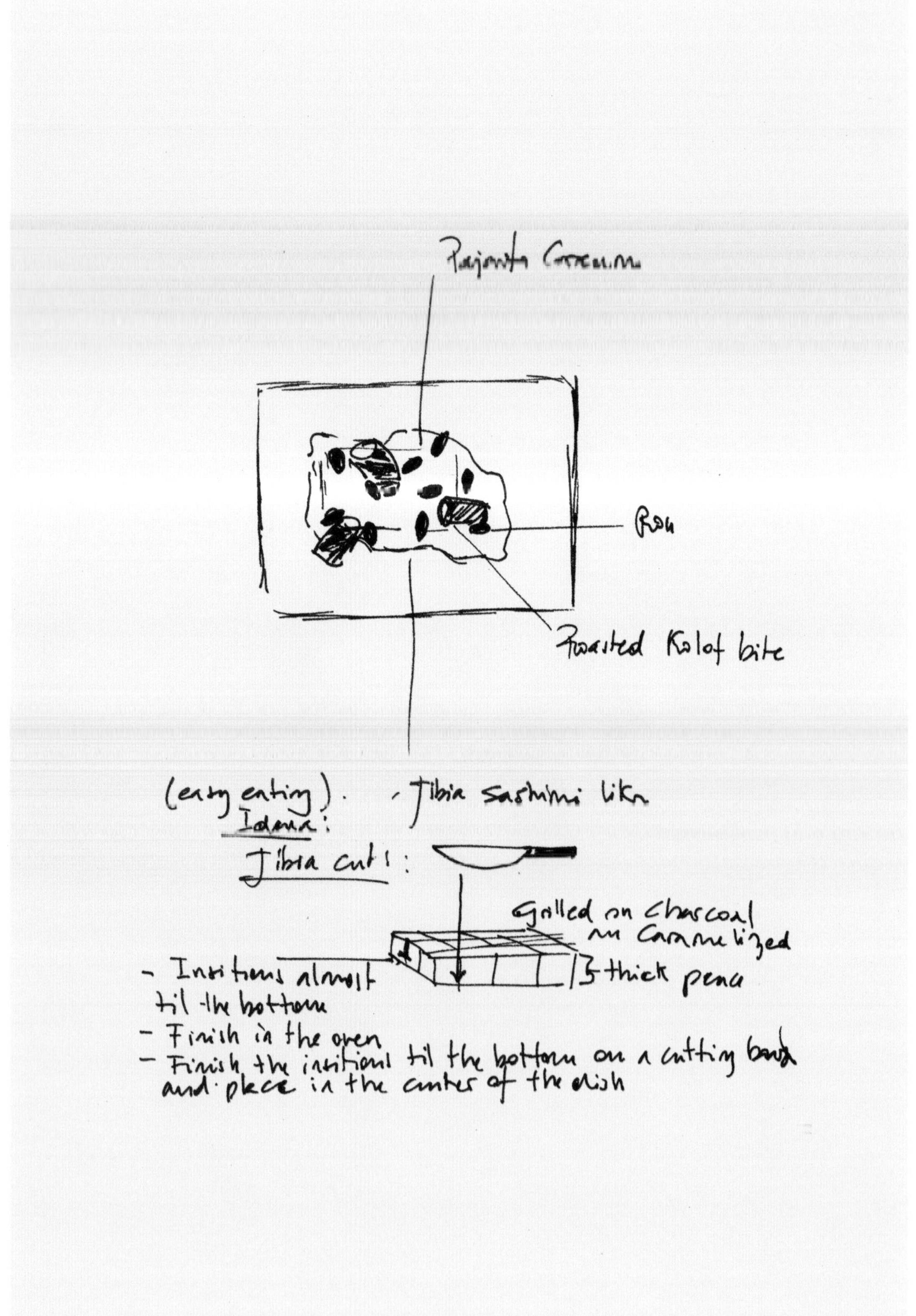

Aged and Steamed Jibia with Pajaritos Cream and Roasted Kolof → 229

Jibia Cooked Over Espino Embers with Chilean Coconut Yogurt, Mandarin Orange, and Rue → 244

Fermented Pewén Chupe → 258

TREE LEAVES

INFUSIONS WITH TREE LEAVES IN LIQUID

Certain fruit trees—especially during the summer and part of the fall—have aromatic leaves, which are included in preparations at Boragó in many different ways, such as infusions, extracts, and oils. However, many of these leaves also work well as cold infusions in pajarito yogurt whey, after allowing the leaves to settle for several days. We vacuum pack the leaves with the liquid that we want to infuse—often removing the main veins to avoid bitterness. We break up the leaves in small pieces to enable the absorption of essential oils. Some of the leaves we work with are tepa, melí, pink pepper leaves, eucalyptus, Chilean laurel, fig, lemon, and avocado, among many others.

INFLUENCE FROM OTHER CULTURES: GRAPEVINE LEAVES

In Chile there are many immigrants from the Middle East, mainly Palestine. I remember that during my childhood, several of my friends came from this background and I was fortunate to be invited into their homes and eat some of the most spectacular food I have ever tried. Some of these preparations require an astonishing combination of skill and knowledge. I believe that this is the root of my fascination with the applications and treatment of grape leaves. I have always been a fan of these leaves, particularly their texture. We have been working with them for years at the restaurant, both directly and indirectly. Thanks to my contact with this culture through my childhood friends, vine leaves and other kinds of leaves have always been as important as any other seasoning or ingredient. I feel that they haven't been explored as thoroughly as they could be in the world of cooking.

We have learned that the traditional way to work with them is to soak the leaves in brine with 8 percent salt and different types of spices for two months or longer. Considering that this is a large amount of salt, the pH is inverted and the structure of the leaves breaks down. They are normally scalded or steamed, or even placed in boiling water wrapped around the traditional spiced rice filling.

INSECT WINGS

Insect wings are probably one of the finest textures you can get in terms of crunchiness. There are several reasons why we don't cook insects at the restaurant. One is that they aren't a part of our culture and I feel there's no point in doing so, given the large number of unique and unexplored ingredients in Chile, some of them with equally high protein content.

I mention the texture of insect wings because during the year, we treat certain leaves in a way that results in a thickness similar to insects wings, and often with interesting flavor. Many of the leaves are stored in different types of vinegar for about a week, and are then left to dry between two nonstick surfaces at 195°F (90°C) for thirty minutes. Some of the leaves aren't edible due to their high concentration of toxins and acid pH, which is easily noticeable because of the astringent and acid flavor. Some years ago, we began to try getting rid of this astringency and bitterness, and we achieved excellent results because many of these leaves had truly unique aromas that are not normally found in edible leaves.

Our process is fairly simple but protracted, because it requires boiling the leaves up to ten times, changing the water each time. They are then scalded, depending on the type of leaf, to change their pH. Once this is done, many of them are pickled in vinegar for a few months—the most astringent for up to one year. The thickest and most difficult to treat are left in a strong brine with 8 percent salt for a month before pickling.

SPEAKING OF LEAVES

Lately we have perfected the drying of leaves. There is a large difference between dry leaves and raw leaves, as there is even more crunchiness when they are dry and the leaves can also be seasoned with other flavors. In addition, this method sets the pigmentation of the leaves.

For achieving the crunchiness and the setting of the pigmentation, it is necessary to keep the leaves submerged in fat for a one-week period. This can be vegetable oil, specifically oil infused with mushrooms, herbs, or aromatic leaves, or it can be animal fat. We often smoke this fat before packing it with the leaves, which gives it a special aroma. Finally, we extract all the oil and water from the leaves by putting them between sheets of smooth paper towels and placing a steam iron on top for 30 seconds.

Wild radish leaves during the drying process

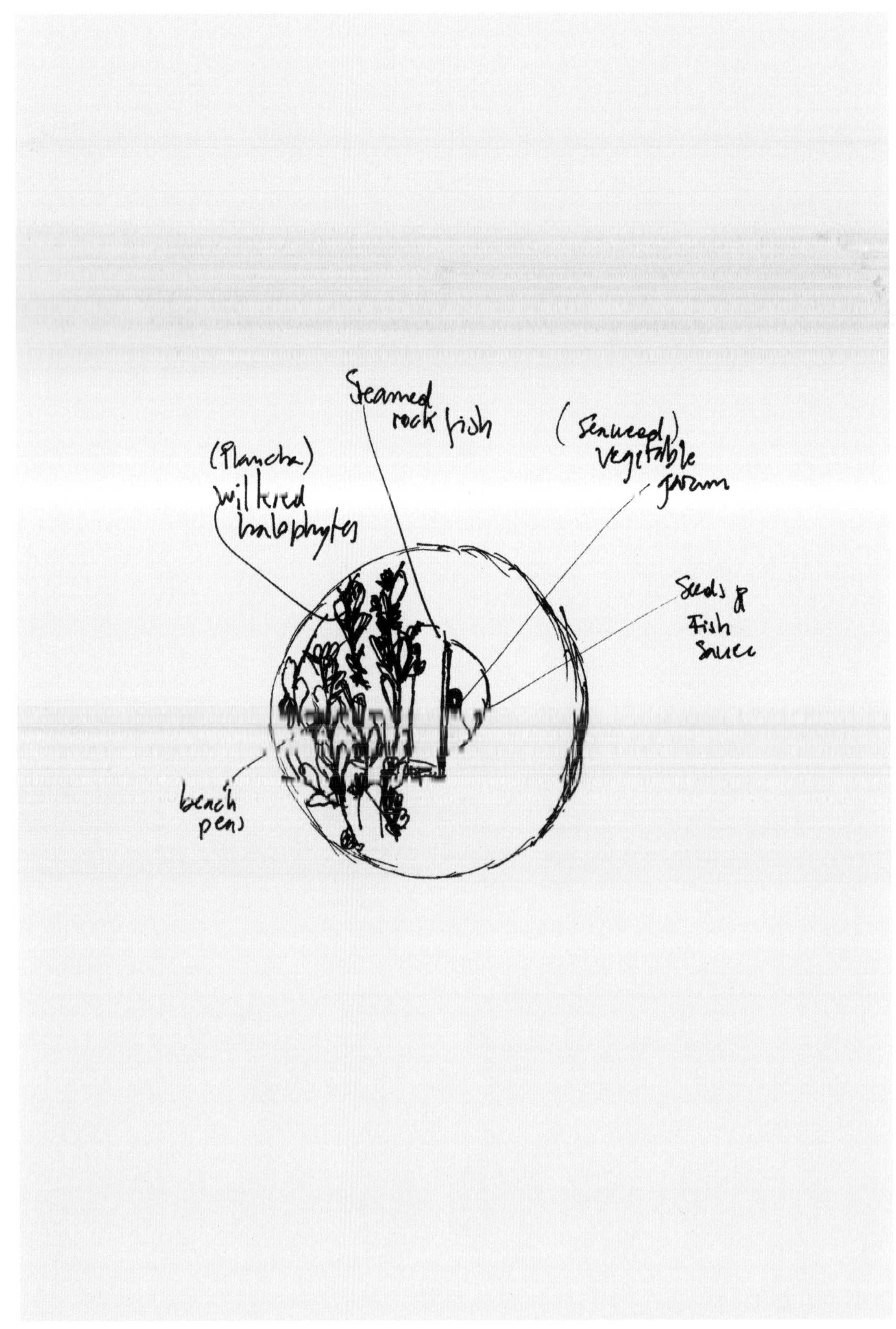

Steamed Baúnco Fish and Wilted Rock Plants on the Grill with Vegetable Garum → 243

Copao Chilenito → 220

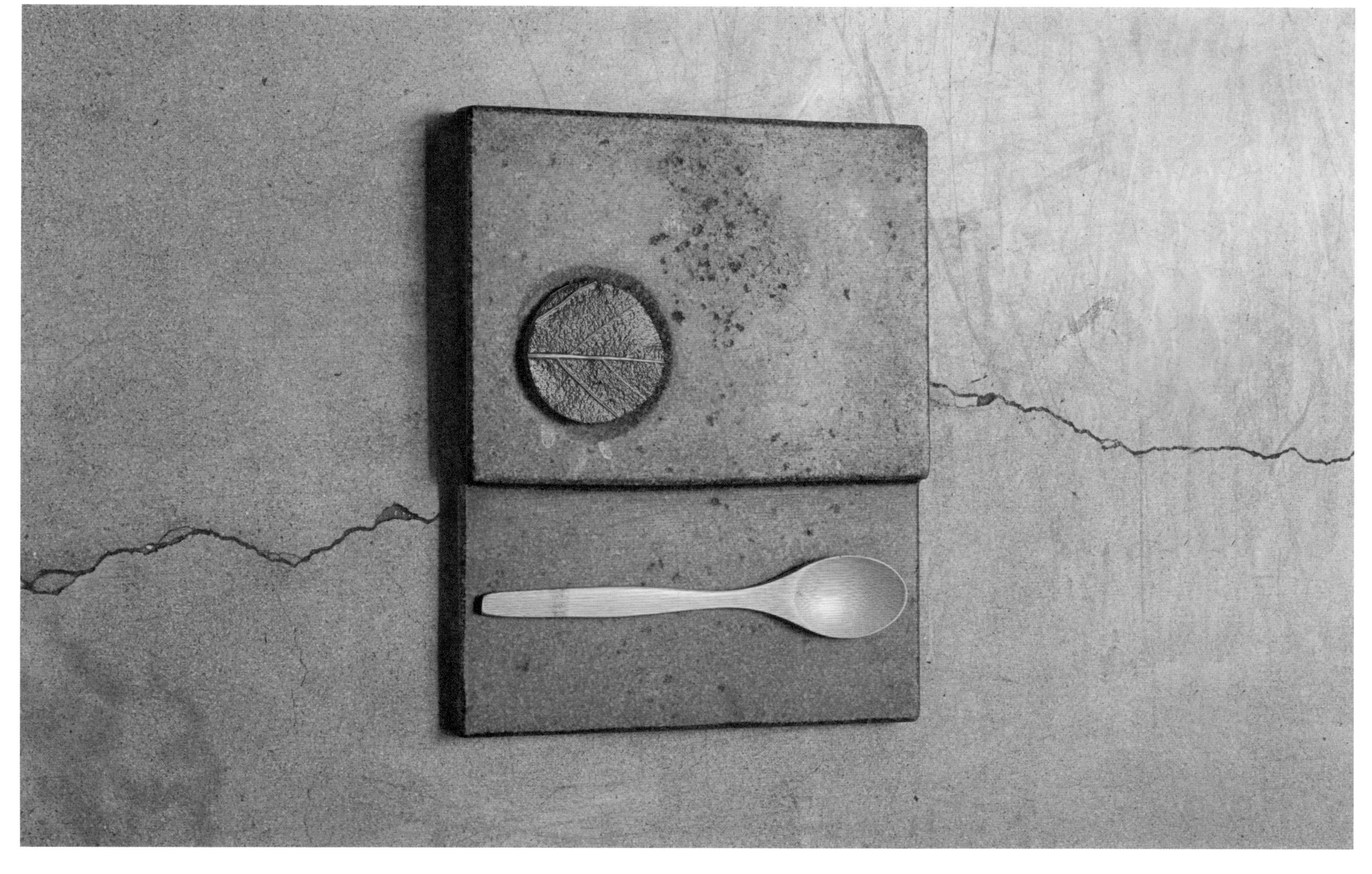

ICE CREAMS

Ice cream has been important for the restaurant since the day one. It is true that there are different options for making ice cream, and I would like to make an important distinction. Making true ice cream requires not only dexterity and knowledge but also the control of several factors, among which are important aspects such as controlling the infrastructure of a kitchen and the conditions and moment in which the ice cream will be served, in addition to the way it will be served. Good ice cream cannot have a temperature that is too low and at the same time it must have a structure that is sufficiently resistant to retain bubbles and have perfect emulsion. This way it can melt easily with the temperature of the mouth. This may sound basic, but on several occasions different mixtures we have made have had such low temperatures that when we ate them there was no aroma.

There are many homogenizers capable of transforming frozen juice or cream, by means of pressure and the friction of blades, and the result is good and makes life easier for restaurants. However, for us that is not ice cream; we consider it cold cream. The structure and texture are fragile and they melt quickly in the mouth, and it is impossible for them to retain bubbles. I've always thought that the best possible ice cream is the one that has just come out of the ice-cream machine after spinning, and that is the ice cream we try to offer at our restaurant every day. Beyond developing the recipes we use on a day-to-day basis, we have become almost obsessed about the texture one can achieve in ice cream. In our case, we obtain great results by starting the ice-cream machine when the dinner service has just begun.

It is worth mentioning that all the recipes we have designed are specifically planned for the equipment at the restaurant. We use an ice-cream machine with a 5-quart (5-liter) capacity, and we perform artisanal pasteurization according to the types of milk we use—vegetable, donkey, goat, Chiloé sheep, and cow's milk. The storage of the ice cream is as important as the preparation: we store it at barely 27°F (-3°C) and for no longer than three hours. When scooping up the ice cream for the machine, it is important to avoid breaking the bubbles or the structure. Likewise, the container plays an important role: we store it only in ⅓-inch (1 cm)-thick, 6⅔-inch (17 cm)-diameter Styrofoam containers. Then, when serving the ice cream on the plate, we soak the spoon in very cold water first, to avoid leaving a double texture on the ice cream that hot water tends to create. Because of this, it is essential that the *quenelle* or scoop has a regular shape, so that when putting the ice cream inside the mouth, it still gives the sensation that it was just taken out of the ice-cream machine and you can even bite it.

LESS SUGAR

One of the most problematic aspects of this type of preparation is the absence of sugar. When ice cream does not contain sugar, the temperature decreases quickly and crystals might form as a result. Lately we have discovered excellent methods to reduce sugar—in some cases down to 0 percent—by adding ingredients that have high umami concentration, such as mushroom powder or algae. We use seaweed as a sort of natural stabilizer; sometimes we deodorize the seaweed, and on other occasions we use it as a fantastic flavor contrast. In Chile there is a large variety of seaweed, some of which adds a touch of sweet umami taste. The same happens with the mushrooms that we use. I think it is important to understand these criteria to gain a better understanding of our ice cream recipes in this book.

Rica Rica Ice Cream and Chañar Concentrate → 220

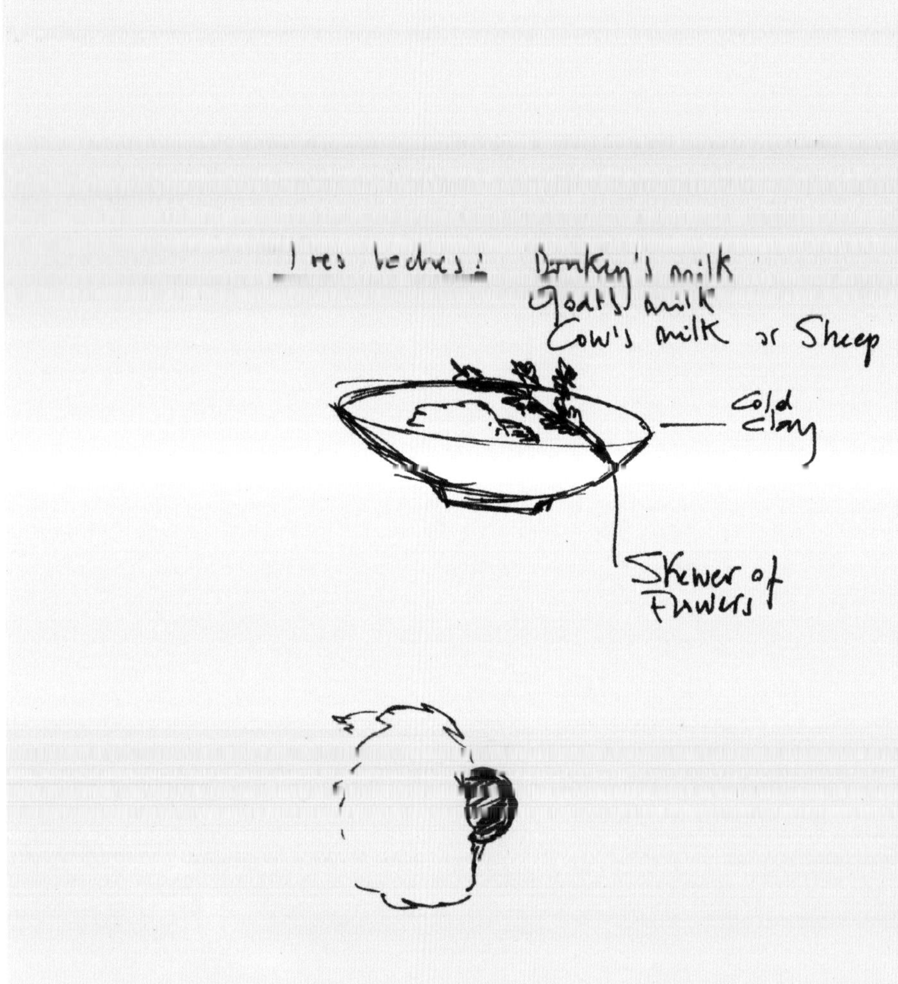

Table side: beet juice and lemon juic
plus olive oil and salt.

Version 2: Tres Leches and Three Wild Fruits → 261

Version 1: Tres Leches and White Strawberries from Purén → 260

Version 3: A Year Around the Peumo → 262

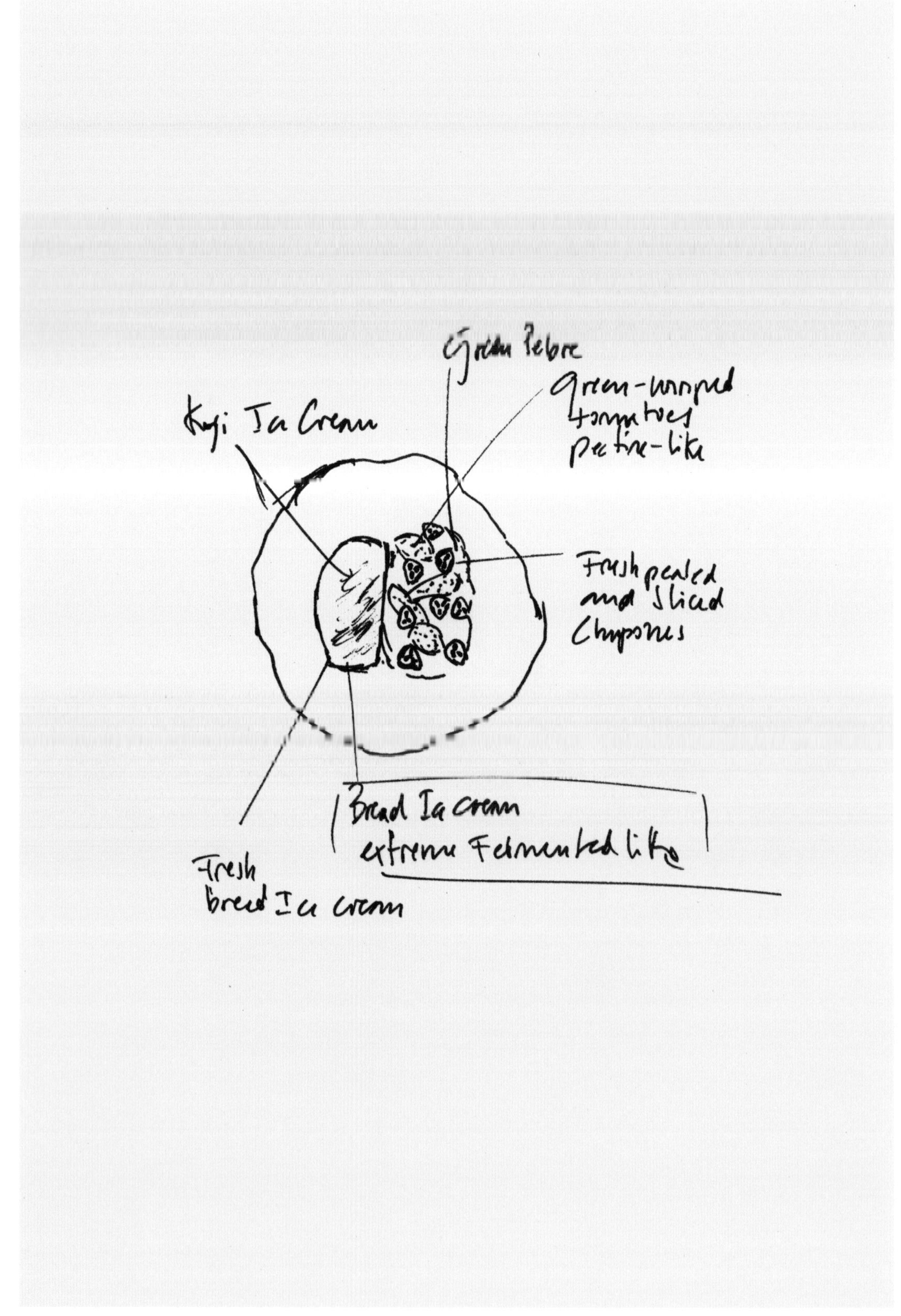

Overly Fermented Bread Ice Cream with Green Pebre → 263

Gigantic Macaron with Rica Rica Ice Cream and Chañar → 222

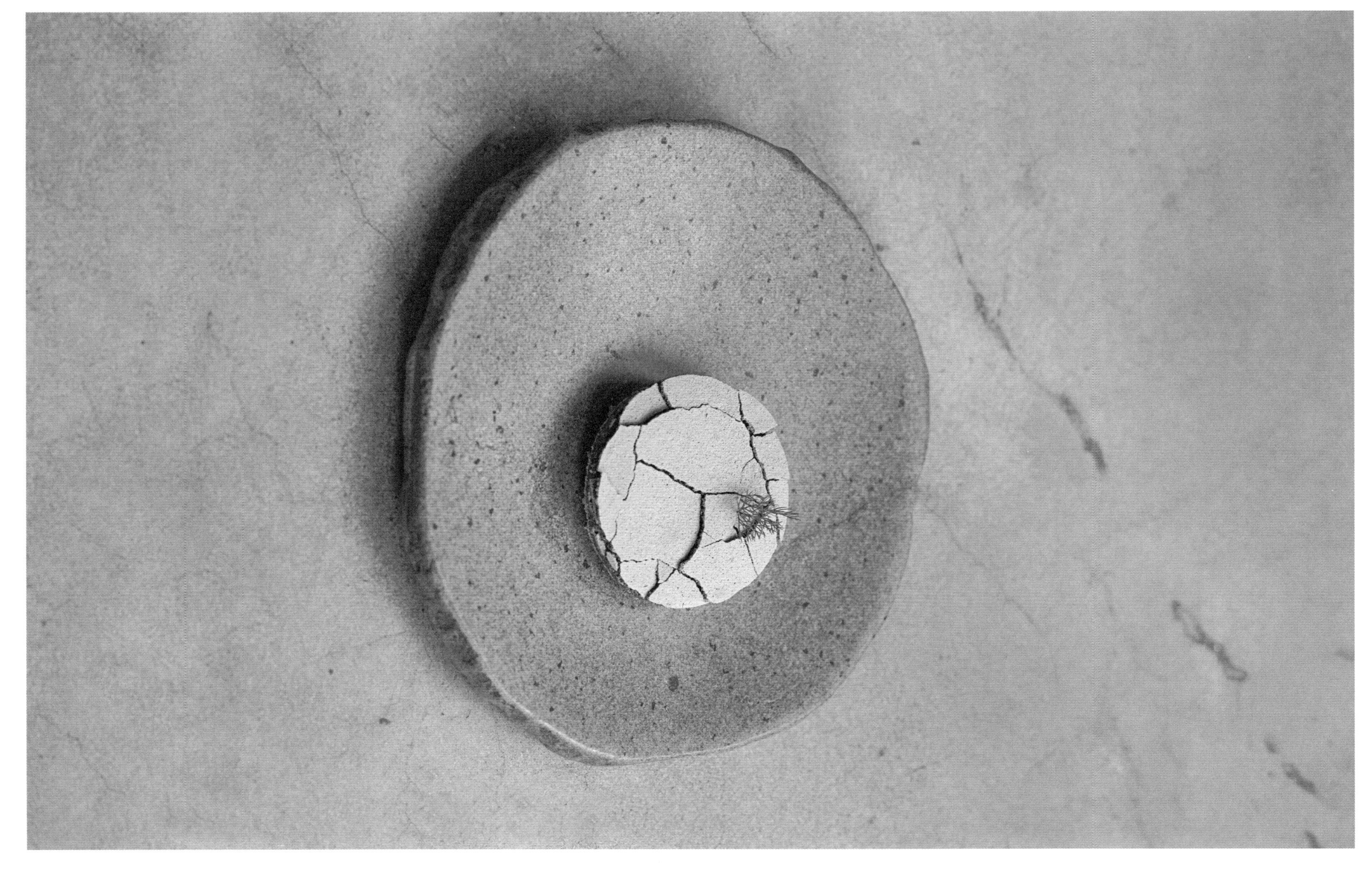

SEAWEEDS NOW!

It is clear that all over the world large fish have been dragged out of the sea with no thought to their reproductive cycles. This is why we now have to pay the price, not only in the economic sense, but also in terms of availability. In Chile, we have an exceptionally long coast but the harvesting of seaweed has been focused on a few species. However, there are thousands of other species in the sea that have never been harvested from the ocean for human consumption. One of these is seaweed, of which there are more than 750 types. They were once eaten mostly by the aboriginal inhabitants but are currently ignored. Many of the seaweeds have unique flavors, which has sparked our curiosity regarding all their possibilities and this is the reason we use them in most of the food we serve. The different texture that can be achieved is interesting, as well as the fact that they can be used to enhance meats and vegetable stocks, and can even be the main ingredient in a course. We use almost every part of the seaweed in our preparations, using different processes such as ripening, aging, cooking over charcoal, or smoking over native woods.

123

One of the simplest procedures we do is for the types of algae that are thin and have a more vegetable-like color. We call it the 123. It has 1 part sugar, 2 parts vinegar, and 3 parts water. If the algae are too thick, we first scald them, and soak them in the 123 preparation for a couple days to bring out their floral qualities. We often mix algae with vegetables and other wild plants, and with mushrooms.

FERMENTATION

We have obtained the best results with the roots of certain algae, such as kolof and black huiro. Despite the fact that the flavors are completely different, fermentation can be achieved by adding koji, a mold commonly used for making miso, soy sauce, and also fermented drinks. The koji we use for this is inoculated with Chilean mote, a type of wheat commonly used in Chile. We let it ferment for around three months, and even though black huiro stock has a super strong earthy flavor compared to kolof, interesting results can be obtained. Other fresh algae can be added to this and it will absorb the features of the fermentation after some weeks. Another way we achieve fermentation is through misos. We have a specific method for seaweeds where we place layers of miso between layers of algae. The fermentation can be ready in around six months.

INFUSIONS AND JUICES FOR PAIRING, AS IF THEY WERE TEA

I believe the way tea is prepared in Japan is interesting and I must acknowledge that I'm addicted to teas, particularly green tea. Once when Melinda Joe, a food journalist from the United States who lives in Tokyo, came to Chile, she brought me an incredible green tea—it was the best tea I'd ever tasted. One of the things that caught my attention was the quantity of umami in it; it tasted almost as if it were seaweed. Since then, we started looking for short infusions made of seaweed with a process similar to the one used for tea in Japan; we thought this would be an excellent way to offer warm beverages as a nonalcoholic pairing with food at the restaurant. In many cases, it is a perfect complement to the ingredients in our courses, since we have algae with highly complex flavors. We often mix the algae with wild fruit to provide acid notes, or with other ingredients, and serve them cold in the summer.

ALGAE ICE CREAM TO REPLACE SUGAR FOR UMAMI

Most algae, or many of them, have good thickening qualities, especially when used in ice cream, both as a main ingredient and when added as if it were a vegetable. Many algae have a high content of umami, which allows them to replace, together with other ingredients, most of the sugar. The fermentation of seaweed also highlights the flavor; we prepare seaweed miso, which we add to our ice cream to round out the flavors. Furthermore, different textures can be obtained depending on how the algae are treated, whether it is through scalding, dehydrating, and even smoking. Achieving a good result in an ice-cream machine, however, requires a major effort for the machine. We can produce delicious cold creams made with a Pacojet, which are different to ice creams—they have a more liquid and less firm texture—using different types of seaweed, with some excellent results.

BLANCHING AND PIGMENTATION

The treatment we generally give to seaweed, including those with strong flavors, is to blanch them. There are several species for which blanching eliminates the sliminess, giving the seaweed a texture similar to pasta, and it works when combining the seaweed with mushroom broths, different types of milk, vegetables, and meat broths. When serving some preparations that use this algae, we glaze many of the seaweeds with various stocks and other preparations, and when they reach a medium temperature, they quickly absorb these flavors, especially with animal and vegetable fat.

There are many types of seaweed with different colors and textures, most of which can be fixed through blanching. Taking into account the length of the Chilean coastline, understanding the seasonality of seaweeds has taken us several years, because when a particular season ends during spring in the central zone, another could be just starting farther south. As with vegetables, understanding the seasonality is crucial to serve them when they taste best at their seasonal peak. Another important aspect to keep in mind is their reproductive phase, because this completely alters the temperature and time required to cook the seaweed. When they are reproducing, depending on the time of the year and the type of seaweed, the cooking time must be only a few seconds; otherwise, at least with Chilean seaweed, it becomes so slimy that it is uncomfortable to eat.

SEAWEED ROASTED AT A HOT TEMPERATURE

The use of seaweed has allowed us to expand the flavors of the restaurant and has changed the way we cook. One of these changes is roasting at hot temperatures. This can only be done with more succulent seaweeds, but we are able to create exceedingly crunchy textures and flavors that are completely foreign to what algae usually look and taste like. With most of the seaweed we roast, it is important to plan the time spent between harvesting and roasting. If the seaweed is cut and roasted on the same day, the result is flawless. However, if it is left for a few days, it becomes increasingly harder to achieve a nice even roast and complex flavor.

SMOKE IN ALGAE

Smoke is probably the main ingredient of Chilean food because it can be used as a technique to preserve food and also because it is an excellent element in which to cook. In the case of luche, we scald, compact, and then hang it over smoke—the traditional method used in the *rukas* (Mapuche huts). This is done at a very low temperature, which is ideal for fermentation to occur while it is being smoked. The results after six months are stunning. We have applied this same method to hundreds of different seaweeds: We press and then smoke them over low embers. The seaweed turns to a paste with a texture resembling black garlic, and we use it in many of our preparations.

Version 1: Punta de Tralca Wild Food, Organized by Layers → 233

Version 2: Punta de Tralca Rock Salads, Organized by Layers → 234

KOLOF ROOTS

SORT-OF SOY SAUCE MADE IN CHILE WITHOUT FERMENTATION

There are more than 750 species of algae in the different geographic areas of Chile, and many of them can grow only in those specific areas and environmental conditions. Unfortunately, Chileans generally use only four of these, which is quite the opposite of what the native peoples of Chile do.

Probably the most popular algae currently eaten in Chile is known as cochayuyo. Its real name in Mapudungun is kolof, which is the word we use for it at the restaurant. You can find kolof at any of Chile's fish markets; it grows in large quantities along the coast, from the northernmost area to Patagonia. It looks like some sort of mutant: it can grow up to 10 feet (3 meters) long and has a unique rubbery texture. It is the only honeycomb algae. Furthermore, its flavor and texture change vastly in accordance with its age.

Kolof has infinite uses in the kitchen. The stem of the kolof is called ulte. It can be eaten raw or cooked. Most remarkable of all is its similarity to hearts of palm—you could say it is a hearts-of-palm sea vegetable of sorts. The stems of the biggest specimens can be 3 inches (8 centimeters) in diameter.

The root of the kolof looks exactly like a stone and is as hard as one too. It has always been considered waste because the waves wash them up on the shore. In general, this algae reproduces quickly and contains large amounts of protein and other nutrients. Not long ago, we discovered something that not even the Lafquenches—Mapuche people who used to live along the southern coast of Chile—knew about: using the root of the kolof to make soup. The result is truly fantastic. It seems to have a high fermentation rate but that is simply the natural flavor of the root. It reminds us of soy sauce, possessing its same umami, but is much lighter: you can drink large amounts of it.

Cooking kolof root is a technical process. During the first cooking, the roots must be blanched completely to obtain a thick, bright, and light brown soup. We take 22 pounds (10 kilos) of kolof roots and blanch them in 21 quarts (20 liters) of water, yielding 16 quarts (15 liters) of broth. Then the broth is strained and cooled. This process takes several hours, and depending on the type of energy or fire used, there are important variations in the cooking time that do not, however, impact the final result. This first broth is set aside.

After having softened the roots at least a little in the first cooking, we repeat the process, using the same 10 kilos of roots in 20 liters of fresh water. You could say that this second broth, on first sight, is of better quality than the first: it has an even shinier, darker, and smoother texture. It has a significantly different flavor but is also delicious and can be used for the same purpose as the first broth. Another difference with the first broth is that for the second we must reduce the amount of water from 20 to 12 liters. We strain it and then let it cool. To obtain the intense flavor of the first cooking and the characteristics of the second, we mix the two broths together.

This has become one of the foundations of several of the flavors that we use in the restaurant, almost like a Chilean version of soy sauce. At first we used it as a hot stock, and later we started using it to cook, glaze, ferment, and even as a cold dressing, with different concentrations giving us extraordinary results that even included floral notes. For now, we have the foundations of this element, but new windows of opportunity have opened to expand all the flavors we use in the kitchen.

SOY SAUCE WITH KOLOF ROOT

We have also hydrated mote koji in kolof broth and achieved something very similar to soy sauce, letting it age for two weeks into an exceptional flavor, which perfectly matches soy sauce. This gives it even more floral tones than the kolof broth, but also brings the umami flavor in a meaty direction.

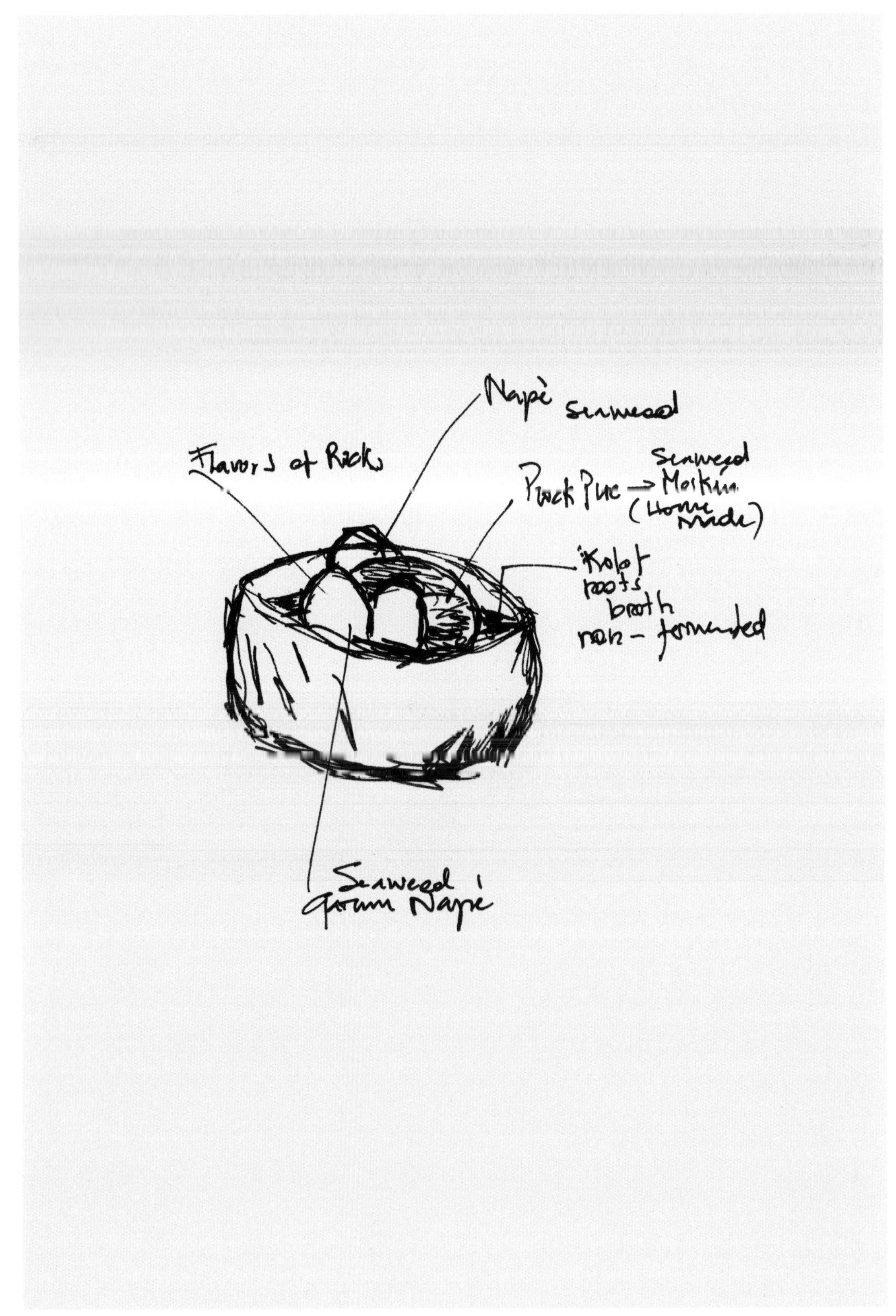

Seaweed Roots Pulmay and Some Rock Flavors → 235

AGING

MEAT

Currently, almost all the meat we use has been previously aged, because when it contains more amino acids and less water, it acquires a concentration of flavor that affects the manner of preparation, especially when cooking over embers. We use very cool embers in order to cook slowly and gradually.

IN ULMO BEESWAX

Aging fish in beeswax with a small amount of ulmo honey—which comes from bees pollinating the flower of the ulmo, a native tree—adds pleasant aromatic caramel notes, almost like a perfume, especially in fish with a high amount of collagen, such as conger eel. Wonderful results can be obtained by doing this regardless of the chosen cooking method.

AGING LAMB: HOW WE STARTED
AND OUR PROGRESS

We have successfully aged some types of meat, such as Patagonian lamb, which has a strong flavor, in beeswax with ulmo honey. This technique preserves the honey's peculiar aroma, which in turn gives the lamb a bold character; we serve it in small portions so it is not too rich and cloying. Also the way of cooking it "à l'inverse" melts all the fat during cooking, which perfectly complements the process of aging of the animal.

SEA CREATURES

In general, and just as with fish, aging different sea creatures turns out well because it helps us concentrate the flavors. We maintain good convection in our aging chamber, and therefore we can cook thoroughly and gradually. Regardless, we always choose light cooking methods, such as steaming or simply a progressive glazing with different types of emulsion or even butter. Cooking must always be done at a low temperature; we believe this is essential in the aging process of these species. Some examples include jibia and different fishes from the coasts of Chile. We hang them at 37°F (3°C) with adequate air circulation, either in beeswax or covered in seaweed.

Guanaco Crudo and Arrayán → 265

KATSUOBUSHI
AND ITS INFLUENCE ON OUR KITCHEN

Without a doubt, one of the most fascinating things about our trip to Japan was learning how to prepare katsuobushi. It seems simple, but it is actually quite complex; and it can be one of the most delicious preparations of all. We wanted to apply a similar method to our version, maybe a little simplified, but reaching a similar result. In our case, we use bluefish instead of bonito, in addition to sardines and anchovies, which we smoke in a clay oven for a month with light embers. For the smoking process, we use equal amounts of the native trees tepú and luma. In addition to the wood, we place aromatic leaves from the Valdivian forest—such as melí, Chilean laurel, or tepa—in the oven, and on occasion we use plants from the Atacama Desert, which gives it a completely different flavor. Once the smoking process has finished, the fish has lost all its liquid and dried up completely while keeping the aromatic properties of the smoke. We use this as an excellent seasoning.

There are truly delicious sea urchins on the central coast and along the rest of Chile's coastline; the most outrageous kind for making katsuobushi come from Quintay. We also make katsuobushi using conger eel, jibia, and rock fish.

Snail and Calendula Salad → 230

Crudo Beef Seasoned with Sea Carrots → 243

MISO

OUR KOJI

To produce high-quality miso, it is essential to have well-made koji (a mold used to ferment soybeans commonly used to make soy sauce or miso). To do this, we inoculate koji into two types of grain and that allows us to obtain a floral result. The first grain is Chiloé quinoa, and the second is Chilean mote, a different variety of wheat that we call mote wheat. In both cases, we steam them at 212°F (100°C) for 25 minutes. Then we spread the grains over a table and put a fan in place to air them out thoroughly until the temperature goes down to 86°F (30°C). We then inoculate the grains with koji and store them in wooden boxes, piling up the grain in the center like little sand piles. The grain is covered with a wet cloth and finally topped with a wooden lid that allows air circulation. The following day, we barely stir it. The second day, we stir it three times and spread it out to dehydrate at room temperature. The more it oxygenates, the more uniform its inoculation.

OUR MISO

Miso is one of the most traditional preparations of Japan. For us, fully understanding how miso works has opened the possibility to create miso with several other ingredients—from Chilean mote to sea asparagus—instead of just soybeans. In general, miso only has one problem: it takes a long time to achieve a truly high quality that is floral and complex. So the fermentation takes at least one year, which means the logistics for a restaurant like ours require a lot of planning.

Mainly to accommodate the needs of the restaurant, we use young miso—fermented between three and six months, depending on the preparation for which it is needed—which has aromatic alcohol notes due to it being at the initial stage of fermentation. The expelling of alcohol notes happens at three, six, and nine months. These three maturation milestones have completely different uses and all of them have interesting aspects, taking into account the mixtures we make with other ingredients and various cooking methods.

We prepare miso by cooking legumes and then crushing them, using a ratio of 2 pounds (1 kilo) of legumes—which can be beans—to 1 pound (0.5 kilo) of koji and 3 percent salt. Once the mixture is homogeneous, we store it in a thick transparent glass jar. It is important to prevent air bubbles forming, which might allow the growth of molds, so it is essential to apply weight on the surface, especially at the beginning. Then, during the first two or three weeks, we must adjust the pressure. The method we use is to fill a double vacuum bag with stones that are approximately 2 inches (5 centimeters) in diameter. Because the lids of the containers we use are pressure-based, these stones add weight when closing the jar so it becomes almost hermetically sealed. The fact that the jar is transparent enables us to observe the miso's progress every month.

Raw Beef, Mother of Kombucha, and Nalca Candy → 259

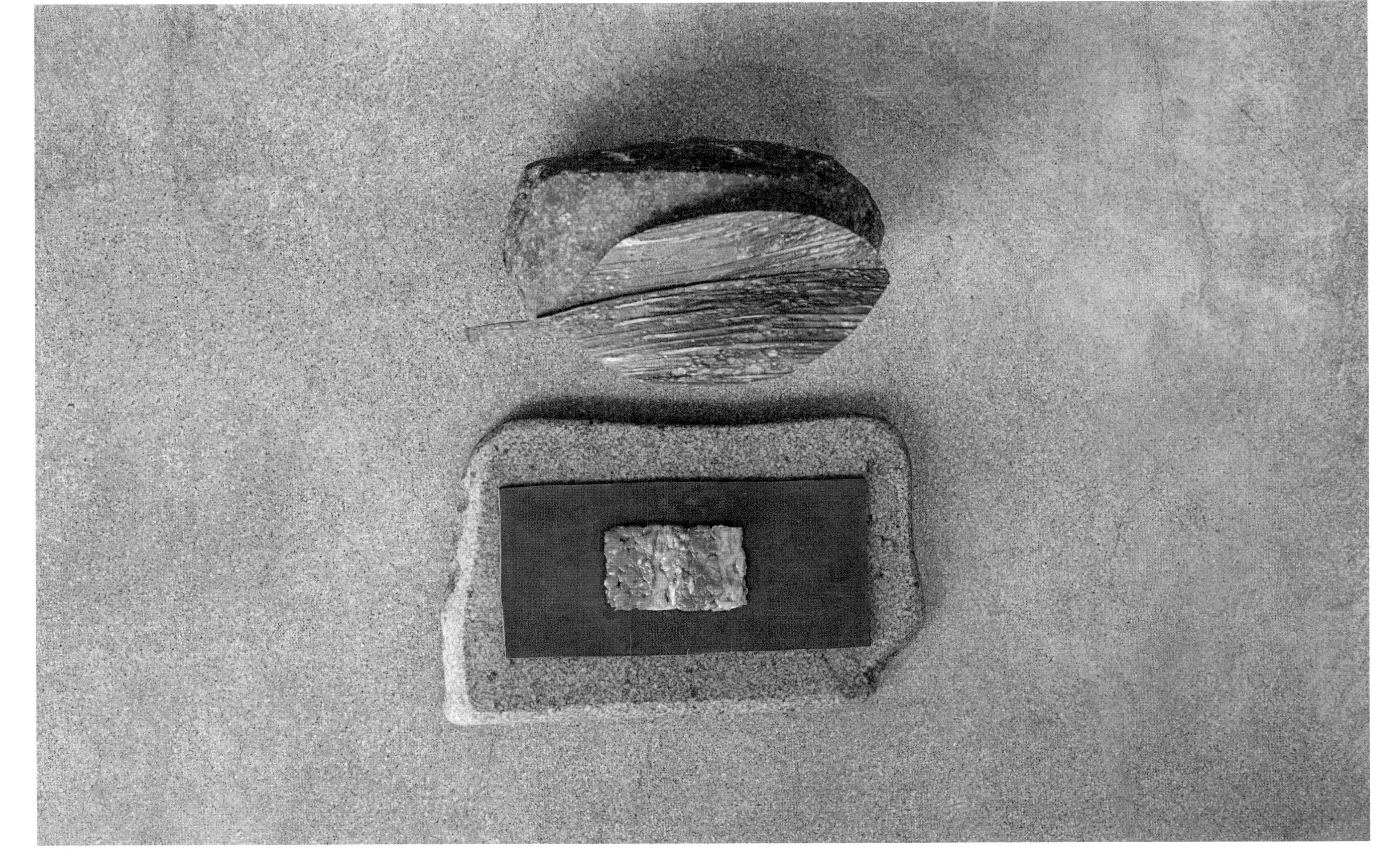

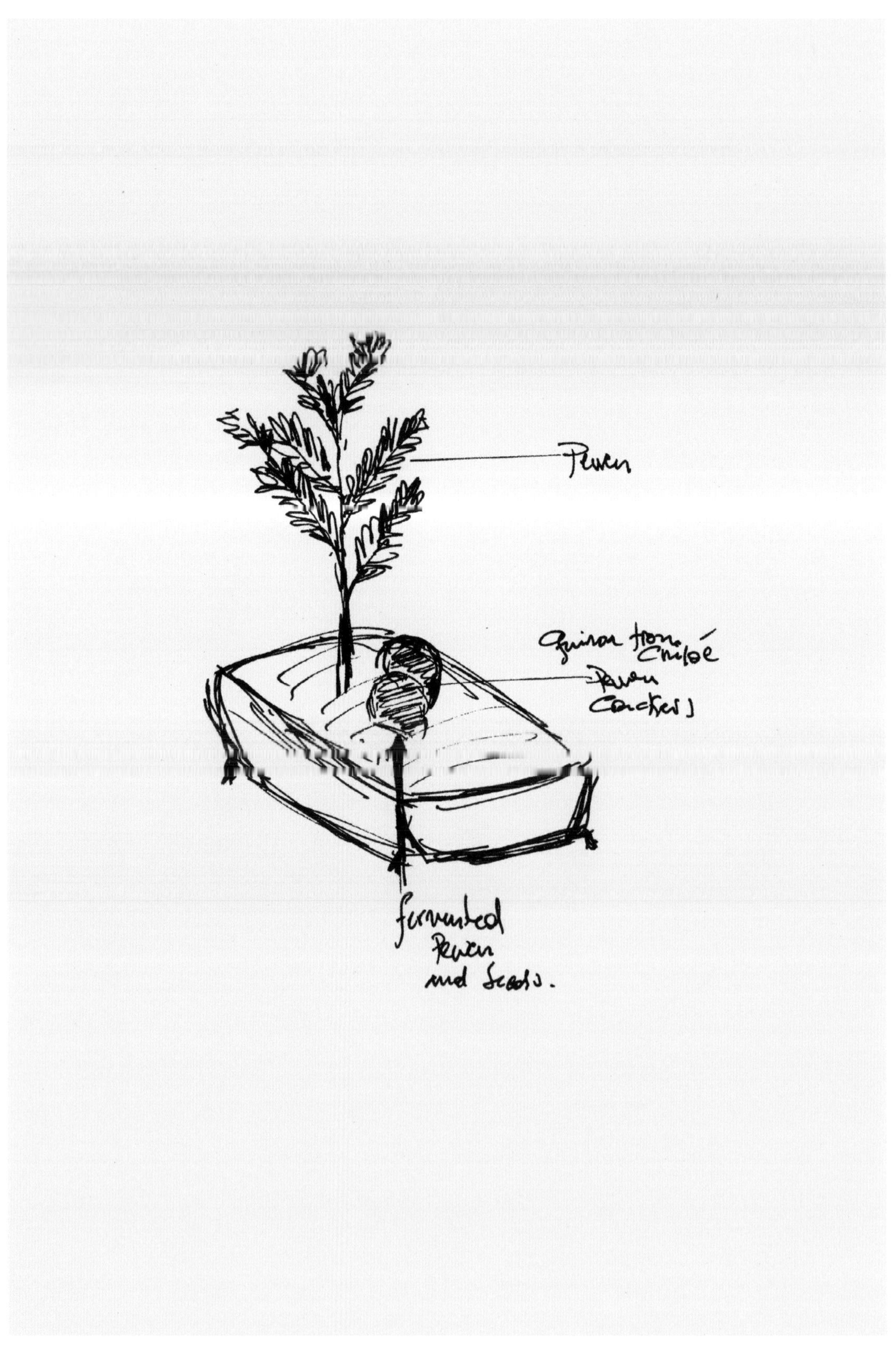

Quinoa Chilota and Pewén Cookies → 251

Muchay and Koji Cake → 255

Snowy Quinoa Koji Milk and Wild White Apples → 269

THE FIFTH ELEMENT

In 2015, Andrea Petrini invited me to talk at the European Lab forum about the future of restaurants. I told him the name of my presentation was going to be "The Fifth Element," like the movie.

Many people say that times have changed, that everything has become more expensive. The cost of renting a place to establish a restaurant in a major city has skyrocketed, and food has become more costly while our free time has decreased. It is also common to hear that luxury restaurants will disappear and that most people will eat at bistros or at cheaper but still sophisticated places.

For me this is confusing and contradictory because many aspects seem subjective. First of all, what is luxury? How do fine dining restaurants around the world operate? These are important factors to consider, and they function differently depending on the context and the culture. I like to think that most revolve around four elements, regardless of location.

In the first element, there are several types of restaurants. They thoroughly understand the territory and are capable of carrying out everything in a sustainable manner. This is not as simple as it seems because it is necessary to understand the geography on a large scale, and this can also drive the discovery of new possibilities at some restaurants.

In the second element, there are restaurants that also tie their food to culture. Some do this centering on origin and others on tradition.

The third element refers to restaurants that rely on technique, which sometimes turns out to be a little more complex, because it is necessary to have skilled cooks and a deep knowledge of the evolution of cooking. In most cases this element requires a learning process.

The fourth element can seem simple at first but can turn out to be highly complex when using each of its components in coordination with the seasons. Using seasonal products, for example, and growing vegetables in the field, requires an understanding of agriculture. This can be even more complicated because each vegetable has its own cycle that happens slowly on a farm, but then also has to coincide with the logistics of a restaurant. On the other hand, using native ingredients requires understanding the territory and the seasons, as well as learning about how they grow, how they're harvested, and their possibilities. Establishing a connection with the cycles, whether they are natural in a larger territory or simply particular to an area, can be troublesome because it involves many aspects that are hard to control. It is even more difficult when considering the complexity of establishing a supply network surrounding one of these two options, or both. At the same time, the sea plays an important role in this type of restaurant. Therefore, if it is possible to form a relationship with the fishermen, they learn about the requirements of the kitchen. Likewise, it is important for this type of restaurant to learn about the animals that are available during the seasons, as well as other related aspects. In any case, this fourth element can have important consequences, especially on the social level, in addition to positively affecting local communities because the restaurants that are able to relate to them can produce changes in local economies, agriculture, and neighboring markets, and in some cases they can even influence supermarkets and completely modify the perception of the environment.

And there are other restaurants that use what I refer to as the fifth element, which is to interact with the other four elements in a perfect manner. This means that they are capable of modifying an environment and an entire community, as well as altering or improving the perception of food, communicating a message through the food that is consumed daily. They are also capable of generating knowledge and transmitting it, enriching traditions, and interacting with the territory in a seasonal fashion. They have a perfect understanding of the possibilities of seasonality and establish a strong bond with farmers and fishermen. There are not many of these restaurants, but they can change and improve their surroundings, and it doesn't really matter if it is in a predetermined way or if they follow a specific pattern; the important part is that they should never cease to exist, because they are singularly capable of improving the lives of people and generating and disseminating knowledge.

Cheese and Mushrooms Alfajor → 250

THE TASTING MENU

AS THE WAY TO EAT AT BORAGÓ

There are as many ways to serve food as there are restaurants. The method that makes most sense to us is the tasting menu. For most of the world, Chile might be the most distant country in Latin America, and for Chileans, due to the country's geography, many places within the country lie far away. Because of this it is important for us to present as many flavors as possible. The existence of a number of seasons and pre-seasons—as we like to call the small windows of time when certain ingredients appear around the country—enables us to offer a large variety of preparations inspired by our territory. At the same time, we have the feeling that there is a great deal of curiosity about these flavors that most of our guests have never tasted before. It is an important opportunity for both sides to become satisfied and happy, and happiness always leads to positive things, especially around a table.

When the restaurant opened, we first operated with a tasting menu called Endémica, as well as with an à la carte menu. However, à la carte was restrictive in several ways because it didn't allow us to show everything that happens during the seasons in Chile's complex geography. Finally, in 2013, when the restuarant started to be fully booked for the first time, most of our diners were choosing the tasting menu, so we decided to remove the à la carte option altogether. It was a change driven by our diners, and therefore was more like a natural process than anything else.

ENDÉMICA

Our tasting menu has kept the same name since we opened the doors of the restaurant, although its format has changed over the years. We try to use it to gather and combine the best endemic products of the Chilean territory, which evolve during the year.

The menu currently contains between sixteen and eighteen preparations, depending on the time of year, as well as the proportion and amount of food and plates used. It is important to keep in mind that we are open only at night, which is why the menu must always be very vegetal. This doesn't mean that we don't serve meat. On the contrary, many of our preparations include meat but sometimes not in the traditional way as a main ingredient; it is just that the percentage of vegetables on the menu is a lot higher.

WE CALL THEM EE

In the past, the period from the second half of December to the end of March was the time when the restaurant tended to have fewer guests. So we took advantage of this quieter time and concentrated on coming up with the preparations. Nowadays, there isn't much difference between these months and the rest of the year; we have the same number of guests all year round. One difference persists though: at least 30 percent of the next season's menu is designed during this period. This lets us have a new pool of ideas to start with after March.

Our range of ingredients is so large and ever changing—depending on what is in season—that we can have hundreds of possible preparations to choose from to create a menu every night. In order to be able to quickly devise a menu from these hundreds of options, we created a system that we call *EE*. On a blackboard in our test kitchen, we draw two E's opposite each other: E Ǝ. This creates the start of a grid shaped like a ladder with a hole in the middle of the rungs. Then we continue adding rungs to the EE's ladder until we have one for each possible preparation. We classify our preparations into two categories: snacks and dishes, and list the dishes on the left side and the snacks on right side of the EE's. When we want to assemble or adapt a new tasting menu, we then simply have to link pairings of dishes and snacks between the two sides so that we can visualize a balanced and dynamic sequence of preparations in a simpler and more organized way, in accordance with the season and the number of preparations we want to present.

MOVEMENTS

The tasting menu is an option that allows us to show plenty of flavors and preparations, as well as the things we have learned and discovered about our ingredients and cooking processes. Most importantly, it lets us show ways to think about food that are deeply rooted in our culture.

Nevertheless, when we talk about the tasting menu, there are several contradictions. I always like to start from the understanding that we are cooking for other people and not for ourselves, and this pushes us to give our best day after day. On the other hand, it opens the possibility to certain aspects that can be truly uncomfortable for a guest. In a restaurant that serves many courses, a lot of time can go by from the start to the end of the meal. Take, for example, the time spent waiting for food, wine, change of cutlery, cups, explanations, and so on. It could result in endless interruptions. So we realized that we had to develop a system of dynamic service that reduces these interruptions, makes our guests feel at ease, but also reflects the nature of the cooking. After all, it would be unfair to not show all the fascinating things that happen in Chile during specific times of the year just because of time limitations.

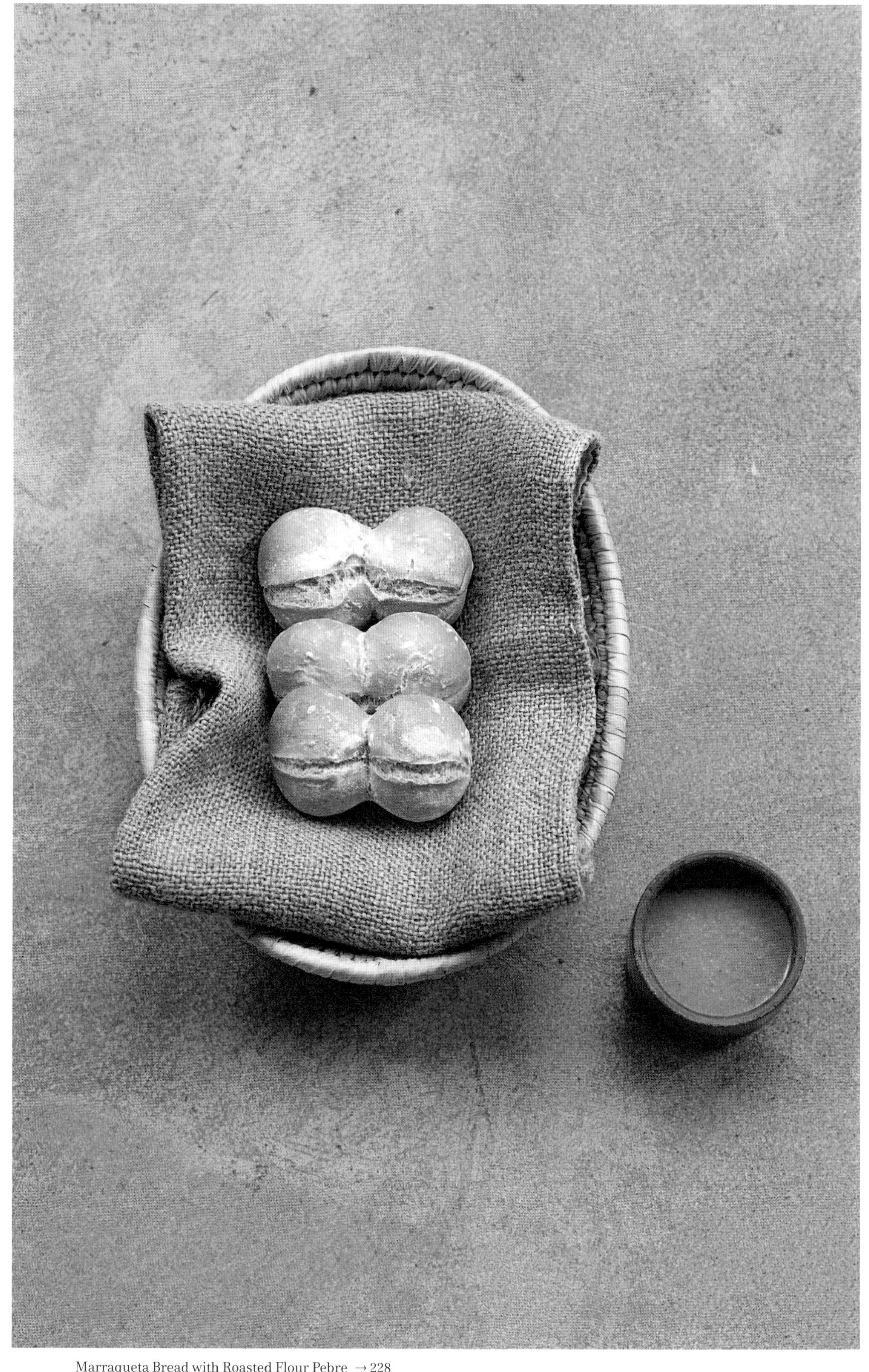

Marraqueta Bread with Roasted Flour Pebre → 228

When it is time to create a menu, one of the most complex aspects is having the abstract capacity to visualize the full tasting menu in our minds, in order to keep the focus to design and place the preparations in a proper position throughout it. One of the considerations at a restaurant like ours, which presents many small preparations (sometimes all together as one dish), is the time it takes for the guest to eat what we serve. Regardless of the nature of each person, there is a point at which tension and attention is lost, and things that are fantastic could become dull. To me, there is a fine line between enjoying the whole meal and being tedious, which could happen after more than three hours have gone by, with some exceptions. That is why we aim to serve the tasting menu within a period of two and a half hours. We try to maintain their attention without becoming invasive, allowing us to keep surprising them so that the general feeling is good and not boring.

We decided to design a new kind of dinner service experience for our diners, which would take into account time restrictions, the fact that there could be very delicate ingredients on the plate, and the diner's enjoyment. We came up with a system that we call Movements.

Our Movements method represents an agile system that uses our dinnerware to serve a number of dishes in quick succession in a fluid way that is unobtrusive to the diner. The diversity of our dinnerware—its shapes and textures—means that it can be used in a modular fashion, removing the need to completely clear and reset a place setting between each course. So the meal is broken down into several "movements" that link a number of dishes and snacks, serving one after another in a very dynamic way, while also keeping the tension between dishes and holding the diners' attention.

For us, Movements provides the momentum to the meal, and shapes the way in which the guests perceive the food on the table—the way the food is shaped and the time it will take to taste it. The dinnerware, therefore, also becomes an important part of the meal. Our plates are made from a native river stone from an area called Bío-Bío and are very tactile. I am convinced that at a certain point, food not only has to be delicious, but also show a real care to be beautiful and desirable to all the senses. At Boragó, it has become very important for the aesthetics of the dish and the materiality of the dinnerware to perfectly match the flavors of what we serve, so that all of of these aspects combine into one experience.

Ten years of serving Endémica, the tasting menu, has taught us to cook and understand the territory in a manner we never thought possible. And finally, after that long learning process, we still have the same feeling as when we opened the doors for the first time: we feel like we are just beginning to cook—because now we know where we are, where we come from, and what we have around us.

Cold Welcome Pulmay → 227

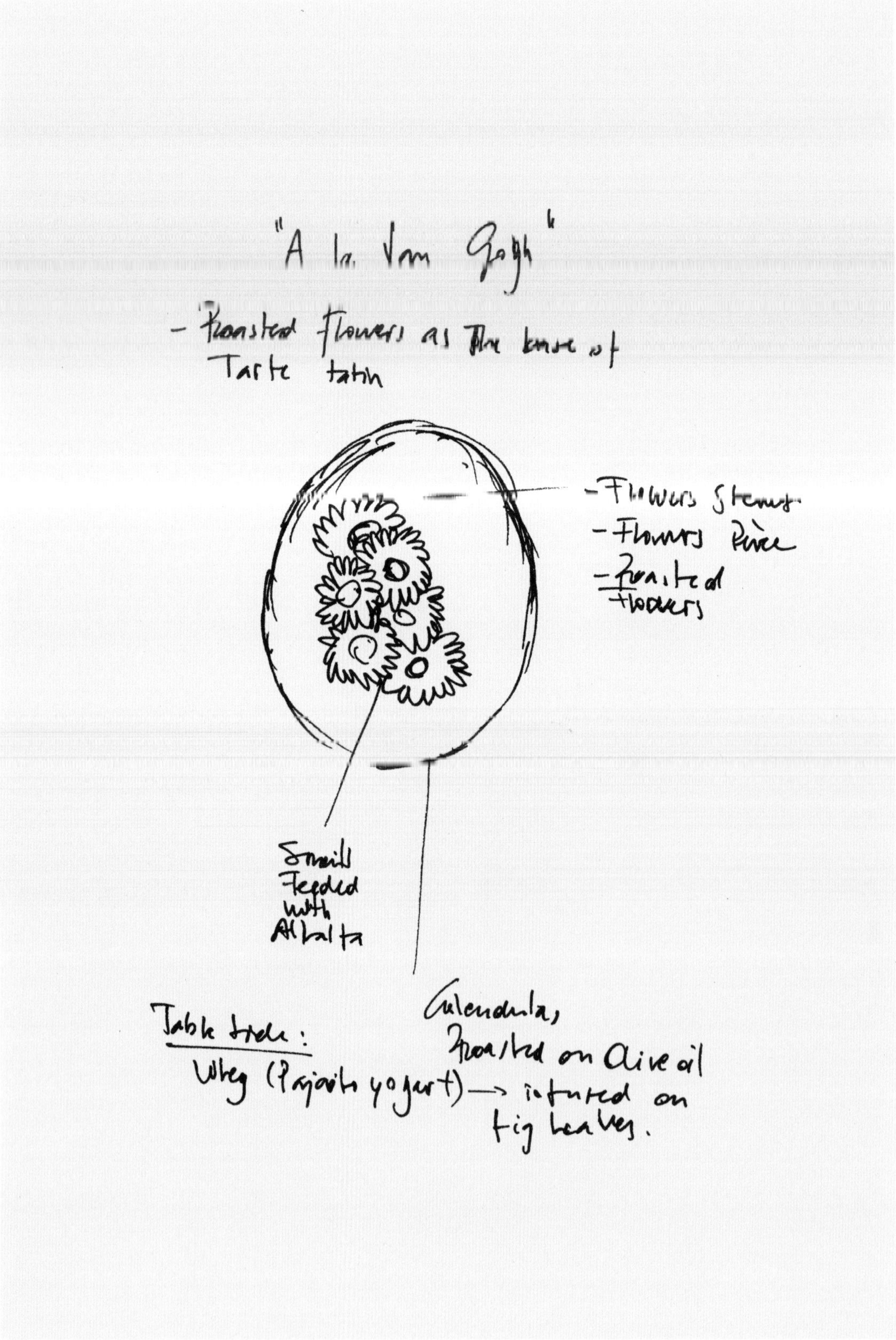

"A la Van Gogh"

- Roasted flowers as the base of Tarte tatin

- Flowers Stems
- Flowers Rice
- Roasted flowers

Snails Feeded with Alfalfa

Calendula, Roasted on Olive oil

Table side:
Whey (Prajita's yogurt) → infused on fig leaves.

Lukewarm Flowers Chupe à la Van Gogh → 245

Topinambour and Changles from Oncol → 257

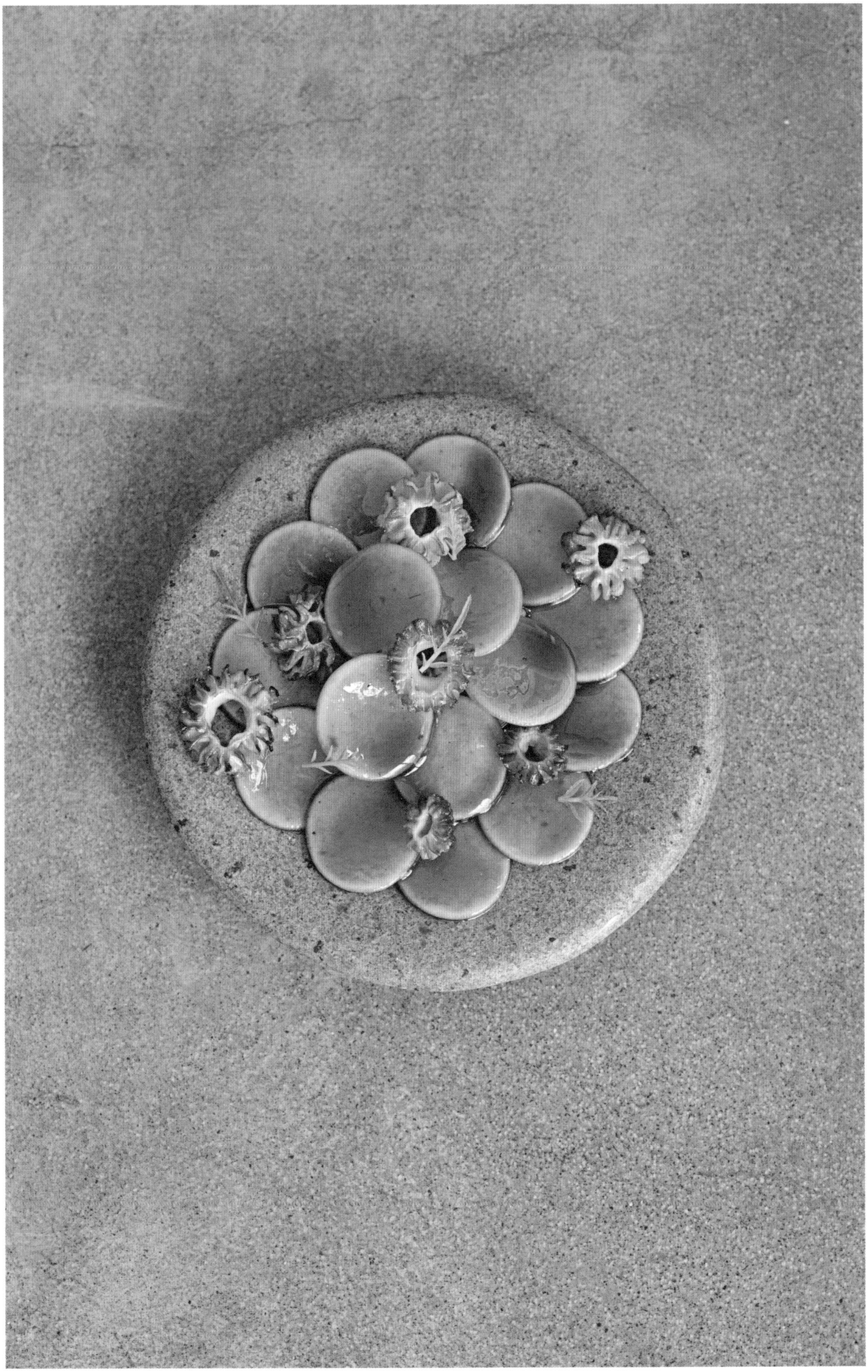

Pantrucas Cooked in Meat Broth with Morels →254

Guanaco and Murtillas → 268

Tarte-Tatin of Rock Vegetables → 242

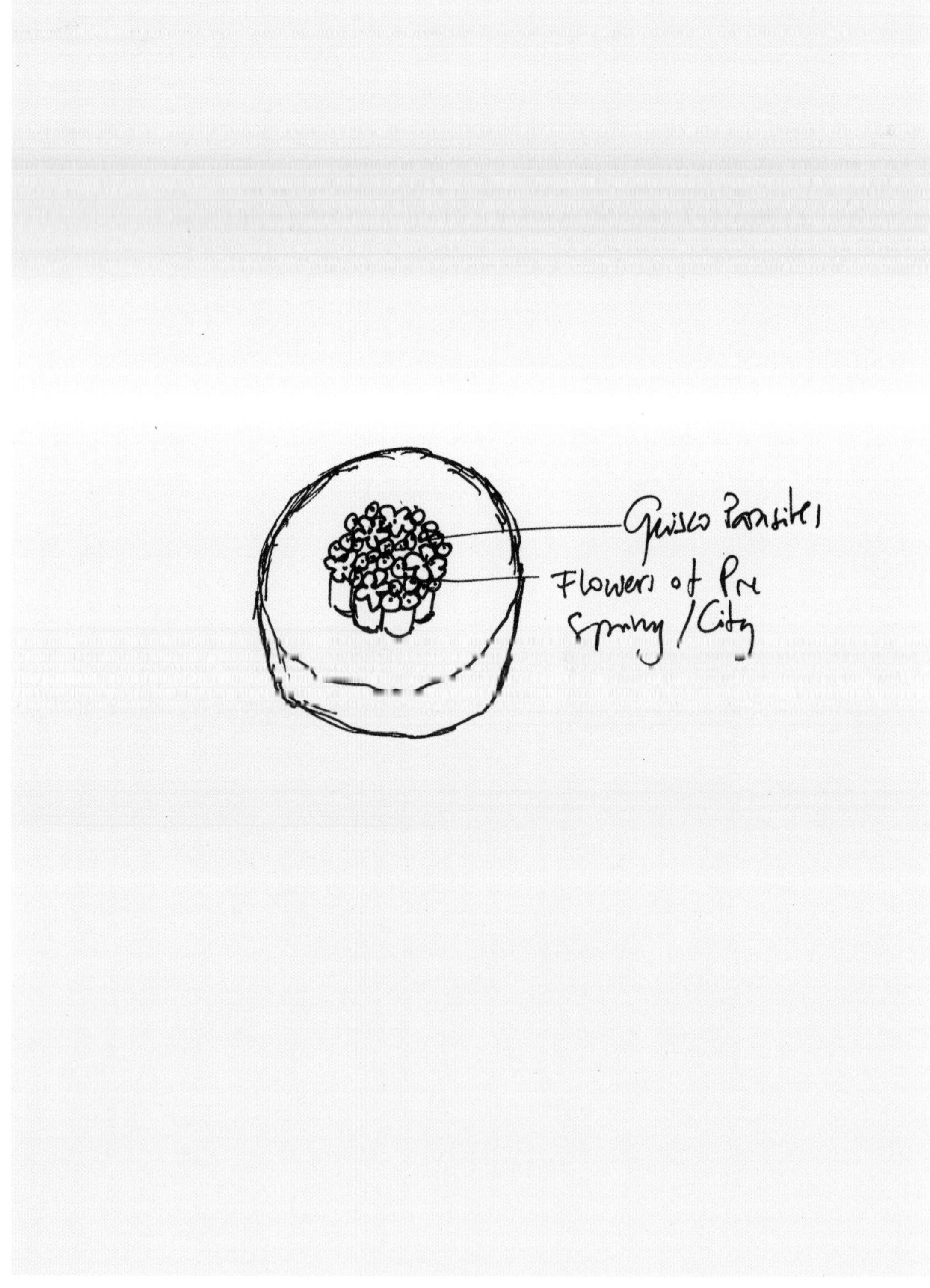

Ice Cake and Pre-Spring Quisco Parasites →247

City Chocolate Mushroom Cake → 247

Wild Boar in a Clay Oven with Nettle Meringue → 254

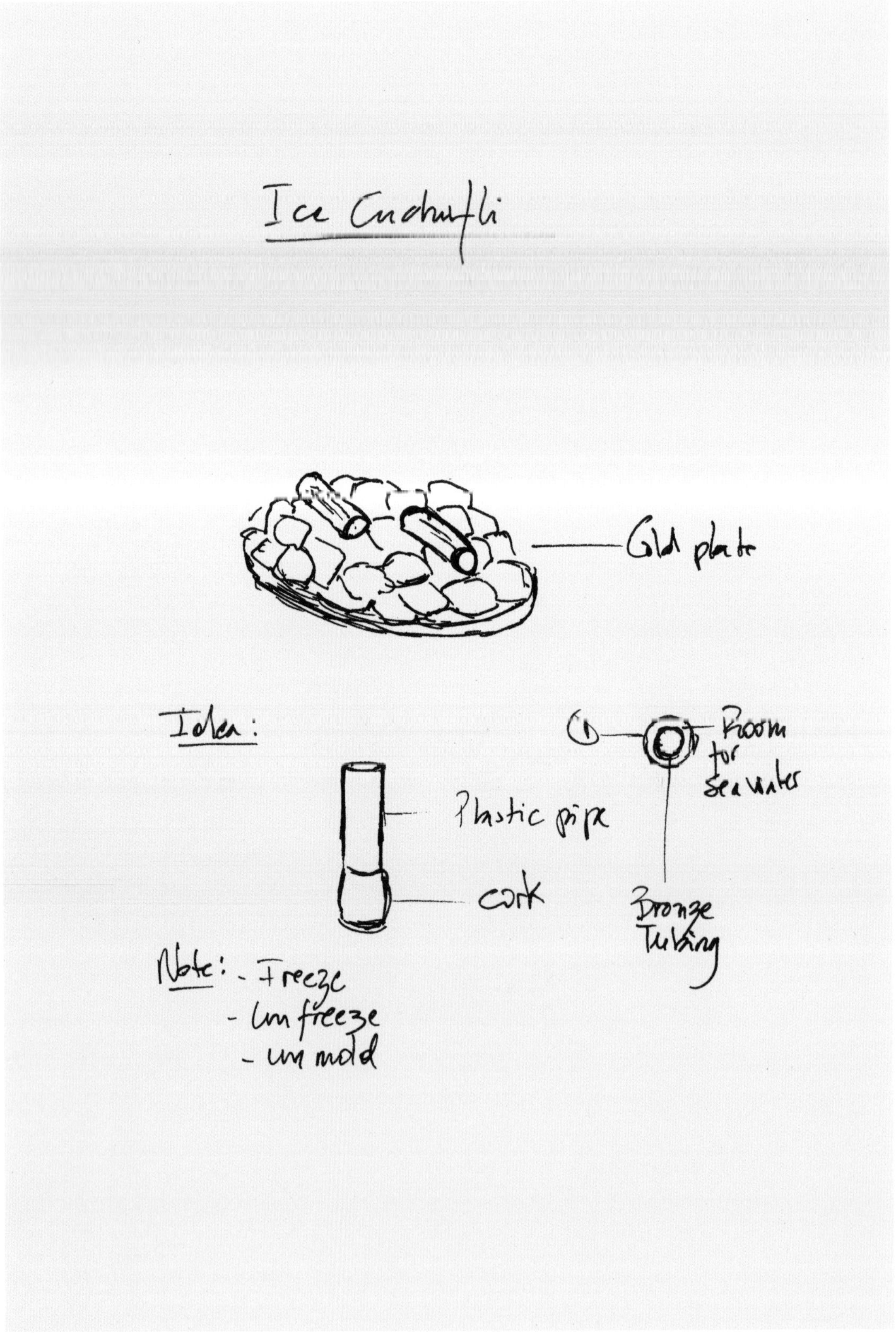

Ice Cuchufli

Cold plate

Idea:

①

Room for Sea water

Plastic pipe

cork

Bronze Tubing

Note: - Freeze
- un freeze
- un mold

Ice Cuchuflí Stuffed with Calbuco Black-Bordered Oysters → 265

Granado Beans with Tomatoes from Limache → 245

Veal from Parral Cooked in its Own Milk → 259

Flowers Grissini → 265

Warm Chilean Macha Ceviche in Its Own Cooked Blood → 222

Jibia and Apple → 256

RECIPES

ATACAMA

→162

Copao Chilenito

Serves 4

For the grapevine leaves:
1 grapevine leaf
100 g apple cider vinegar
50 g sugar

For the chilenito rounds:
62.5 g all-purpose (plain) flour, sifted
1 egg
15 g egg yolk
7.5 g pisco
3.7 g solid vegetable shortening

For the sunflower seed praline:
125 g shelled unsalted sunflower seeds
6 g sugar
1 g fine sea salt
62.5 g sunflower oil

For the copao pulp:
half of a copao fruit

To serve:
1 g Cáhuil fleur de sel

GRAPEVINE LEAVES

Using a 2½-inch (6 cm) round cookie cutter, cut 4 rounds out of the grape leaf, making sure the leaf veins are centered within the rounds. In a pan, combine the vinegar and sugar with 150 g water, and set aside. Bring another pan of water to a boil. Blanch the cut-out leaves in the boiling water for 2 minutes. Then transfer the leaves to the pot containing the vinegar solution, just until boiling. Remove from the heat and let the leaves cool completely in the liquid. Then vacuum-seal the leaves in the solution and set aside for 2 weeks.

CHILENITO ROUNDS

Preheat the oven to 425°F (220°C/Gas Mark 7). In a bowl, mix the flour, egg, and egg yolk until you obtain a firm dough. In a small pan over low heat, combine the pisco and the shortening, and warm until the shortening has melted. Add the flour-egg mixture to the shortening-pisco mixture, and mix until a thoroughly mixed, smooth, and firm dough form. Roll the dough out between 2 silicone baking mats until paper-thin (1 mm); the dough should be nearly translucent. Using a 2½-inch (6 cm) round cookie cutter, cut out 8 rounds; remove and discard the excess dough. Using a fork, perforate each round in 4 places, leaving a space between the marks. Put the dough rounds on a silicone sheet and bake for 6 minutes or until light brown. Transfer to a cooling rack and let cool completely on the silicone sheet. Lower the oven temperature to 400°F (200°C/Gas Mark 6).

SUNFLOWER SEED PRALINE

Toast the sunflower seeds on a baking sheet in the oven for 5 minutes or until lightly browned. Transfer the seeds while hot to a food processor, add the sugar and salt, and process together until smooth. With the processor running, gradually add the oil and process until the praline is smooth and emulsified. Transfer the praline to a pastry (piping) bag and set aside.

COPAO PULP

Remove the pulp and seeds from the copao half with a spoon. In a food processor or blender, puree the pulp and seeds slightly, until the fruit becomes mucilaginous. Transfer to a covered bowl and set aside.

TO SERVE

Using one of the chilenito rounds as a base, dot a quarter of the sunflower seed praline at 7 points, placing them apart from each other. Spoon a quarter of the copao pulp over the chilenito round, and sprinkle with a quarter of the fleur de sel. Repeat with 3 more chilenito rounds. Remove the grapeleaves from the pickling solution and while slightly damp adhere each leaf to one of the remaining chilenito rounds. Then put the leaf-covered rounds on top of the chilenito filling to make 4 "sandwiches." Serve immediately.

→165

Rica Rica Ice Cream and Chañar Concentrate

Serves 4

For the rica rica ice cream:
2 g unflavored gelatin sheet
2 rica rica twigs
787.5 g whole (full-fat) milk
312.5 g heavy (double) cream
3.7 g ice-cream stabilizer
135 g powdered milk
125 g sugar
168 g glucose powder
33.7 g dextrose powder

For the chañar concentrate:
1 kg chañar fruit

To serve:
4 water balloons
200 g liquid nitrogen

RICA RICA ICE CREAM

Fill a shallow dish with cold water and submerge the gelatin sheet in it. Set aside. Remove the leaves from the rica rica twigs. Set the twigs aside, and grind 7.5 g of the leaves in a coffee grinder. Pour the milk and the cream into a pan and warm it to 175°F (80°C). Add half the ground rica rica leaves and infuse in the warm mixture for 2 hours.

Next, leave the mixture with the leaves to set. Pour the mixture into a food processor and add the remaining ground rica rica leaves. Blend for about 5 minutes until it is smooth and thoroughly mixed. Then strain the mixture in a bowl. Set the pan in an ice bath and cool the mixture to 120°F (50°C). In a separate bowl, mix the stabilizer, powdered milk, sugar, glucose, and dextrose together, and add this mixture to the cooled infusion. Return the pan to the heat and, whisking constantly, heat the mixture to 185°F (85°C). Then remove it from the heat, place in the ice bath, and cool to 120°F (50°C) again. Once the mixture has cooled, add the hydrated gelatin sheet and stir. Refrigerate the mixture at 39°F (4°C) until the following day.

CHAÑAR CONCENTRATE

Soak the chañar in a bowl of cool water for 24 hours. Then fill a pan with 3 kg water, bring it to a simmer, add the drained chañar, and simmer for 4 hours.

Remove the skin and the seeds from the fruit, return just the fruit to the remaining cooking water in the pan, and simmer for 1 more hour or until the liquid has the consistency of a syrup. Strain and reserve the syrup at room temperature.

TO SERVE

Fill a 50-ml (2 oz) syringe with rica rica ice cream, fill each water balloon with 15 g of the ice cream, and tie them closed. Set aside at room temperature.

Heat a pan of water to 100°F (40°C). Fill a bowl with the liquid nitrogen. Immerse an ice-cream–filled balloon in the liquid nitrogen for 28 seconds. Then use a sharp knife to cut an X in the top of the balloon, and immerse the balloon in the hot water for only 2 seconds; immediately remove the balloon and immerse it once again in the liquid nitrogen for 1 second. Repeat with the remaining 3 balloons.

Cut open the balloons, remove the ice cream balls, immerse them again in the liquid nitrogen for 3 to 5 seconds and serve immediately, resting the ice cream balls on the reserved rica rica twigs, with the chañar concentrate alongside for dipping.

→129

Llama Crudo

Serves 4

For the tolilla cookie:
4 g freshly cut tolilla
142 g semolina
2 g fresh yeast
2 g fine sea salt

For the crudo:
140 g llama meat, preferably whole sirloin pieces, aged for 2 weeks
10 g cachiyuyo
0.5 g tola
1 g Cáhuil fleur de sel
3 g olive oil

For the rica rica mayonnaise:
1 egg
2 g fine sea salt
10 g dried rica rica leaves
250 g canola (rapeseed) oil
40 g lemon juice

For the rica rica tartara sauce:
10 g rica rica
80 g Pajaritos Cream (see Basic Recipes → 274)
3 g brine packed capers
4 g liquid mustard

For the radish leaves:
100 g radish leaves
100 g llama fat

For the roasted muña muña:
100 g muña muña branches with leaves

To serve:
80 g chopped copao flesh

TOLILLA COOKIE

Preheat the oven to 425°F (220°C/Gas Mark 7). Grind the tolilla in a coffee grinder, and sift it into a bowl. Add the semolina, yeast, salt, and 70 g water, and knead vigorously until a soft, firm dough. Place the bowl on top of the warming oven, and let the mixture proof covered for 30 minutes.

Roll the dough out until paper-thin (1 mm) thickness. Using a 2 × 3-inch (5 × 8 cm) oval cookie cutter, cut out 4 ovals. Put the ovals on a baking sheet between silpats and bake for 5 minutes. Remove and transfer inmediately to a cooling rack.

CRUDO

Remove the excess fat from the llama meat and store it in the refrigerator. Grind the meat in a manual meat grinder. Cut the cachiyuyo into thin ribbons and the tola into small pieces. In a large bowl, mix the ground (minced) meat with the fleur de sel, tola, and cachiyuyo. Stir in the olive oil, cover, and refrigerate at 39°F (4°C) until ready to serve.

RICA RICA MAYONNAISE

In a blender, mix together the egg, salt, and rica rica. With the blender running, gradually add half of the canola oil. Next, add the lemon juice and finish with the remainder of the canola oil. Use a spatula to carefully push the mayonnaise toward the center of the blender, and blend gently again to make sure the mayonnaise is aerated. Save 26 g for the rica rica tartara sauce.

RICA RICA TARTARA SAUCE

Process the rica rica in a coffee grinder for 7 seconds and repeat 3 times, until it forms a very fine and intensely green powder.

In a bowl, stir the pajaritos cream with the powdered rica rica, capers, mustard, and 26 g of the rica rica mayonnaise. Pass the mixture through a fine-mesh sieve into a bowl, discarding any chunks. Place the tartara sauce in a small plastic pastry bag and refrigerate at 39°F (4°C).

RADISH LEAVES

Using a 1-inch (3-cm) oval cookie cutter, cut out the radish leaves so that the central vein is in the middle of each oval.

Preheat the oven to its lowest setting. Put the llama fat in a baking dish and heat it to 115°F (45°C). Put the radish leaves and the melted llama fat in a vacuum bag, and vacuum at least 6 times. Arrange 5 radish leaves between sheets of paper towel, and press with an iron set on low steam until the leaves caramelize and become perfectly translucent and dry. Repeat with the remaining leaves. Store in an airtight container.

ROASTED MUÑA MUÑA

Preheat a nonstick skillet (frying pan) over high heat, add the muña muña, and stir constantly until roasted, about 10 minutes. Remove and allow to cool to room temperature.

TO SERVE

Fill each tolilla cookie with crudo, and cover the meat with copao flesh. Pipe 13 dots of the rica rica tartara sauce over the copao flesh in an irregular pattern. Sprinkle with the roasted muña muña, and then cover with the radish leaves, letting them overlap. Serve immediately.

→ 112

Rose-of-the-Year Cuchuflí

Serves 4

For the almond milk yogurt:
500 g almonds, skin-on
65 g lactose
13 g pajaritos starter

For the cuchuflí:
200 g sugar
1 green apple, cored
1 g rose of the year petals

To serve:
40 small rocks

ALMOND MILK YOGURT

Soak the almonds in 2 kg water overnight. Then grind the mixture in a food processor for 10 minutes. Filter it through a fine cheesecloth placed over a container for at least 5 hours, and reserve the resulting almond milk.

Add the lactose and the pajaritos to 5½ cups (1.3 liters) of almond milk in a plastic or glass container and cover. Ferment for 2 days.

After the whey has separated from the almond milk yogurt, reserve it for other preparations, strain the yogurt through a fine cheesecloth into a bowl for 4 hours, and then filter that yogurt through a fine-mesh strainer. The result should be a thick, shiny yogurt. Stir well and place in a plastic pastry bag in the refrigerator.

CUCHUFLÍ

Preheat the oven to 350°F (180°C/Gas Mark 4). In a pan, combine 100 g of the sugar with 100 g water, and cook over medium heat until a thick syrup forms; then pour into a bowl and let cool. Slice the green apple with a mandolin, and submerge the slices in the sugar syrup for 5 minutes. Then put the bowl in a vacuum machine, and vacuum the apples in syrup 3 times.

Bake the apples on a nonstick baking sheet in the oven for 10 minutes or until they are gently browned.

Remove the apples from the oven and quickly roll them around the ½-inch (1 cm) diameter metal rods to form cuchuflís; let cool to room temperature.

In a pan, make a thinner sugar syrup with the remaining 100 g sugar and 200 g water, heating it to 243°F (117°C). Let the syrup cool slightly and paint the syrup all over the outside of the cuchuflís. Stick the rose petals on them to cover the apple completely.

TO SERVE

Put a napkin on a rectangular plate and place the rocks on top. Fill the rose-of-the-year cuchuflís with the almond yogurt, and arrange them on the rocks. Serve immediately.

→ 216

Warm Chilean Macha Ceviche in Its Own Cooked Blood

Serves 4

For the Chilean machas:
240 g fresh Chilean machas
12 g olive oil
40 g lemon juice
1 g dry molle fruit

For the cooked Chilean macha blood:
1 kg fresh Chilean machas
2 g fine sea salt
1 Black Fermented Lemon
(see Basic Recipes → 273)

To serve:
12 macha shells
Petals from 8 society garlics

CHILEAN MACHAS

Clean and remove the guts; cut them into very tiny dice approximately 0.04-inch (1 mm) cubes. In a medium bowl, emulsify the olive oil with the lemon juice; add the cubed machas and toss to season them. Grind the dry molle fruit in a coffee grinder and sprinkle over the machas.

Clean the Chilean macha shells, trying not to cut the muscle that holds the two halves together. Set them aside in the refrigerator.

COOKED CHILEAN MACHA BLOOD

Pack the machas, without their guts, in a vacuum bag and freeze it. Next, cook it in a sous vide machine at 144°F (62°C) for 8 minutes. Strain into a small pan, pressing gently and taking care that no pieces fall in, then discard the machas. Stir the resulting broth over low heat until it reaches 145°F (63°C). Grind the lemon in a coffee grinder to a fine powder and add 1 g of it and the salt to the broth. Once it turns pink, use it immediately.

TO SERVE

Divide the cubed machas among the reserved shells, taking care that the muscle does not break so the shell can be held in the hand for eating. Season the macha meat with the society garlic petals, and place 3 filled shells on each plate. Fill the center of the plate with the cooked macha blood.

→ 172

Gigantic Macaron with Rica Rica Ice Cream and Chañar

Serves 4

For the gigantic macarons:
150 g sugar
100 g egg whites
150 g powdered sugar
150 g almond flour
2 drops squid ink

For the rica rica fermented ice cream:
0.75 g powdered agar agar
1 rica rica sprig,
soaked in 540 g water pajarito
with half a peeled apple for
1 month
30 g pulverized dried rica rica
3 g ice-cream stabilizer
62 g liquid glucose
54 g dextrose powder

To serve:
30 g chañar syrup
1 g powdered rica rica
4 wild dill sprigs

GIGANTIC MACARONS

Combine 150 g water and the sugar in a pan and heat over medium heat. Meanwhile, beat 50 g of the egg whites until soft peaks form. When the sugar syrup reaches 244°F (117.5°C), gradually add it to the egg whites in a thin stream, with the mixer running. Beat at full speed until the mixture temperature decreases to 104°F (40°C). Stop the mixer and fold in the powdered sugar, almond flour, squid ink, and remaining 50 g egg whites. Put the mixture in a pastry (piping) bag.

Line a baking sheet with a silicone baking mat. Use the pastry (piping) bag to form four 4 ½-inch (12 cm)-diameter macarons. Rap the tray against a work surface to remove any bubbles in the batter. Let stand at room temperature for 10 hours.

Preheat the oven at 290°F (145°C/Gas Mark 2) for 15 minutes. Bake the macarons for 15 minutes. Remove from the oven and let cool on the baking sheet for 4 hours. Then remove them from the silicone mat and cut them out with a 3¾-inch (9.5 cm) round cookie cutter. Crack the surface of each macaron with the back of a spoon. Store in an airtight container at room temperature.

RICA RICA FERMENTED ICE CREAM

In a pan, dissolve the agar agar in 100 g water and then boil for 5 minutes, stirring continuously. In another pan, warm the water pajarito mixture and the rica rica branch over medium heat (reserve the apple). When it reaches 104°F (40°C), add the pulverized rica rica, boiled agar agar, ice-cream stabilizer, liquid glucose, and dextrose powder. Heat to 185°F (85°C). Remove from the heat and cool in an ice bath; let set for 12 hours in the refrigerator. Spin the mixture in an ice-cream machine for 5 minutes before serving.

TO SERVE

Chill the plates in the freezer for 30 minutes. Cut the reserved apple into small cubes. On each plate put some chopped apple followed by a scoop of the rica rica fermented ice cream on top. Slightly cover the ice cream with the chañar syrup. Put a cracked macaroon on top, pressing it down slightly. Sprinkle with the powdered rica rica. Finally, insert a sprig of wild dill in one of the cracks of each macaron.

→ 128

Rica Rica Cold Cream, Cachiyuyo, and Cucumber Salad

Serves 4

For the aloe vera:
1 aloe vera leaf

For the rica rica ice cream:
4 g unflavored gelatin sheets
10 g dried rica rica
1.4 kg whole (full-fat) milk
720 g heavy (double) cream
9 g ice-cream stabilizer
216 g powdered milk
360 g glucose powder
28 g dextrose powder

For the parsley oil:
500 g parsley
1 kg canola (rapeseed) oil

For the cucumbers:
1 cucumber

For the lemon verbena gel:
20 g grated lemon zest
50 lemon verbena leaves
20 g powdered agar agar
10 g xanthan gum
50 g sugar
150 g lemon juice

For the algarrobo powder:
200 g algarrobo fruit, dehydrated at 185°F (85°C) for 12 hours

To serve:
6 g cachiyuyo leaves
1 g grated lime zest

ALOE VERA

Remove and discard the skin from the aloe vera, and cut it into julienne strips; soak in water for 2 days, changing the water each day. Then cook in boiling water for 5 minutes and cool in an ice bath.

RICA RICA ICE CREAM

Fill a shallow dish with cold water and submerge the gelatin sheets in it. Set aside.

Grind the rica rica in a coffee grinder; then combine it with the milk and the cream and infuse at 175°F (80°C) for 2 hours. Grind with an electric handmixer and strain the mixture into a bowl. Lower the temperature to 120°F (50°C) by cooling the mixture in an ice bath. Mix the stabilizer, powdered milk, glucose, and dextrose together, and add to the rica rica mixture. Pour into a pan and, using a whisk, stir over medium heat until it has warmed to 185°F (85°C) again; then remove from the heat and cool in the ice bath. When the temperature of the mixture drops to 120°F (50°C), add the hydrated gelatin sheets and stir. Set the mixture aside at 39°F (4°C) until the following day. Pass the mix through the ice-cream machine, place the ice cream inside an expanded polystyrene container, and keep at 28°F (–2°C).

PARSLEY OIL

Blend the parsley with the canola oil at maximum power at 150°F (65°C) for 15 minutes. Strain through a cheesecloth (muslin) into a bowl for 12 hours at 39°F (4°C). Separate the oil from the liquid below it and store it at room temperature in a dark place.

CUCUMBERS

Peel the cucumber and put it through a low-speed extruder, keeping the juice. Slice the cucumbers into thin lengthwise slices and then cut them into ⅔-inch (1.5 cm) squares; put half the cucumber squares in the cucumber juice in a bowl. Arrange the bowl inside a vacuum sealing machine and vacuum 6 times.

LEMON VERBENA GEL

Infuse the lemon zest and lemon verbena in 950 g water in a bowl at 140°F (60°C) for 2 hours. Strain the infused water into a pan, and mix in the agar agar, xanthan gum, and sugar. Boil for 5 minutes, whisking continuously with a balloon whisk. Remove from the heat and let it cool, stirring it slowly. Finish the cooking process while blending at minimum speed for 20 minutes. Add the lemon juice and place in a plastic pastry (piping) bag.

ALGARROBO POWDER

Grind the dehydrated fruit at maximum power until it forms a smooth powder. Sift and store in an airtight container.

TO SERVE

Pass the rica rica ice cream through an ice-cream machine at top speed right until it is creamy yet still firm.

Place 3 dots of lemon verbena gel in the center of each plate, slightly separated from one another, and sprinkle with the algarrobo powder. Using a scoop, place a quenelle of the ice cream on the powder. On top of this, arrange both types of cucumbers over the ice cream, interleaving them to cover the ice cream. At the same time, add the cachiyuyo between the cucumbers. Arrange the aloe vera on one side; add a drop of parsley oil to the aloe vera and, after 1 minute, sprinkle lime zest on top. Serve immediately.

→ 127

Parfait of Bitter Plants

Serves 4

For the parfait:
2 g unflavored gelatin sheet
1 kg whole (full fat) milk
600 g heavy (double) cream
160 g glucose powder
240 g powdered milk
240 g sugar
60 g dextrose powder
4 g guar gum
4 g gellan gum
8 g copa copa leaves
8 g muña muña leaves
8 g lampaya leaves
8 g chichicandia leaves

For the chañar powder:
200 g fresh chañar

For the Chilean carob powder:
300 g Chilean carob fruit

PARFAIT

Fill a shallow dish with cold water and submerge the gelatin sheet in it. Set aside.

Mix the milk, cream, and glucose in a pan and heat to 105°F (40°C). Add the powdered milk, sugar, dextrose, and guar gum. Heat to 185°F (85°C) and add the gellan gum. Cool the mixture to 150°F (65°C) in an ice bath, and then add the hydrated gelatin. Strain the mixture and divide it into 4 equal parts. Add the copa copa to the first part, the muña muña to the second part, the lampaya to the third part, and the chichicandia to the fourth part. Spread each mixture on parchment paper into even rectangles, and freeze for at least 4 hours, until it reaches a firm texture. Cut them into irregular pieces, from 6 g to 8 g, making sure they have a flat base so they don't roll on the plate. Store in the freezer.

CHAÑAR POWDER

Remove the pit from the unpeeled fruit. Dry the pulp at 150°F (65°C). In a food processor, blend until it forms a fine powder; then sift the powder into an airtight container and store at room temperature.

CHILEAN CAROB POWDER

Remove the pit from the fruit. Dry the pulp at 150°F (65°C). In a food processor, blend until it forms a fine powder; then sift the powder into an airtight container and store at room temperature.

TO SERVE

Chill 4 irregularly shaped stone plates. Arrange the chañar powder in a container and the Chilean carob powder in another one. Pass the copa copa parfait pieces, and then the muña muña parfait pieces, through the chañar powder. Pass the lampaya parfait pieces, and then the chichicandia parfait pieces, through the Chilean carob powder. Arrange the parfaits irregularly on each plate, grouping 8 pieces per plate so they lean one over the other, and serve immediately.

→ 146

Tru-trum and Chochas

Serves 4

For the grape umeboshi:
1 kg unripe green grapes
80 g salt

For the tru-trum:
1 kg tepú wood
500 g white Michuñe potatoes from Chiloé
2 g fine sea salt
50 g pig skin
100 g pork lard
1 tepú wood branch, 20 inches (50 cm) long and 2¾ inches (7 cm) in diameter

For the chochas:
1 fresh chocha

To serve:
16 dry espino twigs
4 chochas

GRAPE UMEBOSHI

Pack the grapes and the salt in a vacuum bag; seal at maximum pressure and store for 6 months before using it.

TRU-TRUM

Burn the tepú wood in a deep metal pan until you have red-hot embers.

In a large pan of boiling water, cook 300 g of the Mechuñe potatoes until completely cooked. Then drain and mash them, forming a rustic mash, and add the salt. Let cool to room temperature.

Grate the remaining 200 g uncooked potato and mix it with the mashed cooked potato to form a paste. Let stand for about 1 hour.

Chop the pig skin into small cubes. Heat the lard in a skillet (frying pan) over low heat, add the cubes, and caramelize them, stirring occasionally, for 1 hour. Then drain the pig skin, reserving the fat. Mix the caramelized skin into the potato paste. Wrap the paste around the tepú wood branch and let it rest horizontally on two supports over the hot embers. Cook, turning the branch continuously for 5 hours, regardless of how gently the fire turns. Every 15 minutes, brush the surface that is exposed to the heat with the reserved pig fat, in order to prevent it from drying excessively. Additionally, blow on the fire every 20 minutes in order to prevent it from extinguishing.

CHOCHA

Remove the chocha from the shell and cut it into thin pieces, as for sashimi. Arrange them symmetrically, matching the size of the tru trum.

TO SERVE

Arrange 4 espino twigs in a parallel formation on each plate.

Carefully remove the caramelized tru-trum from the tepú wood branch by slicing it horizontally. Cut 4 pieces, 2¾ x 2½ inches (7 × 6 cm) each. Leaving a ¾-inch (2 cm) border, arrange the chocha sashimi on the tru-trum pieces. Thinly slice the grape umeboshi and intersperse it with the chochas, covering the center of the tru-trums. Press the edges over, and serve immediately over the espino twigs.

→ 133, 134

Ice Brûlée of Plants and Rose-of-the-Year Ice Cream Sandwich

Serves 4

For the pears cooked in tola:
1 g tola
1 pear

For the rica rica cold cream:
1.4 kg whole (full-fat) milk
720 g heavy (double) cream
10 g rica rica
360 g glucose powder
216 g powdered milk
28.3 g dextrose powder
6 g ice-cream stabilizer

For the lemon verbena foam:
7.6 g unflavored gelatin sheets
5 g fresh lemon verbena
200 g lemon juice
100 g sugar

For the tolilla foam:
9.5 g unflavored gelatin sheets
2 g tolilla
100 g sugar
100 g tolilla vinegar

For the rica rica oil:
100 g canola (rapeseed) oil
100 g spinach
2 g rica rica

For the ice disk:
100 g purified water
1 g rose of the year petals
10 g sugar

For the rica rica powder:
10 g rica rica

For the muña muña ash:
10 g muña muña

For the cookies:
100 g unsalted sunflower seeds
100 g all-purpose (plain) flour

For the kombucha syrup:
1 kg rose-of-the-year kombucha

For the rose-of-the-year ice cream disks:
4 g unflavored gelatin sheets
1 kg whole (full-fat) milk
500 g heavy (double) cream
134 g glucose powder
12 g rose-of-the-year petals
240 g powdered milk
90 g sugar
60 g dextrose powder
4 g ice-cream stabilizer

For the rose-of-the-year ice cream sandwich:
4 Cookies
2 Rose-of-the-Year Ice-Cream Disks
8 g Kombucha Syrup
2 g cachiyuyo leaves

For the sugared rose of the year:
50 g sugar
5 g rose-of-the-year petals

PEARS COOKED IN TOLA

Combine the tola with 200 g water in a pan and infuse for 1 hour at 115°F (45°C).

With a melon baller, create 20 pear spheres. Pour the tola infusion into a bowl, add the pear spheres, and use a vacuum machine to vacuum 10 times. Remove the pears and dehydrate at 115°F (45°C) for 1 hour.

RICA RICA COLD CREAM

Mix the milk, cream, glucose, and rica rica in a pan and heat it to 120°F (50°C). Then add the powdered milk, dextrose, and stabilizer and stir continuously until it heats to 185°F (85°C). Cool the mixture in an ice bath, strain it, and freeze it in a beaker to 10°F (–12°C) and pass through the Pacojet until it has a whipped cream texture. Store at 25°F (–4°C).

LEMON VERBENA FOAM

Fill a shallow dish with cold water and submerge the gelatin sheets in it. Set aside.

Combine the lemon verbena and 300 g water in a pan and heat to 175°F (80°C); infuse for 1 hour. Let the mixture cool to room temperature, add the lemon juice and sugar, and strain it into another pan. Add the gelatin, heat the mixture to 120°F (50°C), and stir until the gelatin is completely dissolved. Strain again. Add the mixture to an N_2O siphon. Charge it with two N_2O siphon cartridges and store in the refrigerator.

TOLILLA FOAM

Fill a shallow dish with cold water and submerge the gelatin sheets in it. Set aside.

Combine the tolilla and 300 g water in a pan and infuse at 175°F (80°C) for 1 hour. Let the mixture cool to room temperature, add the sugar and tolilla vinegar, and strain it into another pan. Add the gelatin, heat the mixture to 120°F (50°C), and stir until the gelatin is completely dissolved. Strain again. Add the mixture to an N_2O siphon. Charge with two N_2O siphon cartridges and store in in the refrigerator.

RICA RICA OIL

Combine the canola oil, spinach, and rica rica in a pan and heat to 150°F (65°C); infuse for 15 minutes. Strain the oil through a fine cloth into a container, and store in a dark place at room temperature for up to 2 weeks.

ICE DISK

In a pan, mix the purified water, rose-of-the-year petals, and sugar. Infuse at 185°F (85°C) for 2 hours. Let cool to room temperature, and strain. Place 5 g of the mixture in silicone molds that measure 3 inches (8 cm) in diameter to form a disk of 0.06 inches (1.5 mm) in thickness, and freeze. Store in the freezer, arranged between plastic bags to avoid sticking.

RICA RICA POWDER

Blend the rica rica in a coffee grinder until it forms a fine powder. Set it aside in an airtight container at room temperature.

MUÑA MUÑA ASH

Burn the muña muña in a skillet (frying pan) until it is a uniform black color and has an intense scent. Let it cool to room temperature and then grind in a coffee grinder to make a fine powder. Store in an airtight container at room temperature.

COOKIES

Preheat a skillet over medium heat, and toast the sunflower seeds. Blend the seeds and 200 g water at 185°F (85°C) for 10 minutes or until it forms a smooth paste. In a bowl, combine the flour, 150 g water, and 40 g of the sunflower seed paste. Whisk by hand until smooth.

Preheat a panini grill, making sure that the plates are smooth and can be in full contact. Pour a full tablespoon of the sunflower mixture onto the grill, close the grill, and press evenly with a cloth for about 25 seconds, until the dough expands. Remove the wafer immediately. Repeat to make 4 cookies. Store in an airtight container at room temperature.

KOMBUCHA SYRUP

In a pan over medium heat, reduce 1 kg rose-of-the-year kombucha for approximately 3 hours until it measures 200 g. Set aside in an airtight container at room temperature.

ROSE-OF-THE-YEAR ICE CREAM DISKS

Fill a shallow dish with cold water and submerge the gelatin sheets in it. Set aside.

Mix the milk, cream, glucose, and rose-of-the-year petals in a pan and infuse at 175°F (80°C) for 2 hours. Then strain the liquid and reduce the temperature to 120°F (50°C) in an ice bath. Add the powdered milk, sugar, dextrose, and stabilizer and stir continuously over heat until the mixture reaches 185°F (85°C). Reduce the temperature again to 120°F (50°C) in the ice bath; then add the hydrated gelatin sheets and stir until they are completely dissolved. Let the mixture stand for 12 hours.

Pass the mixture through an ice-cream machine at full speed until it forms a firm but creamy texture. Spread the ice cream over a baking sheet, forming a ⅓-inch (1 cm)-thick layer, and freeze for approximately 1 hour until the ice cream is firm. Using a 3-inch (8 cm) round dough cutter, cut out 2 disks. Return to the freezer until firm. Then use a melon baller to cut half-sphere holes in the ice cream disks, and fill them with kombucha syrup. Store in the freezer until ready to serve.

ROSE-OF-THE-YEAR
ICE-CREAM SANDWICH

Put a cookie on a flat surface. Spread a thin layer of kombucha syrup over the cookie, and arrange the cachiyuyo leaves to cover the surface, letting them overlap. Put the rose-of-the-year ice cream disk over a cookie and cut in half. Cut the cookie covered by cachiyuyo in half and cover the top of the ice cream sandwich. Cover in the same way the edges of the sandwich with cachiyuyo leaves and store at –4°F (–20°C) until the moment you serve it.

SUGARED ROSE OF THE YEAR

Preheat a nonstick skillet over medium heat.

Add the sugar and heat it to 245°F (121°C). Then add the rose petals and stir continuously with a wooden spoon until the pieces are crystallized. Store in an airtight container at room temperature.

TO SERVE

Chill four 3¼-inch (8.5 cm)-diameter bowls. Place the tola-infused pear balls in the center of the bowls, and put a scoop of rica rica ice cream on top of them. Press the top of the ice cream with a spoon to create an indent and pour the rica rica oil over it. Pour the tolilla foam on the left side and the lemon verbena foam on the right side. Cover the bowl with the ice disk. Sprinkle with the rica rica powder and muña muña ashes.

Place the sandwich on the edge of the bowl over the ice disk without letting the sandwich touch the ice disk.

Explain that the sandwich must be left on the side; so you first eat the ice brûlée, and then the sandwich with hands. (It is important that the sandwich is really cold when served, so it has the optimum temperature when eaten by hand.)

SANTIAGO

→ 137

Cheese Carrot Chilenito and Sea Strawberries

Serves 4

For the sea strawberries:
1 kg sea strawberries
1.5 kg rose vinegar

For the cheese carrots:
1 large carrot, 2 inches diameter
1 g *Penicillium candidum* mold spores

For the chilenito rounds:
63 g all-purpose (plain) flour, sifted
1 egg
15 g egg yolk
3.7 g solid vegetable shortening
8 g pisco

For the seaweed pajaritos cream:
500 g Pajaritos Cream (see Basic Recipes→ 274)
50 g reduction of Kolof Root Broth (see Basic Recipes → 273)

To serve:
2 g Cáhuil fleur de sel

SEA STRAWBERRIES

Remove the skin from the sea strawberries, taking care not to break the inside, and put them in a jar. Add the vinegar, seal the jar, and set aside at room temperature for 2 months. During the first week, take the sea strawberries out of the jar and dry them in the sun for 2 days; then put them back in the jar and leave them for the rest of the 2 months.

CHEESE CARROTS

Cut the carrot into 4 rounds that are 2 inches (5 cm) in diameter and ¼ inch (7 mm) thick.

Bring a large pot of water to a boil, add the carrot rounds, and blanch them. Drain and spread the carrots out on a rimmed stainless steel sheet to cool to room temperature.

Inoculate the carrots with *Penicillium candidum* by sprinkling it over the carrots with a plastic mesh strainer. Let the carrots ferment for 2 days at 55°F (13°C) with 57% humidity.

CHILENITO ROUNDS

Preheat the oven to 425°F (220°C/Gas Mark 7). Put the flour, egg, and egg yolk in a bowl. In a small pan over low heat, melt the shortening. Mix it with the pisco and add it to the flour mixture. Knead vigorously until you have a uniform, slightly elastic dough. Wrap in plastic wrap (clingfilm) to prevent dehydration.

Roll the dough out until it is paper-thin and almost translucent. Using a 2½-inch (6 cm) round cookie cutter, cut out 4 rounds of dough. Prick each round at least 5 times with a fork so it won't inflate. Put the dough rounds between 2 silicone baking mats on a baking sheet, and bake for 6 minutes. Remove the dough rounds and let them cool on a wire rack.

SEAWEED PAJARITOS CREAM

Beat the pajaritos cream in an electric mixer at medium speed. With the mixer running, add the kolof root reduction in a thin stream. Store the seaweed pajaritos cream covered at 39°F (4°C).

TO SERVE

Warm the cheese carrots on top of the oven or a hot surface before serving. Pipe some seaweed pajaritos cream onto each chilenito round. Cut each sea strawberry into 4 pieces, arrange them in the center of the chilenito, and pipe more pajaritos cream over them. Place a carrot on top, to resemble the top crust of a pie. Sprinkle fleur de sel over the surface of the carrot, and serve to be eaten by hand.

→ 199

Cold Welcome Pulmay

Serves 4

For the pulmay:
4 branches of tepu wood
100 g onion
15 g Chilean green chile (pepper)
7 magellanic sea scallops
300 g lemon juice
15 g olive oil
5 g 40% alcohol pisco
60 g cilantro (coriander)
7 ice cubes
2 g Cáhuil fleur de sel

To serve:
4 cow horns
Stone base for a platter

PULMAY

Light the wood in a deep metal pan. Place it over an open fire until it starts to expel yellow smoke. Place the onion and chile in a perforated metal pan and place it on top of the deep metal pan to make a smoker. Cover with aluminum foil and smoke the onion and chile for 7 minutes. Remove the vegetables from the smoker and store in the refrigerator.

In a food processor, blend the scallops with the lemon juice. Add the olive oil and pisco, and blend again until the mixture is smooth; remove half and refrigerate it. To the remaining half add the cilantro, onion, chile, and ice cubes; blend again. Reincorporate the reserved half and blend for 5 seconds. Season with the fleur de sel, strain it through a fine cloth into a container, and store in the refrigerator until ready to serve.

TO SERVE

Place the cow horns on the stone base, and serve the cold welcome pulmay immediately in the horns.

→ 89

Pâté Berlín

Serves 4

For the pâté:
250 g chicken livers
250 g whole (full-fat) milk

5 g sea salt
50 g unsalted butter
60 g muscovado sugar
1 white onion
0.5 g black pepper
1 g Cáhuil fleur de sel
30 g port wine

For the Berlín dough:
28.4 g whole (full-fat) milk
5 g sugar
6 g fresh yeast
8 g unsalted butter
1 egg yolk
65 g all-purpose (plain) flour
0.5 g sea salt
1 kg canola (rapeseed) oil

To serve:
8 small bunches yuyo flowers
2 g olive oil
1 g powdered sugar

PÂTÉ

Remove any excess fat from the chicken livers. Pour the milk into a baking dish, stir in the salt, and let the livers soak in the milk at 91°F (33°C) for 5 hours; press on the livers with your hands every hour to help the blood flow. Then drain the livers, rinse them well, and set them on a perforated tray to drain for 1 hour, until completely dry.

Preheat a skillet (frying pan) over medium high heat. Add the butter and the muscovado, and brown the livers. Combine the browned livers with the onion, pepper, fleur de sel, and port in a blender and grind at maximum power at 175°F (80°C) for 10 minutes. Freeze the mixture until it reaches 10°F (–12°C) and pass it twice through a Pacojet. Pour the pâté into a pastry (piping) bag fitted with a metal tip.

BERLÍN DOUGH

Form the leavening by combining the milk, half of the sugar, and the yeast in a bowl at room temperature. In a large bowl, mix the remaining sugar with the butter and egg yolk. Add the leavening, and then the flour and salt. Knead until obtaining a soft and firm dough, cover with plastic wrap (clingfilm) and set it aside at room temperature for 45 minutes.

Cut out 20 1½-inch (3.5 cm) squares of wax (greaseproof) paper. Form Berlines—or doughnuts—of 8 g each, and put each one on a square of waxed paper. Place the Berlines, separated from one another, on a baking sheet, cover with plastic wrap, and let them rise at room temperature for 15 minutes.

Deep fry in canola oil at 350° (180°C) until each Berlín is golden brown and set aside until cooled to room temperature.

TO SERVE

Make a cut in the top of each Berlín, cutting almost halfway through, and pipe the päte inside. Season the yuyo flowers with the olive oil, and set 2 flowers on top of the pâté on each Berlín. Place the Berlín on the plate and sprinkle with the powdered sugar. Serve immediately.

→ 197

Marraqueta Bread with Roasted Flour Pebre

Serves 4

For the roasted flour pebre:
100 g summer tomatoes
50 g onion
50 g fresh Chilean green chiles
50 g cilantro (coriander) stems
100 g roasted flour
80 g olive oil
0.5 g seaweed merkén
5 g fine sea salt

For the marraqueta bread:
1.8 kg all-purpose (plain) flour
42 g fresh yeast
1.6 g water, heated to 175°F (80°C)
48 g fine sea salt

ROASTED FLOUR PEBRE

Chop the summer tomato, onion, chiles, and cilantro stems in irregular pieces. Add them to a food processor and blend until it forms a liquid sauce. Add the roasted flour, olive oil, seaweed merkén, and salt. Blend again and store covered in the refrigerator.

MARRAQUETA BREAD

In a bowl, mix the flour, yeast, and lukewarm water. Add the salt on the borders of the bowl, preventing it from touching the yeast. Knead on a floured surface for 30 minutes or until obtaining a soft and firm dough. Brush the dough with water, cover it with plastic wrap (clingfilm), and let rest at room temperature for 2 hours. Meanwhile, on a work surface, arrange 1-inch (2.5 cm) diameter PVC tubes in parallel rows with a 1½-inch (4 cm) gap between them.

Preheat the oven to 500°F (260°C/Gas Mark 9). Form 40 buns of 20 g of the dough. Place 2 dough buns in contact with each other on a work surface, and smash them horizontally, right in the center, with a flour-covered towel. While carrying out this process, continually brush the dough with water in order to prevent the surface from dehydrating. Place each piece of dough between the tubes so that it it will rise upwards and not sideways. Repeat with the remaining buns.

Heat a baking sheet in the oven for 30 minutes. Then bake the bread for 15 minutes, applying touches of moisture every 5 minutes. Remove from the oven and allow the bread to cool just a little inside a flour-covered cloth. Serve as soon as possible.

TO SERVE

Place the hot marraqueta bread in a cloth-lined basket. Distribute the roasted flour pebre among 4 clay bowls, and serve immediately to accompany the bread.

Unripe Green Tomato Pebre with Savory Leche Asada

Serves 4

For the leche asada:
200 g whole (full-fat) milk
20 g chili powder
1 g fine sea salt
2 eggs

For the green tomato pebre:
2 green tomatoes
5 g fresh Chilean green chile
20 g white onion
4 g cilantro (coriander) leaves
5 g green cilantro (coriander) seeds
1 g Cáhuil fleur de sel
10 g olive oil
5 g lemon juice

To serve:

24 cilantro (coriander) flowers
40 small lemon balm leaves
0.5 g Cáhuil fleur de sel

LECHE ASADA

Combine the milk, chili powder, and salt in a pan and cook at at 140°F (60°C) for 5 minutes. Remove from the heat and let the mixture cool to 77°F (25°C); then strain it into a bowl and add the eggs. Whisk until evenly mixed. Pour 50 g of the mixture into 4 small clay containers each.

Preheat the oven to 194°F (90°C/Gas Mark ¼). Put the clay containers in a metal baking dish and add water to the dish until it reaches the level of the mixture within the clay containers; cover with aluminum foil and bake for 40 minutes. Remove from the heat and the water, let the leche asada cool to room temperature, and then store covered in the refrigerator.

GREEN TOMATO PEBRE

Cut the green tomatoes in half and remove the cores; reserve the cores for serving. Finely dice the firm flesh of the tomatoes, chile, and white onion. Cut the cilantro leaves into fine slivers, and toss the mixture together in a bowl.

Using a mortar and pestle, crush the green cilantro seeds with the fleur de sel and olive oil to form a rustic paste. Add the lemon juice and toss with the tomato mixture.

TO SERVE

Cut each of the tomato cores in half.

Arrange 25 g of the green tomato pebre on top of each leche asada. Then add a piece of tomato core, 6 cilantro flowers, and 10 small lemon balm leaves. Sprinkle the fleur de sel over the tomato cores and serve immediately.

→ 87

Quail's Nest with Autumn Mushrooms

Serves 4

For the mushroom cookie:
10 g clarified butter
50 g pink changle
20 g all-purpose (plain) flour
1 g fine sea salt
20 g corn flour

For the mushroom paste:
80 g small Chilean morel mushrooms
80 red pine mushrooms
40 g clarified butter
1 g fine sea salt

For the enoki nests:
50 g enoki mushrooms

For the quail eggs:
5 g mushroom paste
4 quail eggs

To serve:
5 g Mushroom Oil (see Basic Recipes → 273)
0.5 g Cáhuil fleur de sel
2 dead bonsai

MUSHROOM COOKIE

Preheat a skillet (frying pan) over medium heat and add the clarified butter. Cook the changles until soft and then blend it to a rustic paste in a food processor.

In a bowl, mix together the flour, salt, corn flour, 30 g water, and the changle paste. Preheat both sides of a flat panini griddle, making sure that the plates are smooth and can be in full contact. Pour a spoonful of the mixture onto the griddle, close the griddle, and press it evenly with a cloth until the dough expands. Open the griddle a little for approximately 15 seconds (depending on the heat) to let in a bit of humidity. Remove the cookie and place it in a tubular silicone mold that is 1½ inches (4 cm) in diameter and ¾ inch (2 cm) deep. Then dehydrate for 30 minutes at 131°F (55°C) and store at room temperature in an airtight container. Repeat to make a total of 4 cookies.

MUSHROOM PASTE

Cut the morels into into 0.2-inch (0.5 cm)-thick rings. Cut the red pine mushrooms into a medium dice. Preheat a skillet over medium heat, add the clarified butter, and cook the mushrooms until the texture is no longer firm. Sprinkle with the salt and set aside.

ENOKI NESTS

Preheat the oven to 150°F (65°C/Gas Mark 2).

Fry the enoki stems in a pan and, with the aid of fine-point tweezers, separate the filaments. Place them on a nonstick surface and dehydrate at 122°F (50°C) for 1 hour. Store in an airtight container at room temperature.

QUAIL EGGS

Fill a fine-needle syringe with the mushroom paste. Inject the paste into the yolks of the quail eggs, making perforations through the shells, until each egg yolk is filled with 0.1 g mushroom paste.

Bring a pan of water to a gentle boil and cook the eggs one at a time, because they're so fragile, for 1 minute. Immediately transfer them to an ice bath to cool. Remove the shell, being careful not to damage the egg when doing so. Keep the eggs in a warm-water bath at 118°F (48°C) until serving.

TO SERVE

Spread the mushroom paste over the cookies and form a nest of mushroom filament over it. Remove the quail eggs from the bain-marie and arrange one in the center of each nest. Season with the mushroom oil and sprinkle fleur de sel on top. Place the nests on the adjacent branches of the bonsai trees, and serve immediately.

→ 154

Aged and Steamed Jibia with Pajaritos Cream and Roasted Kolof

Serves 4

For the jibia:
130 g fresh jibia
1 kg Chilean espino coal
4 g olive oil

For the roasted kolof:
10 kg fresh kolof, harvested the day of cooking

To serve:
1 g Cáhuil fleur de sel
50 g Pajaritos Cream (see Basic Recipes → 274)
1 Chilean mandarin
36 small rue leaves

JIBIA

Chop the jibia into rectangles measuring 3½ inches (9 cm) long, 2 inches (5 cm) wide, and ½ inch (1.3 cm) thick. Allow the jibia to age, uncovered, in the refrigerator for 2 days.

Light the coal in a metallic container and burn until it forms red-hot embers.

Arrange the jibia on a rack and set it over the embers. Pour the olive oil onto the embers to simulate what happens when animal fat falls directly on the embers, and cover the jibia with a metal pan; smoke for 1 minute. Then let the jibia cool to room temperature and store covered at 30°F (1°C).

ROASTED KOLOF

Preheat the oven to 485°F (250°C/Gas Mark 9) with convection at maximum power. Put the kolof in a roasting pan and roast for 5 minutes. Allow the kolof to cool to room temperature before storing in an airtight container.

TO SERVE

Cook the jibia in a bamboo steamer over a medium heat for 20 minutes in order to prevent the outside from dehydrating.

Place the jibia on the center of each plate and add fleur de sel. Stir the pajaritos cream well and spread it over the jibia. Grate the mandarin zest over the pajaritos cream, then scatter the rue leaves randomly on top. Finish by placing a piece of roasted kolof in each corner of the plates. Serve immediately.

→185

Snail and Calendula Salad

Serves 4

For the snails:
40 live land snails
500 g fresh alfalfa

For the snail eggs:
10 g Chilean espino coal
5 g salt
20 g snail eggs
10 g olive oil

For the sea carrot sediment:
100 g sea carrot
100 g canola (rapeseed) oil

To serve:
10 lemon verbena leaves
3 lovage leaves
5 rue leaves
10 g katsuobushi-style mackerel
1 g Cáhuil fleur de sel
Petals of 8 calendula flowers, freshly picked

SNAILS

Feed the snails with the alfalfa for 2 weeks.

Fill a large pot with 3 kg cold water. Add the snails, place the pot over medium-high heat, and bring to a boil. When the water starts boiling, set the timer for 30 minutes.

Remove the snails and shell them, using a piece of wire.

SNAIL EGGS

Light the espino coal in a metal container and burn until it forms red hot embers. Prepare a brine by mixing 200 g water with the salt in a bowl; immerse the snail eggs in the brine for 7 minutes. Then remove the eggs and place them on a rack in a metal pan. Cover the pan with aluminum foil and set it over the hot embers. Pour the olive oil directly onto the embers and smoke the eggs for 10 seconds. Then remove and store them in the refrigerator.

SEA CARROT SEDIMENT

Preheat the oven to 465°F (240°C/Gas Mark 9). Roast the sea carrot for 7 minutes.

Heat the canola oil in a pan. Remove the sea carrot from the oven and deep fry it in the canola oil at 356°F (180°C) for 3 minutes. Blend the sea carrot with a stint of oil in a food processor to form a rustic paste. Vacuum pack the paste and let it settle for 2 weeks in the refrigerator.

TO SERVE

Cut out 4 brown cardboard rectangles measuring ¾ inch (2 cm) wide, 6 inches (15 cm) long, and fold into a concertina shape, folding every ½ inch (1.5 cm). Cut the lemon verbena, lovage, and rue leaves into thin slivers. Grate the mackerel and mix it with the snails, sea carrot sediment, and snail eggs; season with the fleur de sel. Distribute the snail mixture over the rectangles and place one on the right side of each plate; finish the dish with a sprinkling of calendula petals.

→150

Version 1
Creamy Rock Clovers and Other Plants from Isla Negra

Serves 4

For the rock spinach puree:
1 kg rock spinach
100 g ice cubes

For the ember-grilled rock spinach:
30 g reduction of Kolof Root Broth
(see Basic Recipes → 273)
50 g olive oil
80 g rock spinach

For the rock plants cream:
5 g olive oil
40 g beach asparagus
10 g beach beans
20 g beach Swiss chard
16 g organic unsalted butter
18 g mantecoso cheese
5 g rock clover stems
8 g Smoked Luche
(see Basic Recipes → 274),
cut into small pieces

For the sea-spiced bread mix:
75 g cilantro (coriander) seeds
15 g merkén
150 g fresh parsley sprigs
140 g squid ink

For the sea-spiced bread:
35 g whole (full fat) milk
12.5 g fresh yeast
10 g sugar
600 g all-purpose (plain) flour
600 g whole wheat flour
15 g fine sea salt

For the sea wafer:
100 g all-purpose (plain) flour
30 g squid ink
10 g walnut miso sauce

For the sea carrot sediment:
100 g Roasted Sea Carrots
(see Basic Recipes→ 274)
250 g canola (rapeseed) oil

To serve:
15 rock clovers

ROCK SPINACH PUREE

Bring a pan of water to a boil, add the rock spinach, and blanch for 2 minutes. Drain, and cool in an ice bath. Then combine the rock spinach and ice cubes and blend in a food processor at high speed for 8 minutes or until smooth. Drain in a very fine-mesh strainer (sieve) set over a bowl to remove the excess water. Freeze the puree in a beaker until 10°F (–12°C) and then pass it through a Pacojet. Let it reach room temperature, freeze it again, and pass it through the Pacojet again.

EMBER-GRILLED ROCK SPINACH

In a bowl, emulsify the kolof reduction with 40 g of the olive oil.

Bring a pan of water to a boil, add the rock spinach, and blanch for 2 seconds. Drain, and cool in an ice bath. Dry the rock spinach well and brush it with the remaining 10 g olive oil. Pass it through the previously prepared embers in a metallic container on 1 side only, for 1 minute. Marinate the rock spinach in the kolof root emulsion until serving.

ROCK PLANTS CREAM

Heat the olive oil in a skillet (frying pan), and sauté the beach asparagus until tender and it reaches a light brown color. Add the beach beans and sauté until light brown. Cut the beach Swiss chard into thin slivers and add them to the skillet. Add the butter, 15 g rock spinach puree, the mantecoso cheese, rock clover stems, and smoked luche. Stir continuously until the melting butter and cheese create a smooth and shiny cream.

SEA-SPICED BREAD MIX

In a food processor, blend the cilantro seeds with the merkén; then add 1 kg water. Add the parsley and the squid ink, and grind until the mixture forms a homogenous juice.

SEA-SPICED BREAD

Form a leaven by mixing the milk with the yeast and sugar in a bowl and let sit for 30 minutes. In a large bowl, stir together the all-purpose flour, whole wheat flour, and salt, and shape the mixture into a "volcano." Incorporate the leaven into the crater of the "volcano" and knead it in. Finally, add the sea-spiced bread mix and knead until the dough is homogenous. Place the dough in a bowl, cover it with plastic wrap (clingfilm), and let it stand on top of the oven to ferment for 45 minutes.

Preheat the oven to 350°F (180°C/Gas Mark 4) with 90% humidity. Bake the bread for 20 minutes; then raise the oven temperature to 425°F (220°C/Gas Mark 7) and bake without moisture for 10 minutes.

Allow the bread to cool to room temperature, and then break the loaf into small pieces. Bake the pieces at 175°F (80°C) for 3 hours in the oven, then blend at maximum speed in a food processor.

SEA WAFER

Preheat both sides of a flat panini griddle.

Mix the flour, 180 g water, the squid ink, and the walnut miso together in a bowl. Pour 1 tablespoon of mixture onto the griddle, close the griddle, and press on the surface with a cloth so that the wafer becomes light, airy, and dry through the process of dextrinizing. Repeat to make 6 wafers altogether. Store between sheets of paper towels in a dry place.

SEA CARROT SEDIMENT

Blend the roasted sea carrots at 185°F (85°C) in a food processor for 5 minutes, then slowly add the canola oil while they are grinding.

TO SERVE

Preheat 4 plates.

Put a spoonful of the rock plants cream on each plate as a base. Cover it slightly with the ember-grilled rock spinach. Arrange the rock clovers on top in an irregular patters, leaving space between them, and season with the sea carrot sediment underneath some of the clovers. Break the wafers into small irregular pieces and add them on top. Sprinkle randomly with the sea-spiced bread crumbs. Serve immediately.

→ 149

Version 2
Creamy Rock Plants with Mushrooms from the Same Place

Serves 4

For the rock spinach puree:
1 kg rock spinach
100 g ice cubes

For the rock plants cream:
5 g olive oil
40 g beach asparagus
10 g beach beans
20 g beach Swiss chard
16 g organic unsalted butter
18 g mantecoso cheese
5 g rock clover stems
8 g Smoked Luche (see Basic Recipes → 274), cut into small pieces

For the sea-spiced bread mix:
75 g cilantro (coriander) seeds
15 g merkén
150 g fresh parsley sprigs
140 g squid ink

For the sea-spiced bread:
35 g whole (full-fat) milk
12.5 g fresh yeast
10 g sugar
600 g all-purpose (plain) flour
600 g whole wheat flour
15 g fine sea salt

For the sea wafer:
100 g all-purpose (plain) flour
30 g squid ink
10 g walnut miso sauce

For the grilled red pine mushrooms from Quintay:
20 g molle tree leaves
70 g melted clarified butter
2 red pine mushrooms
30 g lemon juice
30 g Mushroom Oil (see Basic Recipes → 273)

To serve:
1 g Cáhuil fleur de sel
24 oxalis from the forest of Quintay
16 oxalis flowers from the forest of Quintay
15 rock clovers

ROCK SPINACH PUREE

Bring a pan of water to a boil, add the rock spinach, and blanch for 2 minutes . Drain, and cool in an ice bath. Then combine the rock spinach and ice cubes in a food processor and blend at high speed for 8 minutes or until smooth. Strain the rock spinach through a very fine-mesh strainer (sieve) set over a bowl to remove the excess water. Freeze the puree in a beaker until it reaches 10°F (–12°C) and then pass it through a Pacojet. Let it reach room temperature, freeze it again, and blend one more time.

ROCK PLANTS CREAM

Heat the olive oil in a skillet (frying pan), and sauté the beach asparagus until light golden brown. Add the beach beans, and sauté until just tender. Cut the beach Swiss chard into thin slivers and add to the skillet. Add the butter, 15 g rock spinach puree, mantecoso cheese, rock clover stems, and smoked luche. Stir continuously until the melting butter and cheese create a smooth and shiny cream.

SEA-SPICED BREAD MIX

In a food processor, blend the cilantro seeds with the merkén; then add 1 kg water. Add the snipped parsley and the squid ink, and grind until the mixture forms a homogenous juice.

SEA-SPICED BREAD

Form a leaven by mixing the milk with the yeast and sugar in a bowl and let sit for 30 minutes. In a large bowl, stir together the all-purpose flour, whole wheat flour, and salt, and shape the mixture into a "volcano." Incorporate the leaven into the crater of the "volcano" and knead it in. Finally, add the sea-spiced bread mix and knead until the dough is homogenous. Place the dough in a bowl, cover it with plastic wrap (clingfilm), and let stand on top of the oven to ferment for 45 minutes.

Preheat the oven to 350°F (180°C/Gas Mark 4) with 90% humidity. Bake the bread for 20 minutes; then raise the oven temperature to 425°F (220°C/Gas Mark 7) and bake without moisture for 10 minutes.

Allow the bread to cool to room temperature, and then break the loaf into small pieces. Bake the pieces in the oven at 175°F (80°C) for 3 hours, and then blend at maximum power in a food processor.

SEA WAFER

Preheat both sides of a flat panini griddle.

Mix the flour, 180 g water, squid ink, and walnut miso together in a bowl. Pour 1 tablespoon of the mixture onto the griddle, close the griddle, and press on the surface with a cloth so that the wafer becomes light, airy, and dry through the process of dextrinizing. Repeat to make 6 wafers altogether. Store between sheets of paper towels in a dry place.

GRILLED RED PINE MUSHROOMS FROM QUINTAY

Break the dried molle leaves with your hands, and vacuum-pack them with the clarified butter. Cook at 175°F (80° C) for 20 minutes; then strain, reserving the butter.

Cook the red pine mushrooms on a Chilean espino coal grill on soft embers for 2 hours, hydrating constantly by spreading the butter over the mushrooms, including over their sides. Turn them over every 20 minutes. Cut the red pine mushrooms into slices 1/5-inch (0.4 cm) thick. In a bowl, make an emulsion of the lemon juice and mushroom oil.

TO SERVE

Preheat 4 plates. Place a spoonful of the rock plants cream on the left side of each plate; on the right side, arrange the red pine mushrooms, placing them irregularly, leaving space between them. Sprinkle with the fleur de sel and cover with the oxalis and its flowers. In the same manner, cover the left side with the rock clovers. Cut the sea wafers into small irregular pieces and put them on the left side, and then sprinkle over the sea-spiced bread crumbs. Add a few drops of the emulsion on the rock clovers and oxalis.

Conger Eel and White Roses

Serves 4

For the conger eel:
800 g fine sea salt
400 g red conger eel sirloin
700 g Ulmo honey beeswax

For the rose oil:
10 earliest white roses of the year
5 kg canola (rapeseed) oil

For the marinated roses:
70 g apple cider vinegar
10 pink roses

For the rock clover salad:
16 g rock clover
100 g seawater

For the black luga:
2 g black luga
20 g Mushroom Oil
(see Basic Recipes → 273)

For the sliced nalca:
1 nalca stem
20 g lemon juice

To serve:
160 g conger eel
500 g clarified butter
50 g honey
1 earliest fresh white rose of the season
1 g Cáhuil fleur de sel

CONGER EEL

Put the salt in a bowl. Place the red conger eel sirloin in the bowl and cover it with the salt; let it stand for 7 minutes. Then remove from the bowl and rinse the eel to remove the salt. Put the eel in a metal container

Melt the honey beeswax in a small pan, and pour some over the eel to cover; allow it to cool, and then cover the eel with a new layer. Repeat this procedure until there are 4 layers of melted honeycomb. Mature the fish at 39°F (4°C) for 1 week.

ROSE OIL

Vacuum pack and infuse in a sous vide machine the petals of the white roses in the canola oil at 158°F (70°C) for 1 week. Let it sit in a dark place.

MARINATED ROSES

Emulsify 100 g of the rose oil with the vinegar in a bowl. Remove the petals from the pink roses and marinate them for at least 1 hour before serving.

ROCK CLOVER SALAD

Compress the rock clovers in seawater inside a vacuum-sealing machine 3 times, until they remain translucent.

BLACK LUGA

Bring a pan of water to a boil, add the black luga, and blanch for 5 minutes. Cool in an ice bath. Drain, and cut the black luga into four 1½ x ½-inch (4 × 1.5 cm) rectangles. Season with the mushroom oil.

SLICED NALCA

Slice the nalca stem with a mandoline to make 1/5-inch (0.4 cm)–thick slices. Pour the lemon juice into a container and add the freshly cut nalca, in order to prevent it from oxidizing.

TO SERVE

Cut the eel into 4 medallions of 40 g each. Heat the butter and honey in a skillet (frying pan) until it reaches 158°F (70°C) and cook the eel in it for 6 minutes. Put a piece of mushroom oil–brushed luga in the center of each warmed plate; place a nalca slice in the center, and 4 rock clovers on top. Slightly drain the rose petals and arrange 4 petals on the clovers, so that they stick perfectly. Add the fleur de sel and set 8 fresh white rose petals on top of this in a line putted between. Exactly at the moment of serving, remove the fish from the butter, add the fleur de sel, let drain briefly over absorbent paper, and then place it on one side of the plate.

→ 88

Rockfish, Sea Lettuce, and Violet Garum

Serves 4

For the sea lettuce merkén:
10 luma twigs
1 kg sea lettuce
1 green (unripe) cacho de cabra chile
1 g ground cilantro (coriander) seeds

For the rockfish:
Four 12-inch (30 cm) sea lettuces
200 g rockfish

For the phyllo (filo) paste:
80 g all-purpose whole wheat flour
8 g apple vinegar
1 g fine sea salt

For the fermented wild radish:
200 g wild radish
4 g fine sea salt

For the garum and violets:
10 g garum
0.5 g violet flower distillate
4 g olive oil

SEA LETTUCE MERKÉN

Cut the luma twigs into 2-inch (3 cm)–thick pieces. Burn the luma wood in a clay oven until it is red-hot. Place the the sea lettuce and the chile on a rack, set it in the oven, and close the lid so it is airtight—so the fire goes out and the wood smokes intensely. Repeat this procedure daily for 3 weeks. Dehydrate the smoked sea lettuce and chile at 115°F (45°C) for 5 hours. Then grind them in a coffee grinder and combine with the ground cilantro seeds. Sift, then store in an airtight container in a dry place.

ROCKFISH

Dehydrate 4 pieces of sea lettuce that are at least 12 inches (30 cm) in diameter (note this is irregularly shaped seaweed) at 104°F (40°C) for 3 hours.

Cut the rockfish into 4 pieces, each 4½ inches (11 cm) long and 2 inches (3 cm) wide. Wrap each piece in dehydrated sea lettuce and store at 39°F (4°C) for 2 days to allow the fish to age.

PHYLLO PASTE

Preheat the oven to 120°F (50°C/Gas Mark ½). Mix the flour, vinegar, 50 g water, and the salt in a bowl to form a dough; work it vigorously for 15 minutes, developing the gluten. Wrap the dough in plastic wrap (clingfilm) and bake for 20 minutes. Allow the dough to cool to room temperature and then, on a floured working surface, stretch it by hand thinly. Cut the dough into 5 × 3-inch (13 × 3 cm) rectangles and dehydrate at 185°F (85°C) for 20 minutes.

FERMENTED WILD RADISH

Cut the radish into thin rounds; toss with the salt and place in a vacuum bag. Cook at 100%, at 77°F (25°C) for 5 days. Remove and blend in a food processor at top speed; pass through a fine-mesh strainer (sieve) in order to obtain a smooth paste. Put 20 g inside a plastic pastry (piping) bag.

GARUM AND VIOLETS

In a bowl, mix the garum with the violet flower distillate and the olive oil, creating an emulsion where the oil and garum remain slightly separated.

TO SERVE

Cook the rockfish in a steamer at medium heat for 30 minutes, so the cooking is easy on the meat. Remove when it is rare.

Place the fish on the left side of each plate and sprinkle with the sea lettuce merkén. Brush the surface of the fish with the garum-violet emulsion. Add 2 dots of fermented radish paste on the fish, then place the phyllo dough on top and serve immediately.

→ 176

Version 1 Punta de Tralca Wild Food, Organized by Layers

Serves 4

For the paco crab:
10 g fine sea salt
4 paco crab claws

For the locos:
2 locos
60 g tepú wood
1 g Cáhuil fleur de sel

For the rock spinach puree:
1 kg rock spinach
100 g ice cubes

For the luche cream:
10 g organic unsalted butter
8 g Smoked Luche
(see Basic Recipes → 274)
5 g mantecoso cheese
0.5 g fine sea salt

For the beach asparagus cream:
40 g beach asparagus
5 g olive oil
12 g organic unsalted butter
60 g Rock Spinach Puree
12 g mantecoso cheese
1 g fine sea salt

For the sea wafers:
100 g all-purpose (plain) flour
50.5 g squid ink

To serve:
1 g Cáhuil fleur de sel
8 g rock onions, sliced 1/5 in (5 mm) paper thin

PACO CRAB

Bring 1 kg water to a boil in a pot, add the salt, and dip the crab claws in the boiling water for 45 seconds. Quickly plunge them in an ice bath to chill.

With a strong pair of stainless steel scissors, carefully open the claws on each side; be careful to leave the muscle intact inside to maintain the claw's natural form.

LOCOS

Remove the locos' main muscle (callus) and cut it thinly into ½-inch (1.5 cm)–thick slices. Place them in a perforated metal baking dish and smoke over a small trunk of tepú wood for 15 seconds. Immediately pour the locos into the dish and caramelize each slice evenly for a few seconds on a hot pan. Add the fleur de sel when serving.

ROCK SPINACH PUREE

Bring 1 kg water to a boil in a pan, add the rock spinach, and blanch for 2 minutes. Drain and cool in an ice bath. Then combine the rock spinach and ice cubes and blend at high speed in a food processor for 8 minutes, until smooth. Drain the rock spinach in a very fine-mesh strainer (sieve) set over a bowl to remove the excess water and reserve this water in a bowl. Freeze the puree, then pass it through a Pacojet. Let it reach room temperature, freeze it again, and blend in the Pacojet one more time.

LUCHE CREAM

Heat the butter in a small pan over medium high heat, and caramelize the smoked luches. Then add 80 g of the rock spinach puree, cheese, and salt. Stir continuously and gently, trying to melt the mantecoso cheese completely and evenly. In case the mixture becomes too thick, make it lighter by using water drained from the rock spinach puree.

BEACH ASPARAGUS CREAM

Roast the beach asparagus over the plancha (griddle) with olive oil on both sides for no more than 1½ minutes. Reserve in a covered container until used.

Heat the butter in a small pan over medium high heat and add the beach asparagus. Then add 60 g of the rock spinach puree, cheese, and salt. Stir continuously and gently, trying to melt the cheese completely and evenly. In case the mixture becomes too thick, make it lighter by using water drained from the rock spinach puree.

SEA WAFERS

Mix the flour and 180 g water in a bowl, and divide the batter into 4 portions. Add 45 g of squid ink to the first; 5 g of squid ink to the second; 0.5 g of squid ink to the third; and don't add any ink to the fourth portion.

Preheat both sides of a flat panini griddle, making sure that both plates are smooth and can be in full contact with each other.

One batter mixture at a time, pour a spoonful of the batter on the griddle, close it, and press the top evenly with a cloth for approximately 25 seconds, until the dough expands. Remove the dextrinized wafer immediately.

TO SERVE

Chop the paco claws into ¾-inch (2 cm) chunks, season them slightly with fleur de sel, and arrange them on the upper fourth of each plate. Add the reserved fleur de sel to the caramelized locos, and arrange them in the next fourth of the plate, seasoning with the rock onion. Next, add the luche cream and the asparagus cream on the remaining parts of the plate, forming a line with each cream.

Break the sea wafers with your hands and carefully arrange them, starting with the darkest color at the bottom of the dish to create an ombré effect, so they just barely touch the food and don't moisten.

→ 178

Version 2 Punta de Tralca Rock Salads, Organized by Layers

Serves 4

For the roasted kolof:
10 g kolof (must be roasted on the day it was harvested)

For the kolof root broth reduction:
100 g Kolof Root Broth (see Basic Recipes → 273)

For the kolof root pajaritos cream:
500 g organic heavy (double) cream
100 g pajaritos yogurt

For the grilled beach asparagus:
2 kg Chilean espino coal
80 g beach asparagus
5 g garum

For the rock spinach salad:
40 g rock spinach
20 g lemon juice
8 g Mushroom Oil (see Basic Recipes → 273)
0.5 g Cáhuil fleur de sel

For the sea carrots:
3 g sea carrots (must be roasted on the day it was harvested)

For the chagual salad:
40 g chagual
10 g lemon juice
0.5 g Cáhuil fleur de sel
8 g rock onions

For the sea wafers:
100 g all-purpose (plain) flour
50.5 g squid ink

ROASTED KOLOF

Preheat the oven to 485°F (250°C/Gas Mark 9) with convection at maximum.

Put the kolof in a roasting pan and roast for 5 minutes. Allow the kolof to cool to room temperature. Store in an airtight container.

KOLOF ROOT BROTH REDUCTION

In a pan over medium heat, simmer the broth (do not stir), until it has reduced by 75%. Let it cool to room temperature.

KOLOF ROOT PAJARITOS CREAM

Combine the cream and the pajaritos yogurt in a yogurt maker and process at 104°F (40°C) and 60% moisture for 7 hours; remove and stir vigorously. Mix with 10 g kolof root broth reduction until uniform.

GRILLED BEACH ASPARAGUS

Build an espino coal fire with red-hot embers. Spread out the embers, forming a thin layer to produce slight warmth.

Grill the beach asparagus on a small-hole grill set 12 inches (30 cm) above the embers for 5 minutes, occasionally spreading the garum over them to prevent them from dehydrating. Turn over the beach asparagus and repeat; then remove and use immediately.

ROCK SPINACH SALAD

In a bowl, season the rock spinach with the lemon juice, mushroom oil, and fleur de sel.

SEA CARROTS

Preheat the oven to 485°F (250°C/Gas Mark 9) with the convection at maximum power.

Roast the sea carrots for 10 minutes. Remove and allow to cool to room temperature.

CHAGUAL SALAD

Remove and discard the outer leaves from the chagual and cut it into thin slivers. Combine the chagual with the lemon juice in a bowl, and marinate for at least 1 hour. Add the fleur de sel before using. Finely chop the rock onions and toss with the chagual.

SEA WAFERS

In a bowl, mix the flour with 180 g water; divide the batter into 4 equal portions. Add 45 g of squid ink to the first one, 5 g of squid ink to the second one, 0.5 g of squid ink to the third one, and no ink to the fourth one.

Preheat both sides of a flat panini griddle, making sure that the plates are smooth and can be in full in contact with each other. One batter at a time, pour 1 full tablespoon of the mixture onto the griddle. Close the griddle and press the top evenly with a cloth until the dough expands, approximately 25 seconds. Remove the dextrinized wafer immediately.

TO SERVE

Place a scoop of the pajaritos cream on the upper quarter of each plate and place the roasted kolof on top. Arrange the grilled beach asparagus on another quarter of the plate. Next, add the rock spinach salad and the chagual salad to form a line; set one whole roasted sea carrot on top of the rock spinach salad.

Break the sea wafers with your hands and carefully arrange them, starting with the darkest color at the bottom of the dish to create an ombré effect, so they just barely touch the food and so they don't moisten.

→ 180

Seaweed Roots Pulmay and Some Rock Flavors

Serves 4

For the algae merkén:
300 g luche
500 g black luga
300 g sea lettuce
500 g kolof
1 cacho de cabra chile
4 pieces tepú wood, each one weighing 1 kg
1 g ground cilantro (coriander) seeds

For the rock puree:
200 g dried sea beans
1 red bell pepper
100 g white onion
20 g squid ink
1 g roasted sea carrot
1 g Roasted Kolof (see Basic Recipes → 274)
4 oval rocks, each about 3 inches (8 cm) long

For the pulmay:
20 g pork ribs
20 g longaniza from Chillán
100 g Chilean mussels
100 g clams
50 g chicken drumstick
1 stick tepú wood
100 g dry white wine
1 g merkén
½ Chiloé garlic clove, crushed
113 g purified rainwater

For the clarified pulmay:
1 kg pulmay
1.5 g powdered agar agar

For the stones napped in pulmay:
8 g unflavored gelatin sheets
2 g powdered agar agar
8 misshapen stones with a broad base, frozen overnight

For the sea bread:
35 g whole (full-fat) milk
125 g fresh yeast
10 g sugar
15 g fine sea salt
600 g all-purpose (plain) flour
600 g whole wheat flour
75 g ground cilantro (coriander) seeds
45 g merkén
150 g rock spinach leaves
150 g cilantro (coriander) leaves
150 g parsley sprigs
400 g squid ink

For the beach Swiss chard salad:
80 g beach Swiss chard
10 g lemon juice
25 g Mushroom Oil (see Basic Recipes → 273)
3 g Cáhuil fleur de sel

To serve:
8 g Mushroom Oil (see Basic Recipes → 273)
240 g Kolof Root Broth (see Basic Recipes → 273)

ALGAE MERKÉN

Spread the luche, black luga, sea lettuce, kolof, and cacho de cabra chile over a perforated metal baking pan and place it in a clay oven. Burn one of the sticks of tepú wood in the oven until it gives off yellow smoke; then close the chamber and let it smoke for 7 days. Repeat the process 3 times. Store in an airtight container and leave for 1 month.

After 1 month, remove all the algae and the chile. Blend the smoked ingredients with the cilantro seeds in a food processor.

ROCK PUREE

Soak the beans in warm water overnight. Then cook them in a large amount of water in a pressure cooker for 1½ hours.

Singe the red pepper over a direct flame until charred. Let it sit in a bowl covered with plastic wrap (clingfilm) for 15 minutes. Then remove the skin and seeds.

Cut the onion into thin strips. Preheat a skillet (frying pan) over medium-high heat and slowly caramelize the onions.

As soon as the beans are cooked, drain them, and combine them with the onions, squid ink, red pepper, roasted sea carrot, roasted kolof, and 0.5 g algae merkén in a food processor; grind at full speed. The resulting texture will be a firm, dry puree that can easily be handled to cover the rocks. If the mixture is too liquid, reduce it in a pan.

Cover the whole surface of the rocks with at least ⅓ inch (1 cm) of the thick puree, except for the top of the rocks where it should be ¾ inch (2 cm) thick. Store at 39°F (4°C).

PULMAY

Cut the pork ribs and longaniza into big pieces, and put them in a perforated metal pan. Add the Chilean mussels, the clams, and the chicken. Burn the tepú wood in a clay oven until yellow smoke comes out; then smoke for 20 minutes.

Seal the the chicken, pork, and longaniza with oil in a skillet (frying pan) over high heat until they are golden brown, but being careful not to burn the oil.

Vacuum-pack the chicken, pork, longaniza, white wine, merkén, garlic, and rainwater. Cook at 175°F (80°C) for 48 hours.

Strain and shell the clams and mussels. Bone the chicken, longaniza, and pork, and press them through a very fine-mesh strainer (sieve) to get the best possible concentration of flavor.

CLARIFIED PULMAY

Strain the pulmay through a fine cheesecloth (muslin) into a pan. Add the agar agar and dissolve it in the strained broth while it is cold. Whip it briskly with a balloon whisk and then boil, stirring constantly, for 5 minutes after reaching the boiling point. Cool and freeze in a smooth container.

Unmold the frozen block of broth, place it on a fine cheesecloth, and defrost it in a refrigerator at 41°F (5°C) overnight, allowing the defrost liquid to drip over a container.

STONES NAPPED IN PULMAY

Fill a shallow dish with cold water and submerge the gelatin sheets in it. Set aside.

Combine the agar agar with 400 g clarified pulmay in a pan and boil for 8 minutes. Remove from the heat and let it cool. When it reaches 113°F (45°C), add the hydrated gelatin sheets.

Set the frozen stones on a rack in a baking pan, and pour the pulmay over them. Store them in the refrigerator and be sure they are not moved while stored.

SEA BREAD

In a bowl, mix the milk with the yeast and sugar to form a leaven, and let it ferment for 30 minutes. Add the salt, all-purpose flour, whole wheat flour, and 800 g water, and knead briskly.

In another bowl, combine the cilantro seeds, merkén, rock spinach leaves, cilantro leaves, parsley, squid ink, and 200 g water. Add this to the dough. Continue kneading to get a uniform, elastic texture. Let the dough rest, covered with plastic wrap (clingfilm), at 86°F (30°C) for 45 minutes.

Preheat the oven to 350°F (180°C/Gas Mark 4). Form the dough into a large loaf and bake with 90% humidity for 20 minutes. Then raise the temperature to 425°F (220°C/Gas Mark 7) and bake with no moisture for 10 minutes.

Let the bread cool completely. Then break it into pieces, and dehydrate them at 175°F (80°C) for 3 hours. Cool to room temperature and then grind in a food processor at maximum power.

BEACH SWISS CHARD SALAD

Cut the beach chard into thin slivers. Just before serving, toss with the lemon juice, 25 g of the mushroom oil, the fleur de sel, and 5 g sea bread crumbs.

TO SERVE

Preheat the oven to 350°F (180°C/Gas Mark 4).

Cook the stones covered with 200 g of the rock puree for 15 minutes, until the puree forms a crust and begins to crack. Remove from the oven and serve immediately in the middle of each dish. Place 2 stones napped in pulmay on the side of the coated stone with puree, taking care not to touch the napped pulmay with your fingers. Place 10 g of the beach chard salad on one side of the plate. Emulsify the mushroom oil slightly with the kolof root broth, and pour it over until ¼ of the height of the rocks is covered.

→ 98

End of Autumn Quintay Mushrooms Chupe

Serves 4

For the matico leaves:
2 matico leaves
50 g apple cider vinegar

For the mushroom powder:
1 sea urchin roe
1 stick of lenga wood
100 g pine mushrooms (*Suillus luteus*), picked at the end of autumn

For the mushroom brittle:
100 g rice
0.5 g fine sea salt
20 g dehydrated pine mushrooms (*Suillus luteus*)
150 g sunflower oil

For the butter and pajarito yogurt whey emulsion:
100 g *Suillus luteus* clarified butter
50 g pajarito yogurt whey

For the charcoal-grilled mushrooms chupe:
1 kg Chilean espino charcoal
500 g fresh pine mushrooms (*Suillus luteus*)
100 g white bread
200 g whole (full-fat) milk
100 g onions
50 g salted butter
40 g mantecoso cheese

To serve:
28 matico leaves
20 beach dill sprouts
4 linen cloths 20 × 20-inch (50 × 50 cm)
20 beach dill leaves
1 g Cáhuil flour de sel

MATICO LEAVES

Cut the matico leaves into ¾-inch (2 cm) squares. Soak them in the vinegar for 1 month.

Dehydrate the drained leaves between two nonstick surfaces with weight added on top at 175°F (80°C) for 30 minutes. Remove carefully with a spatula. Set aside in a dry place.

MUSHROOM POWDER

Age the sea urchin for 2 days in a container inside a refrigerator. Then dehydrate it at 120°F (50°C) for 10 hours.

Meanwhile, light the lenga wood in a deep metal tray, set it over a small cooker over direct flame until it releases yellow smoke. Arrange the mushrooms in a perforated tray, place it on top of the deep metal tray to form a smoker, and cover with aluminum foil. Smoke for 10 minutes.

Remove the mushrooms from the smoker and dehydrate at 175°F (80°C) for 12 hours. Let the mushrooms cool to room temperature; then grind at top speed in a food processor to a fine powder and and sift into a bowl. Grate the sea urchin roe over the mushroom powder and mix thoroughly.

MUSHROOM BRITTLE

Cook the rice in a large pan of boiling water until the grains begin to disintegrate. Drain, and combine with 12 g mushroom powder and the dehydrated mushrooms in a food processor; blend to a smooth paste. Roll the paste out on a nonstick surface and dehydrate at 115°F (45°C) for 12 hours. Then cut the brittle into ¾-inch (2 cm) squares.

Heat the oil to 400°F (200°C) in a deep fryer. Deep fry the mushroom brittle pieces in small batches for 20 seconds. Remove the brittle from the oil and let it set and cool slightly, then sprinkle with salt. Fry again for 3 or 4 seconds to let the pieces expand. Set them aside on paper towels.

BUTTER AND PAJARITO YOGURT WHEY EMULSION

In a pan, warm the *Suillus luteus* butter and the pajarito yogurt whey to 105°F (40°C), and stir vigorously with a whisk until emulsified.

CHARCOAL-GRILLED MUSHROOMS CHUPE

Prepare red-hot embers with the charcoal, aerating the embers for at least 20 minutes. Once the embers are ready, distribute some in a single layer, reserving a main pile of red-hot embers. Continue to feed the embers from the pile to maintain a uniform heat throughout the 5-hour cooking process.

Bind the mushrooms with string and suspend over the embers using a structure similar to a mobile for babies, and let them rotate continuously at 3 feet (1 m) over the embers. Cook the mushrooms for 5 hours, regularly hydrating them with the butter–yogurt emulsion.

Soak the bread in the milk for 1 hour. Thinly slice the onions and, in a pan over medium-high heat, slowly caramelize for about 45 minutes. Combine the onions with the bread, milk, and 25 g mushroom powder, and blend in a food processor at 160°F (70°C) for 10 minutes.

Remove the mushrooms from the mobile hanger and let them cool to room temperature. Then thinly slice them into paper-thin (1 mm) dice. Melt the butter in a pan over medium heat, add the laminated mushrooms, and blend with the onion mixture. Add the cheese and stir continuously until it melts, to prevent it from sticking to the pan. Serve immediately.

TO SERVE

Place the chupe on the center of each plate. Sprinkle the mushroom powder on top of the chupe, and arrange the laminated *Suillus luteus* so they cover the chupe. On top, intersperse the mushroom brittle pieces and the matico leaves, forming a contrast with the adjacent colors so both preparations can be appreciated. Finish with a garnish of beach dill, sprinkle the fleur de sel, and wrap each plate with a linen cloth to keep the deep dish warm.

→ 102

Caramelized Pink Cusk-Eel and Sea Stars

Serves 4

For the conger-eel broth:
- 4 conger eel heads
- 500 g onion
- 100 g carrots
- 30 g fennel bulb
- 20 g olive oil
- ½ Black Fermented Lemon (see Basic Recipes → 273), finely diced

For the pink cusk-eel:
- 30 g Chilean espino coal
- 80 g Tiaca honey
- 300 g clarified butter
- 160 g pink cusk-eel
- 10 sea star flowers
- 1 g Cáhuil fleur de sel

For the sunflower conger-eel broth:
- 10 g olive oil
- 10 g Tiaca honey
- 1 kg conger-eel broth
- 100 g unsalted sunflower seeds

To serve:
- 240 sea star (flowers)
- 50 g boiled seawater, chilled

CONGER-EEL BROTH

Clean the conger-eel heads, removing the scales and eyes.

Cut the onion, carrot, and fennel in irregular shapes. In a pot, combine the vegetables and conger-eel heads with the olive oil and 3 kg water, and bring to a boil. Strain through a fine cloth into another pan, lower the temperature to 175°F (80°C), and add the fermented lemon. Cover and chill the liquid in the refrigerator and let infuse until the next day. Then blend in a food processor and strain again through a fine cloth. Discard the conger-eel heads and vegetables.

PINK CUSK-EEL

Build an espino coal fire with red-hot embers, spread them out, and let them die down to a lower temperature of 194°F (90°C). In a pan, melt 60 g of the honey and 30 g of the clarified butter, and emulsify. Cut the pink cusk-eel into 4 equal pieces and brush the emulsion over each piece, making sure to brush all sides. Cook the pink cusk-eel by only one of the sides over the embers.

Infuse the sea star with the remaining 270 g clarified butter in a pan at medium-low heat for about 1 hour. Then strain and add the remaining 20 g Tiaca honey to the infused butter; stir continuously until the emulsion thickens.

Caramelize the other side of the cusk-eel chunks until golden brown in a skillet (frying pan) and deglaze with the sea star emulsion. Glaze the fish continuously to hydrate it. Add the fleur de sel over the fish.

SUNFLOWER CONGER-EEL BROTH

Preheat a skillet over a high heat.

Add the olive oil, then the Tiaca honey. Wait for a few seconds until it caramelizes, and then deglaze with 500 g of the conger-eel broth. Blend with the remaining 500 g conger-eel broth.

In a food processor, grind the sunflower seeds with the broth mixture at top speed for 3 minutes, until it forms a thick sauce.

TO SERVE

Preheat 4 plates and set a piece of the glazed pink cusk-eel at the left side on each plate. Sprinkle the sea star flowers with cold seawater, then completely cover the pink cusk-eel with the flowers so there is no empty space. Pour 40 g of the sunflower conger-eel broth over each plate and serve immediately.

→ 106

Version 1 Flowers Crudo and Cold Conger-Eel Caldillo

Serves 4

For the conger-eel and honey broth:
- 20 g olive oil
- 300 g conger-eel bones
- 20 g canola (rapeseed) oil
- 1 white onion
- 100 g beeswax
- 1 g fine sea salt

For the honey wafers:
- 50 g all-purpose (plain) flour

5 g Ulmo honey
0.5 g fine sea salt

For the fermented lemon:
1 kg lemon
80 g salt

For the salted petals:
1 kg bloomed plum tree flowers (freshly bloomed for stronger aroma)
150 g salt

For the pajarito seasoning:
50 g pajarito

For the chagual salad:
20 g chagual
60 g lemon juice

To serve:
160 sea star flowers

CONGER-EEL AND HONEY BROTH

Preheat the oven to 485°F (250°C/Gas Mark 9). Sprinkle the olive oil over the conger-eel bones in a roasting pan and roast for 10 minutes.

Meanwhile, heat the canola oil in a pan over medium-high heat. Thinly slice the onion and brown it in the oil, then fill the pan with 500 g water. Remove the fish bones from the oven and immediately immerse them in the water. Bring to a boil and cook uncovered over medium-high heat for 2 hours. Remove from the heat and chill in the refrigerator.

Vacuum-pack the fish bones, onions, broth, and beeswax. Cook in a sous vide machine at 185°F (85°C) for 2 hours. Remove the broth from the vacuum bag and strain it; freeze the strained broth in a tray at -0.04°F (-18°C). Set the frozen broth over a cold fine cloth and let it filter for 1 day, until you have a translucent broth. Add the salt and store at 39°F (4°C).

HONEY WAFERS

Preheat both sides of a flat panini griddle, making sure the plates are smooth and can be in full contact.

Mix the flour, honey, and salt in a bowl. Add 80 g water and stir vigorously with a whisk until it forms a sauce consistency.

Pour 10 g of the mixture on the griddle, close it, and press with a cloth for approximately 30 seconds. Remove the wafer and let it cool at room temperature.

Cut each wafer with a 3½-inch (9 cm) round cookie cutter, and then slice off the right quarter of each wafer with a knife. Store in an airtight container.

FERMENTED LEMON

Cut a deep X in the top of each lemon, slicing halfway down the fruit, exposing the core. Vacuum-pack with the salt. Store at 65°F (17°C) for 3 months.

SALTED PETALS

Set a layer of plum tree flowers on the bottom of a glass jar. Cover with a small layer of salt and continue alternating the ingredients until the jar is filled, finishing with a layer of petals. Apply pressure on the top layer and cover with a cloth; secure the cloth with an elastic band. Let stand between 57°F (14°C) and 85°F (30°C) for 50 days—continue applying pressure daily for the first 3 days. Once the storage period is over, remove the flowers and keep in the refrigerator.

PAJARITO SEASONING

Dehydrate the pajaritos at 120°F (50°C) for 12 hours. Then let cool to room temperature and blend to a coarse powder. Store in an airtight container.

CHAGUAL SALAD

Cut the chagual into thin slivers and combine with the lemon juice in a bowl. Let it marinate for at least 5 minutes. Then store it with the liquid in the refrigerator.

TO SERVE

Chill four ¾-inch (9.5 cm) diameter bowls.

Scatter the chagual salad over each honey wafer.

Cut the fermented lemon into tiny dice and distribute over the wafer. Then add the sea star flowers and the salted petals—between the fermented lemon and the sea star flowers. Sprinkle with the pajaritos seasoning as if you were adding salt.

Fit a wafer inside each bowl, pour the very cold conger-eel and honey broth on one side, and serve immediately.

→ 104

Version 2 Flowers Crudo and Cold Fermented Conger-Eel Caldillo

Serves 4

For the fermented lemon:
1 kg lemons
80 g fine sea salt

For the fermented black lemon powder:
1 Fermented Black Lemon (see Basic Recipes → 273)

For the salted petals:
1 kg bloomed plum tree flowers (freshly bloomed for stronger aroma)
150 g fine sea salt

For the pumpkin juice:
5 kg pumpkins
100 g salt

For the cold conger-eel and honey broth:
10 g olive oil
300 g conger-eel bones
20 g canola (rapeseed) oil
1 white onion
100 g beeswax
1 g fine sea salt

For the topinambour:
Two 40-g pieces topinambour
500 g canola (rapeseed) oil

For the penca:
1 penca stem

For the chagual salad:
20 g chagual
60 g lemon juice

To serve:
80 sea star flowers

FERMENTED LEMON

Cut a deep X in the top of each lemon, slicing halfway down the fruit, exposing the core. Vacuum-pack with the salt. Store at 65°F (17°C) for 3 months.

FERMENTED BLACK LEMON POWDER

Place the black fermented lemon in a coffee grinder and grind to a fine powder.

SALTED PETALS

Set a layer of plum tree flowers on the bottom of a glass jar; cover with a small layer of salt, and continue alternating the ingredients until the jar is filled, finishing with a layer of petals. Apply pressure on the top layer and cover with a cloth; secure the cloth with an elastic band. Let stand between 57°F (14°C) and 85°F (30°C) for 50 days. Continue applying pressure on a daily basis for the first 3 days. Once the storage period is over, remove the flowers and keep in the refrigerator.

PUMPKIN JUICE

Vacuum-pack the pumpkin and the salt, and let stand in the vacuum bag at room temperature for 4 weeks. Then freeze the vacuum bag. Open the bag and let it filter over a chinoise with a cheesecloth for 24 hours, until it becomes a translucent juice. Cover and keep chilled in the refrigerator.

COLD CONGER-EEL AND HONEY BROTH

Preheat the oven to 485°F (250°C/Gas Mark 9).

Sprinkle the olive oil over the conger-eel bones in a roasting pan and roast for 10 minutes.

Meanwhile, heat the canola oil in a pan over medium-high heat. Thinly slice the onion and brown it in the oil, then fill the pan with 500 g water. Remove the fish bones from the oven and immediately immerse them in the water. Bring to a boil and cook uncovered at medium-high heat for 2 hours. Remove from the heat and chill in the refrigerator.

Vacuum-pack the fish bones, onions, broth, and beeswax. Cook in a sous vide machine at 185°F (85°C) for 2 hours. Remove the broth from the vacuum bag and strain it, then freeze the strained broth in a tray at –.04°F (–18°C). Set the frozen broth over a cold fine cloth and let it filter for 1 day, until you have a translucent broth. Add the salt and store at 39°F (4°C).

TOPINAMBOUR

Cook the topinambour in a pot of boiling water for 30 minutes. Remove from the water and immediately remove the skin in just one piece with a sharp knife; it is important to do this while the tubers are still hot.

Place the skins between two nonstick surfaces, place a weight on them, and dehydrate at 165°F (75°C) for 12 hours.

Remove and shape them into rustic semicircles, each one at least 5 inches (13 cm) long and 2¾ inches (7 cm) wide. There may be irregularities left on the skin.

Preheat the canola oil in a skillet to 350°F (180°) C. Deep fry the topinambour skins for just 3 seconds; remove, let them cool down slightly at room temperature, and then deep fry again for 4 seconds. Set aside on paper towels.

PENCA

Remove and discard the penca stem bark. Soak the remaining stem in cold salted water for 3 minutes, discard the water, then rinse in cold water until all the salt is removed. Strain, pat dry, and cut into small dice.

CHAGUAL SALAD

Cut the chagual into thin slivers and combine with the lemon juice in a bowl. Let it marinate for at least 5 minutes. Then store it with the liquid in the refrigerator.

TO SERVE

Chill 4 bowls, about 4½ inches (11 cm) in diameter.

Sprinkle 1 g of the fermented black lemon powder over the topinambour skins. Distribute the salted petals and the chagual salad in each bowl, and arrange the sea star flowers on top, facing upwards. Arrange the fermented lemon and penca cubes in the center of each bowl.

Mix 20 g pumpkin juice with 120 g cold conger-eel broth and pour into the bowl.

Place a topinambour skin on the left border of each bowl, preventing it from touching the broth inside the bowl. Serve immediately.

→ 114

Slightly Caramelized Locos from Antofagasta with Kolof and Sea Carrots

Serves 4

For the mushroom powder:
1 lenga branch
100 g pine mushrooms (*Suillus luteus*)

For the roasted kolof powder:
60 g kolof (roasted on the day it is harvested)

For the mushroom and algae wafers:
100 g all-purpose (plain) flour

For the beurre monté:
10 g sea carrots
700 g Noisette Butter (see Basic Recipes → 273), cold and cubed
2 g xanthan gum

For the cured loco:
100 g fine sea salt
1 loco

For the luga salad:
40 g black luga
0.5 g fine sea salt

For the charcoal-grilled beach asparagus:
2 g garum
10 g olive oil
2 kg Chilean espino coal
40 g beach asparagus

For the rock spinach salad:
40 g rock spinach
5 g lemon juice
2 g Mushroom Oil (see Basic Recipes → 273)

To serve:
15 g olive oil
40 g Pajaritos Cream (see Basic Recipes → 274)

MUSHROOM POWDER

Light the lenga branch in a deep metal tray, set it over a small cooker over direct flame until it releases yellow smoke. Arrange the mushrooms in a perforated tray, place it on top of the deep metal tray to form a smoker, and cover with aluminum foil. Smoke for 10 minutes.

Remove the mushrooms from the smoker and dehydrate at 175°F (80°C) for 12 hours. Let the mushrooms cool to room temperature; then grind at top speed in a food processor to a fine powder and and sift into a bowl.

ROASTED KOLOF POWDER

Preheat the oven to 485°F (250°C/Gas Mark 9).

Roast the freshly harvested kolof in a roasting pan for 5 minutes. Remove and let cool to room temperature. Grind only 30 g of the kolof in a coffee grinder to form a fine powder.

MUSHROOM AND ALGAE WAFERS

Mix the flour and 180 g water in a bowl; divide into 4 equal portions. Add 1 g of the mushroom powder and 5 g of the roasted kolof powder to the first portion and mix thoroughly.

Add 2 g of the mushroom powder and 10 g of the kolof powder to the second portion and mix thoroughly.

Add 3 g of the mushroom powder to the third portion and mix well. Add 8 g of the mushroom powder to the fourth portion and mix well.

Preheat a flat panini grill on both sides, making sure that the plates are smooth and can be in full contact. Pour a spoonful of the first mixture onto the grill, close the grill, and press it evenly with a cloth until the dough expands, approximately 25 seconds. Remove the dextrinized wafer immediately. Repeat, making wafers from each of the 4 mixtures. Cut the wafers into squares of different sizes and keep them in an airtight container, separated by color.

BEURRE MONTÉ

Preheat the oven to 485°F (250°C/Gas Mark 9).

Roast the sea carrots in a roasting pan for 5 minutes.

Bring a pan of water to a boil. Portion the frozen noisette butter into cubes. All at once, add the xanthan gum and the noisette butter cubes to the boiling water, and emulsify for 2 minutes, preferably with the food processor.

Infuse the beurre monté with the roasted sea carrots in the emulsion for 30 minutes, trying not to let the temperature drop below 140°F (60°C). Strain and set the beurre monté aside.

CURED LOCO

Make a vertical cut in the loco then skin both halves and cure them in the salt for 7 minutes. Then wash them to remove the salt residue and refrigerate.

CHARCOAL-GRILLED BEACH ASPARAGUS

In a bowl, emulsify the garum with the olive oil by hand. Set aside at room temperature.

Heat the Chilean espino coal until the embers are red-hot. Then spread out the embers into a thin layer to produce a slight warmth.

Put the beach asparagus on a perforated pan and place it about 12 inches (30 cm) above the embers. Grill for 5 minutes, occasionally brushing the garum emulsion over them to prevent them from drying out. Turn the beach asparagus over and repeat the process.

ROCK SPINACH SALAD

In a bowl, season the rock spinach with the lemon juice and mushroom oil.

TO SERVE

Preheat 4 plates and a skillet (frying pan).

Add the olive oil to the skillet over high heat, and caramelize the locos for only a few seconds on each side. Place them on a chopping board and immediately cut them into chunks no larger than 1 inch (3 cm).

Arrange the locos on the upper part of each plate: the first piece at the top center, the second piece slightly to the right side, and the third piece on the left side. Cover all the loco pieces with the beurre monté. Following the line on the plate, arrange the rock spinach salad. In the row, add the grilled beach asparagus, covered with pajaritos cream; and in the last row just spoon pajaritos cream and top it with the roasted kolof chunks.

To finish the dish, arrange the wafers from the top of the dish, starting with the darker and more flavorful ones and descending to the paler and less intense wafers. Serve at once.

→ 100

Pine Mushrooms Wrapped in Sea Lettuce

Serves 4

For the charcoal-grilled mushrooms:
2 kg Chilean espino coal
4 medium pine mushrooms (*Suillus granulatus*)
50 g sea lettuce
100 g clarified butter

For the garum emulsion:
4 g Chilean silverside garum
40 g Mushroom Oil (see Basic Recipes → 273)

To serve:
4 espino small branches
10 g essence of city mushrooms
28 chickweed leaves

CHARCOAL-GRILLED MUSHROOMS

Heat the espino coal until the embers are red-hot. Then spread the embers out to produce a slight warmth.

Wrap the mushrooms completely with the sea lettuce. Then hang them on a rack set about 30 inches (80 cm) above the embers, so they are mobile and can rotate during the cooking. Cook for 3 hours, brushing the mushrooms with clarified butter every 30 minutes. Set aside.

GARUM EMULSION

In a bowl, whisk the garum with the mushroom oil to make an emulsion. Set aside.

TO SERVE

Preheat 4 plates.

Remove the mushrooms from the sea lettuce and thinly sliced. Arrange the slices on the center of each plate. Spread the city mushroom essence over an espino twig and place it at one side of the mushrooms, so it releases its aroma.

Brush the mushrooms with the garum emulsion and scatter the chickweed leaves around them.

→ 107

Sea Urchins from Quintay with Black Luga, Chagual, and Vegetable Milk

Serves 4

For the aged sea urchins:
1 sea urchin
300 g fine sea salt

For the citric vegetable milk:
50 g Chilean palm tree coconuts, shelled
100 g almonds
1 g rue leaves
5 g lemon geranium
2 g fine sea salt

For the sea urchins:
3 sea urchins from Quintay

400 g seawater
200 g ice cubes

For the steamed chagual:
3 kg whole chagual
1 g fine sea salt

For the black luga:
200 g black luga
10 g lamb fat
10 g olive oil

To serve:
8 fresh tender yuyo stems
0.25 g katsuobushi-style mackerel
0.5 g Cáhuil fleur de sel

AGED SEA URCHINS

Cure the sea urchin by covering it with the salt and letting it sit at 39°F (4°C) for 4 hours. Then rinse off the salt and dehydrate at 150°F (55°C) for 12 hours.

CITRIC VEGETABLE MILK

Bring a pan of water to a boil, and add the Chilean palm coconuts and the almonds. Boil for 5 minutes. Then drain them, and with the help of a cloth, remove the skins. Place the coconuts and almonds in a large bowl of water and soak at room temperature for 12 hours.

Drain the coconuts and almonds. Combine them with 700 g water and blend at very high speed in a food processor. Add the rue leaves, lemon geranium, and salt, and grind for around 10 minutes—the mixture forms a white liquid with a milk-like texture. If the mixture thickens too much, add more water, little by little, until you obtain the desired texture. Strain the mixture into a bowl, taking care to remove any foreign bodies from the vegetable milk; if necessary, strain again until the mixture is absolutely smooth.

SEA URCHINS

Open the sea urchins and remove the roe with a spoon.

Bring the seawater to a boil in a pan, then chill it to 39°F (4°C). Strain the water that is inside the sea urchin and mix it with the seawater; add the ice cubes. With utmost care, let the sea urchin roes stand in the cold water for 1 minute just before serving, until they appear tight and firm in texture.

STEAMED CHAGUAL

Remove and discard the most fibrous leaves from the chagual. Cook the tender chagual leaves in a bamboo steamer for 20 minutes. Then let it cool and cut it into thin slivers; toss with the salt and refrigerate.

BLACK LUGA

Cut the black luga into rectangles measuring 4 × 2/3 inches (10 × 1.5 cm). If they are not in their reproductive phase cook them in abundant boiling water for 4 minutes. If they are in their reproductive phase blanch them. Strain and submerge in an ice bath.

Melt the lamb fat and emulsify it manually with the olive oil. Let the cooled black luga sit in this mixture at room temperature until serving.

TO SERVE

Arrange the sea urchin roes in the center of each plate. Arrange the steamed chagual on one side, and place the yuyo stems, 80 g black luga, and the olive oil emulsion over the chagual.

Grate the dehydrated aged sea urchin and the katsuobushi-style mackerel just before serving. Mix them together in equal proportions and sprinkle over the salad. Pour the citric vegetable milk over the salad, and sprinkle fleur de sel on the sea urchin roes.

→ 97

Chupe of Quintay Mushrooms Left Hanging in the Mountain Until the End of Winter

Serves 4

For the 100% almond yogurt whey infused with fig leaves:
500 g 100% almond milk yogurt (see page 222)
3 fig leaves

For the mushroom powder:
1 lenga wood branch
100 g Quintay pine mushrooms, harvested at the beginning of autumn

For the mushroom brittle:
100 g rice
20 g dehydrated mushrooms (*Suillus luteus*)
150 g sunflower oil
1 g fine sea salt

For the Quintay pine oil:
150 g Quintay pine sprouts
100 g canola (rapeseed) oil

For the yuyo leaves:
100 g yuyo leaves
200 g Mushroom Kombucha (see Basic Recipes → 273)

For the mushroom chupe:
100 g white bread
100 g whole (full-fat) milk
100 g onion
half a mushroom aged by the wind
200 g Chiloé sheep's milk
50 g organic unsalted butter
40 g Chiloé sheep's cheese
1 g fine sea salt

100% ALMOND YOGURT WHEY INFUSED WITH FIG LEAVES

Strain the almond milk yogurt through a fine cloth overnight; be careful not to move it, as moving may affect the texture.

Remove the center veins from the fig leaves and discard. Rub the leaves with your hands; then vacuum-pack the leaves with the strained yogurt whey and let it stand in the refrigerator for at least 2 days before serving.

MUSHROOM POWDER

Light the lenga branch in a deep metal pan, and set it over direct fire until it releases yellow smoke. Arrange the mushrooms in a perforated pan, place it on top of the deep metal pan to form a smoker, and cover with aluminum foil. Smoke for 5 minutes.

Remove the mushrooms from the smoker and dehydrate at 175°F (80°C) for 12 hours. Let the mushrooms cool to room temperature; then grind at top speed in a food processor to a fine powder and and sift into a bowl.

MUSHROOM BRITTLE

Cook the rice in a large pan of boiling water until the grains are completely overcooked, about 2 hours. Drain, and combine with 12 g mushroom powder and the dehydrated mushrooms in a food processor; grind to a smooth paste. Roll the paste out on a nonstick surface and dehydrate at 115°F (45°C) for 12 hours.

Then cut the brittle into ¾-inch (2 cm) squares.

Heat the oil to 400°F (200°C) in a deep fryer. Deep fry the mushroom brittle pieces in small batches for 20 seconds. Remove the brittle from the oil and let it cool slightly. Then fry again for another 3 or 4 seconds, so the pieces expand to look like a pork rind. Set them aside on paper towels and season with the salt.

QUINTAY PINE OIL

Dip the Quintay pine in a pot of boiling water, remove it, and grind it with the canola oil at 150°F (65°C) for 10 minutes. Let it drain through a fine cloth into a container, and store inthe refrigerator.

YUYO LEAVES

Clean the yuyo and dry it thoroughly. Cut the yuyo leaves with a leaf-shaped cookie cutter, always trying to center the vein of the leaf in the mold. Vacuum-pack the leaves with the mushroom kombucha; seal it, extracting as much air as possible, and let it stand overnight.

Preheat the oven to 215°F (100°C/Gas Mark ¼). Remove the yuyo leaves, put them on a nonstick surface, and bake for 40 minutes. Remove them from the oven and let cool just a bit, to separate them from the nonstick surface without bending the leaves. (When the leaves are hot, the leaves are easy to handle and are slightly flexible.) Remove them one at a time with an angular spatula and store at once in an airtight container.

MUSHROOM CHUPE

Soak the bread in the milk for 1 hour. Thinly slice the white onion, put it in a pan over medium-high heat, and caramelize it. Combine the onion, bread, milk, and 25 g mushroom powder, and blend at 160°F (70°C) for 10 minutes in a food processor.

Soak the aged half mushroom in 100 g of the sheep's milk until rehydrated. Drain, and cut into approximately 1/5-inch (½ cm) pieces.

Melt the butter in a skillet (frying pan) over medium heat. Add the aged mushrooms and the remaining 100 g sheep's milk, and stir into the bread-onion mixture. Add the cheese and stir until it has melted. Finally, add the salt.

TO SERVE

Preheat 4 bowls.

Spoon 50 g of the mushroom chupe onto the center of each bowl. Sprinkle with mushroom powder and add 2 drops of the Quintay pine oil. Then add the mushroom brittle and the yuyo leaves in uniform vertical arrangement, without letting them touch much with the chupe. Serve the fig leaf–infused almond yogurt alongside.

→ 205

Tarte-Tatin of Rock Vegetables

Serves 4

For the rock spinach puree:
1 kg rock spinach
100 g ice cubes

For the chagual salad:
40 g chagual
10 g lemon juice
0.5 g Cáhuil fleur de sel
8 g rock onions (arrowgrass), finely chopped

For the beach Swiss chard salad:
40 g beach Swiss chard
5 g pine nut miso
10 g Mushroom Oil (see Basic Recipes → 273)
20 g lemon juice
2 g Cáhuil fleur de sel

For the rock spinach salad:
40 g rock spinach
8 g Mushroom Oil (see Basic Recipes → 273)
20 g lemon juice
0.5 g Cáhuil fleur de sel

For the grilled beach asparagus:
2 kg Chilean espino coal
80 g beach asparagus
5 g garum

To serve:
1 chagual root
5 g Mushroom Oil (see Basic Recipes → 273)
4 g pajaritos
10 g olive oil

SPINACH PUREE

Bring a large pan of water to a boil, add the rock spinach, and blanch for 2 minutes. Transfer the spinach to an ice bath. Transfer the cooled spinach to a blender, add the ice cubes, and blend at high speed for 8 minutes, until it forms a smooth texture. Strain, pressing on the spinach to remove all the water. Freeze the puree in a beaker and then pass it through a Pacojet. Blend two times, then let it sit at room temperature.

CHAGUAL SALAD

Remove and discard the exterior chagual layers and use the center. Cut the chagual into thin slivers, and combine with the lemon juice in a bowl. Let it marinate for 1 hour. Then add the salt and rock onion.

BEACH SWISS CHARD SALAD

Cut the Swiss chard into thin slivers. In a bowl, toss the chard with the pine nut miso, mushroom oil, lemon juice, and fleur de sel.

ROCK SPINACH SALAD

Put the spinach in a bowl and season with the mushroom oil, lemon juice, and fleur de sel.

GRILLED BEACH ASPARAGUS

Heat the co†al until you have red-hot embers. Then spread the embers out to produce a faint heat.

Place a rack 12 inches (30 cm) above the embers. Arrange the beach asparagus in a perforated metal pan and set it on the rack. Cook for 5 minutes, brushing the beach asparagus with the garum to avoid dehydration. Remove and use immediately.

TO SERVE

Cut the chagual root into paper-thin (1 mm) sheets, and trim the sheets to form 2 × 1-inch (5.5 × 3 cm) rectangles. Marinade in the mushroom oil for 30 minutes.

In a pan over medium-low heat, combine 100 g rock spinach puree with the pajaritos; stir continuously until the pajaritos are dissolved and binds the mixture to resemble cheese.

Spread the olive oil in a hot pan, put the chagual rectangles on top, cover it with the remaining rock spinach puree, then add the chagual salad, the beach Swiss chard salad, the rock spinch salad, and the grilled beach asparagus in respective layers, caramelize for approximately 1 minute until the rectangles are golden brown. Remove the tart carefully with a spatula so it does not break, and put it upside down in the center of the plate.

→ 186

Crudo Beef Seasoned with Sea Carrots

Serves 4

For the crudo:
100 g beef fillet or a tender cut with a low amount of fat
10 g Roasted Sea Carrots (see Basic Recipes → 274), flaked
10 g olive oil

For the ironed yuyo leaves:
52 yuyo leaves
100 g llama fat

To serve:
1 g rock onion seeds
2 g reduction of Kolof Root Broth (see Basic Recipes → 273)
3 g jasmine essence

CRUDO

Pass the beef through a meat grinder. Mix the beef, roasted carrot flakes, and olive oil in a bowl. Refrigerate.

IRONED YUYO LEAVES

Cut the yuyo leaves with a 1-inch (3 cm) round cookie cutter, centering the vein of the leaf in each round. With the previously pan-melted fat at 115°F (45°C), combine the leaves and the fat in a bowl and vacuum-cook the bowl at least 6 times.

Arrange groups of 5 leaves between sheets of paper towels, and press with an iron on low steam, until the leaves are caramelized, perfectly translucent, and dry. Store in an airtight container.

TO SERVE

Place a piece of leather on a rectangular plate. Season the meat with the rock onion seeds and kolof broth reduction. Spread 25 g portions of the raw meat over the leather, making sure to leave some uncovered spaces. Season each portion with 2 drops of jasmine essence. Place the yuyo leaves in the uncovered spaces. Serve immediately.

→ 160

Steamed Baúnco Fish and Wilted Rock Plants on the Grill with Vegetable Garum

Serves 4

For the butter infused with sea lettuce and alfalfa:
10 g organic unsalted butter
1.5 g sea lettuce
1.5 g alfalfa leaves

For the sunflower seed cream:
100 g unsalted sunflower seeds
150 g conger-eel broth (→ 237)
1 g Cáhuil fleur de sel

For the vegetable garum:
200 g Kolof Root Broth (see Basic Recipes → 273)
5 g 100% pewén or pine nut miso

For the phyllo (filo) dough:
120 g all-purpose (plain) flour
8 g white wine vinegar
2 g Cáhuil fleur de sel

For the roasted watercress puree:
150 g wild watercress
20 g olive oil
2 g Cáhuil fleur de sel

For the baúnco fish:
40 g baúnco fish

For the grilled rock plant salad:
250 g purslane
100 g wild watercress

To serve:
20 g reduction of Kolof Roof Broth (see Basic Recipes → 273)
5 g beach pea flowers

BUTTER INFUSED WITH SEA LETTUCE AND ALFAFA

Melt the butter at 140°F (60°C) in a pan, add the sea lettuce and alfalfa, cover and let it cool to 113°F (45°C) and leave to infuse at room temperature for 3 hours.

SUNFLOWER SEED CREAM

Soak the sunflower seeds overnight in the conger-eel broth. Blend in a food processor at 170°F (75°C) at maximum speed; add 10 g of the infused butter, then the fleur de sel and blend at medium speed.

VEGETABLE GARUM

Simmer the kolof root broth in a pan until it has reduced by 70%. Add the pewén miso and stir until it is thoroughly mixed and the sauce is smooth but light, shiny, and smooth.

PHYLLO DOUGH

Preheat the oven to 105°F (40°C/Gas Mark ¼).

In a bowl, mix the flour with 100 g water, the white vinegar, and the fleur de sel. Form a ball of dough and work it briefly. Cover with plastic wrap (clingfilm) and bake for 8 minutes.

Remove from the oven, remove the plastic wrap from the dough, and roll the dough on an abundantly floured surface until it is almost translucent. Cut it into pieces measuring 4½ × 1 inch (11.5 × 3 cm). Dehydrate the dough at 150°F (65°C) for 10 minutes, and then store in an airtight container.

ROASTED WATERCRESS PUREE

Bring a large pot of water to a boil, and blanch the wild watercress in it for 30 seconds; drain.

Preheat a skillet (frying pan) over medium high heat, add the olive oil, and brown the watercress. Season with the fleur de sel and puree in a food processor at top speed. Freeze the watercress in a beaker to 10°F (12°C) and pass it through a Pacojet. Freeze again and blend again. Heat the puree for 30 seconds at medium heat before serving.

BAÚNCO FISH

Bring a large amount of water to a boil in the bottom of a steamer. Reduce to a simmer, and add the baúnco fish to the steamer for 30 minutes. (Light steam over a long period of time always works very well with this fish, making it possible to achieve a delicate result.)

GRILLED ROCK PLANT SALAD

Sauté the purslane and watercress on a

griddle over medium heat until withered. Use immediately.

TO SERVE

Just before serving, paint the surface of the steamed fish with the kolof reduction. Arrange the roasted wild watercress puree on the left side of the plates, distributing it evenly, and place the grilled rock plant salad on top of the puree. Set the beach pea flowers on the purslane stems. Put the steamed baúnco fish in the middle of the dish and cover with the dehydrated phyllo. Quickly spoon the sunflower seed cream on the right side of the plate and top the cream with the vegetable garum.

→156

Jibia Cooked Over Espino Embers with Chilean Coconut Yogurt, Mandarin Orange, and Rue

Serves 4

For the Chilean palm coconut milk:
300 g Chilean palm coconut, with the shells

For the coconut yogurt:
500 g coconut milk
100 g pajaritos
25 g lactose

For the jibia:
400 g fresh jibia
4 large sea lettuce leaves

For the jibia cuchuflí:
50 g all-purpose (plain) flour
1 g fresh yeast
3 g jibia ink
6.5 g fine sea salt

For the flowers and herbs:
1 Chilean palm coconut
3 sweet alyssum blossoms
12 alfalfa leaves
4 alfalfa flowers
8 wild carrots
5 oxalis flowers
1 chickweed sprigs

For the jibia juice:
4 g olive oil
200 g jibia

For the coconut yogurt whey and jibia:
100 g jibia juice
1 Chilean mandarin orange
0.5 g Cáhuil fleur de sel

To serve:
3 kg Chilean espino coal
50 g Noisette Butter
(see Basic Recipes → 273)
20 small rue leaves

CHILEAN PALM COCONUT MILK

Break the coconuts, remove the nuts, and soak the nuts in water overnight. Then blend the coconut in a food processor for 10 minutes, and strain it through a fine cheesecloth (muslin) to get a smooth milk, without any pieces of coconut. Store in the refrigerator until used.

COCONUT YOGURT

Pour 500 g palm coconut milk, the pajaritos, and the lactose into a rectangular container, stir carefully, and let it sit overnight at a temperature between 82°F and 85°F (28°C and 30°C).

After the yogurt has separated from the whey, pour the yogurt into a fine cheesecloth placed in a strainer (sieve, and let it sit overnight (reserve the whey). Remove the thick yogurt from the fine cheesecloth and put it in a plastic pastry (piping) bag.

JIBIA

Freeze the jibia wrapped in a tray at –20°F (–30°C) for 2 days to break up the fibers and achieve a texture that is both firmer and softer.

Defrost the jibia, wrap each piece in sea lettuce, and allow it to age for 2 days in the refrigerator.

Build an espino coal fire with red-hot embers, spread them out, and let them burn down to a low warmth.

Cut the jibia into ½-inch (1.3 cm)–thick rectangles measuring 3½ × 2 inches (9 × 5 cm). The weight of each piece should be approximately 65 g. Make vertical and horizontal incisions to form perfect deep squares without cutting through the jibia completely.

Cook the jibia on a griddle, pressing with a spatula so that the incisions touch the griddle, until evenly browned. It is very important for the lower part of the jibia to be golden brown, and, the upper part to be to be raw and cold. Set the jibia aside at room temperature.

JIBIA CUCHUFLÍ

Preheat the oven to 350°F (180°C/Gas Mark 4).

In a bowl, mix the flour with 60 g water and the yeast, jibia ink, and salt, forming a dough. Let the dough proof in a cloth-covered bowl at 85°F (30°C) for 30 minutes. Then take out the dough and put it through a pasta machine, working it until it is paper thin. Cut the dough into 4 × 2-inch (10 × 5 cm) rectangles, and roll the rectangles around a ½-inch (1.5 cm)–thick metal tube. Bake at 356°F (180°C) for 10 minutes. Let the cuchuflí cool. Then remove carefully from the cylinder.

FLOWERS AND HERBS

Cut the fruit of the Chilean palm coconut into ½-inch (1 cm) pieces. Coat the outside of each cuchuflí with enough the coconut yogurt to completely cover its surface, following its shape, and attach the flowers and leaves of alyssum, alfalfa, wild carrots, oxalis, and the chickweed sprigs.

Fill the inside of the cuchuflí with the coconut yogurt, using 20 g for each cuchuflí.

JIBIA JUICE

Heat the olive oil in a hot griddle. Grill the jibia, browning it on all sides. Add 500 g water and the browned jibia to a pan and cook over medium heat for 30 minutes. Filter through a fine cheesecloth.

COCONUT YOGURT WHEY AND JIBIA

The reserved whey from the coconut yogurt will be clear, shiny, and thick when cold. Mix it with the jibia juice in a pan. Grate the zest of the mandarin orange into the mixture, and stir slowly over low heat until it reaches 115°F (45°C). Season with the fleur de sel, and use immediately.

TO SERVE

Build an espino coal fire with red-hot embers, spread them out, and let them burn down to a faint heat. Paint the bottom of the jibia generously with the noisette butter, and put it immediately on the grill. Cook for 1 minute, so the fat in the butter burns on the coal and smokes the jibia (moisten the upper part with a brush so it doesn't dry out). Serve immediately, setting the jibia in the middle of each dish, adding 5 rue leaves in between the cuts. Arrange the filled cuchuflí on top of the jibia. Spoon the jibia juice around the jibia and serve immediately.

→ 212

Granado Beans with Tomatoes from Limache

Serves 4

For the fermented pumpkin puree:
500 g camote pumpkin
10 g fine sea salt
100 g organic unsalted butter
80 g white onion, thinly sliced

For the tomato tea:
4 tomatoes from Limache
50 g cilantro (coriander) leaves
20 g basil leaves

For the granado beans:
200 g granado beans in their pods

For the tomato:
1 tomato from Limache
5 g olive oil
1 g Cáhuil fleur de sel
10 g Chilean green chile, finely diced

To serve:
20 g clarified butter
2 g Cáhuil fleur de sel
40 g toasted pumpkin seeds
10 g sheep sorrel

FERMENTED PUMPKIN PUREE

Cut the pumpkin into approximately ¾-inchch (2 cm) cubes and vacuum-pack with the salt. Let it stand at room temperature for 4 days.

Remove the pumpkin from the vacuum bag. Melt the butter in a pan, add the pumpkin and white onion, and simmer for 1 hour. Blend in a food processor at 175°F (80°C) for 15 minutes.

TOMATO TEA

Roast 2 tomatoes over a direct flame until the skin is completely charred. In a food processor, grind the charred tomatoes with the 2 remaining fresh tomatoes, cilantro, and basil for 4 seconds. Then stir and grind again for 4 seconds, leaving chunks of tomato in the mixture, as well as pieces of cilantro and basil. Strain the mixture through cheesecloth (muslin) for 12 hours, until you have a translucent liquid very similar to tea, even in its aroma.

GRANADO BEANS

Shell the beans and cook them in boiling water for 20 minutes. Drain and set aside.

TOMATO

Remove the core from the tomato and slice the tomato horizontally into four ⅓-inch (1 cm)–thick slices. Then cut each tomato slice with a 2-inch (5 cm) round cookie cutter. Combine the olive oil, fleur de sel, and diced chile in a bowl, add the tomato slices, and marinate for 1 hour.

TO SERVE

Warm 4 plates.

Heat the clarified butter in a pan. Put the fermented pumpkin puree in another pan.

Warm the fermented pumpkin puree for 3 minutes. At the same time, warm the beans gently in the pan with the clarified butter, season them with the fleur de sel, and arrange in the center of each dish.

Place a slice of tomato on top of the beans, and cover with the fermented pumpkin puree. Arrange the toasted pumpkin seeds and the sheep sorrel stems evenly over the fermented pumpkin puree so that they point outward. Right before serving, pour 2 spoonfuls of the tomato tea over the top.

→ 200

Lukewarm Flowers Chupe à la Van Gogh

Serves 4

For the almond yogurt whey infused with fig leaves:
40 g 100% almond milk yogurt (→ 222)
1 fig leaf
0.5 g fine sea salt

For the snails:
40 land snails
500 g alfalfa

For the artichokes chupe:
2 artichokes
6 g pajaritos
1 g Cáhuil fleur de sel

For the spring penca stems:
80 g penca stems
10 g lemon juice
5 g olive oil

For the koji salt:
100 g Chiloé quinoa koji
50 g fine sea salt

For the roasted flowers:
16 calendula flowers

For the salted flowers:
10 g olive oil
2 sunflowers
20 calendula buds
0.25 g Cáhuil fleur de sel

To serve:
2 sunflowers, cut in half and caramelized

ALMOND YOGURT WHEY INFUSED WITH FIG LEAVES

Strain the almond yogurt through a fine cloth into a bowl overnight; be careful not to move it, as moving may affect the texture.

Remove the center vein from the fig leaf, vacuum-pack the leaf with the whey and season with the sea salt; let it stand for two days. Strain, then refrigerate.

SNAILS

Feed the snails with alfalfa for two weeks. Then fill a pot with 3 kg cold water, add the snails, and when the water comes to a boil, cook them for 30 minutes. Drain and shell the snails, using a piece of wire.

ARTICHOKE CHUPE

Cook the artichokes in a pressure cooker for 20 minutes, and let them cool to room temperature. Scrape off the edible base from the leaves, separate the heart, and blend the base of the leaves and the heart in a food processor at 150°F (65°C) for 15 minutes. Wrap the artichoke pulp in a beaker and freeze to 10°F (–12°C), and then process it in a Pacojet. Freeze and blend again to achieve a smooth and uniform puree. Heat the puree with the pajaritos in a pan over low heat for a cheese-like elasticity. Add the salt and continue stirring until it is time to serve.

SPRING PENCA STEMS

Peel the penca stems and submerge them in cold water, to remove the bitter taste. Then drain them, change the water, and repeat the process. Dry the stems thoroughly and cut them into ¼-inch (0.5 cm)-thick rounds. Just before serving, marinate the penca in the lemon juice and olive oil for 1 minute.

KOJI SALT

Grind the Chiloé quinoa koji with the fine sea salt in a coffee grinder to create a very fine powder.

ROASTED FLOWERS

Preheat a nonstick skillet (frying pan) over low heat. Place the whole calendula blossoms upside-down in the skillet, so they form a circle of no more than 4 flowers. Fold paper towels on top of them and apply pressure with a stainless steel pan for 1 minute. Roast them for 1½ minutes.

If they are not brittle enough, turn over the flowers and roast on the other side for just 15 seconds. (For the best flavor though, it is best to cook them on only 1 side.) Repeat with the remaining flowers.

SALTED FLOWERS

Heat the olive oil in a skillet. Cut the sunflowers in quarters and sauté the sunflowers and then the calendula buds in a separate pan. After they are caramelized, season the flowers with the fleur de sel.

TO SERVE

Warm 4 bowls.

Heat the chupe and the snails and arrange them in a line on the center of each plate. Add the marinated penca, the caramelized sunflowers, and the salted flowers.

Season the roasted flowers with koji salt and arrange them to look like a Van Gogh painting.

Add 2 spoonfuls of the infused yogurt to each plate and serve.

→145

Pre-Spring Wild Vegetables Wilted on Burnt Butter and Steamed Rollizo Fish

Serves 4

For the duck fat infused in luche:
60 g tepú wood
10 g luche, cut into small pieces
100 g duck fat

For the ironed nettles:
24 nettle leaves

For the alfalfa noisette:
500 g clarified butter
50 g alfalfa

For the pre-spring yuyo stems:
12 yuyo stems, cut during pre-spring season
2 g Cáhuil fleur de sel

For the nettle puree:
500 g sea water
200 g nettles
0.25 g Cáhuil fleur de sel

For the rollizo:
200 g rollizo fillet, cleaned and cut into 4 (50 g) portions

To serve:
5 g anchovy garum
0.5 g Cáhuil fleur de sel
12 yuyo flowers

DUCK FAT INFUSED IN LUCHE

Light the tepú wood in a deep metal pan. Place it over an open fire until it starts to expel yellow smoke. Place the luche in a perforated metal pan and place it on top of the deep metal pan to make a smoker. Cover with aluminum foil and smoke for 1 hour.

Melt the duck fat on low heat, then add the luche and infuse at 122°F (50°C) for 2 hours in the duck fat. Filter. Reserve at room temperature until used.

IRONED NETTLES

Preheat a steam iron at maximum temperature.

Put the nettle leaves in a bowl with 100 g of the duck fat infused in luche; place the bowl in a vacuum machine and vacuum at least 6 times or until they are translucent.

Place the nettles between layers of paper towels and iron them as if they were fabric until they are dry. Transfer to an airtight container lined with paper towels and store for at least 2 days and up to 4 days. It is necessary to prepare them before each serving to obtain better results.

ALFALFA NOISETTE

Infuse the butter with alfalfa for 2 hours at 122°F (50°C), then filter again.

PRE-SPRING YUYO STEMS

Wrap the leaves and the flowers of the stems in aluminum foil. Bring 500 g of the alfalfa noisette to 104°F (40°C) and submerge the stems (but not the wrapped leaves and flowers), until the stems lose their firmness and start to droop, about 5 minutes. Gradually and slowly raise the heat until the plant is completely withered inside the noisette, but not for too long otherwise the vegetable chlorophyll does not become degraded. This process may take up to 25 minutes, depending on the degree of the plant's ripeness. Remove the yuyos and drain the butter on a wire rack. Season with fleur de sel.

NETTLE PUREE

Blanch the nettles for 3 seconds in the boiling seawater; remove and cool in a cold-water bath. Blend in a food processor at 131°F (55°C) for 10 minutes until obtaining a smooth puree. Freeze in a beaker and process it in the Pacojet; season with fleur de sel.

ROLLIZO

Boil water in a pot over high heat and set a bamboo steamer onto the upper part of the pot; reduce the heat to low. Place the rollizo fillets inside the steamer and simmer for 20 minutes until the fish is barely done, then set aside.

TO SERVE

Preheat 4 plates.

Remove the fish from the steamer and place it slightly to the left of center of the dish. Brush it with anchovy garum. Remove the yuyos from the alfalfa noisette, take away the aluminum foil, and drain over a grid. Add the fleur de sel. Stretch the yuyos on the plate so it is possible to get a glimpse of the fish; at the same time, stretch the flowers wilted by the heat plus the leaves, so the leaves can be better appreciated. Pipe 6 dots of hot nettle puree and place the ironed nettles over them, in different directions. Serve immediately.

→ 208

City Chocolate Mushroom Cake

Serves 4

For the liquidambar:
16 medium liquidambar leaves
1 kg apple cider vinegar

For the quince aged in beeswax:
1 quince
2 kg organic beeswax

For the city chocolate mushroom powder:
500 g chocolate mushrooms (recently harvested to maintain the intensity of the chocolate scent)

For the city mushroom ice cream:
6 g unflavored gelatin sheets
1.5 kg whole (full-fat) milk
90 g glucose
450 g heavy (double) cream
12 g ice-cream stabilizer
150 g powdered milk
150 g sugar
180 g dextrose powder

For the chocolate mushroom cookie:
200 g sugar
250 g organic unsalted butter at room temperature
325 g all-purpose (plain) flour

To serve:
1 g distilled grass

LIQUIDAMBAR

Put the liquidambar leaves in a pan of cold water and bring to a boil for 5 minutes; repeat this process 5 times. Vacuum-seal the drained liquidambar leaves with the apple cider vinegar. Store at room temperature in a dark place for at least 6 months.

QUINCE AGED IN BEESWAX

Tie the stem of the quince with a wire. Melt the beeswax in a pot over low temperature. Immerse the quince 13 times in the beeswax, forming a clear, thick layer. Hang it up at room temperature for 2 months.

CITY CHOCOLATE MUSHROOM POWDER

Cut the mushrooms crosswise into paper thin (2 mm) slices. Dehydrate the slices at 115°F (45°C) for 24 hours. Grind the dried slices in a coffee grinder and store in an airtight container at room temperature.

CITY MUSHROOM ICE CREAM

Fill a shallow dish with cold water and submerge the gelatin sheets in it. Set aside.

Blend the milk, glucose, and cream with the city chocolate mushroom powder. Infuse at 175°F (80°C) for 1 hour. Then strain the infusion and reduce the temperature to 120°F (50°C) in an ice bath. Mix the stabilizer, powdered milk, sugar, and dextrose together, and add to the cooled infusion mixture. Stir the mixture in a pan until it reaches 185°F (85°C). Remove from the heat and cool in an ice bath. When the mixture reaches 120°F (50°C), add the gelatin and stir. Let it set for 12 hours at 39°F (4°C).

Just before serving, spin the mixture in an ice-cream machine at full speed, until it is both firm and creamy.

CHOCOLATE MUSHROOM COOKIE

Preheat the oven to 400°F (200°C/Gas Mark 6).

Combine the sugar and butter in a blender; add the cream and blend until the sugar crystals have dissolved. Add the flour and 40 g of the chocolate mushroom cake powder and blend until obtaining a smooth and firm dough. Spread this mixture out on a baking sheet and cut out 2-inch (5 cm) rounds with a cookie cutter. Reserve the scraps of dough. Freeze covered until frozen and bake the rounds for 9 minutes at 356°F 180°C and then at the same termperature the scraps to form a crumble. Let the cookies cool to room temperature and store in an airtight container at room temperature.

TO SERVE

Chill 4 small plates.

Crumble the mushroom cookie scraps, and place them on one side of each plate as a surface to hold the ice cream.

Remove the beeswax from the quince, and cut the quince into slices of 1/10 inch (3 mm) thickness. Cut out 16 rounds with a ¾-inch (2 cm) cookie cutter.

Place a scoop of mushroom ice cream (25 g) on the cookie crumbles. Then add the cookie and the quince rounds and add a few drops of distilled grass. Cover with the liquidambar leaves. Serve immediately.

→ 206

Ice Cake and Pre-Spring Quisco Parasites

Serves 4

For the spinach water:
10 g spinach

For the walnut and Chilean bay leaf milk:
200 g walnuts
10 g Chilean bay leaf
20 g sugar

For the ice cakes:
20 g orange blossoms

For the pica lemon foam:
6 g unflavored gelatin sheet
300 g pica lemon juice
100 g sugar

For the walnut cookies:
50 g all-purpose (plain) flour

For the pre-spring flower distillate:
100 g early flowers of city plum tree
100 g early flowers of city almond tree, using the flowers from the first city blooming, since their flavor is more intense.

For the pre-spring flower vinaigrette:
80 g almond yogurt whey

To serve:
160 quisco parasites, freshly harvested
20 g 100% almond milk yogurt (→ 222)
36 plum tree flowers

SPINACH WATER

In a food processor, blend the spinach with 700 g water; strain and reserve the spinach water.

WALNUT AND CHILEAN BAY LEAF MILK

In a food processor, blend the walnuts and 500 g spinach water for 5 minutes. Filter the mixture through a fine cloth, letting it strain into a bowl for 1 hour. Set aside the walnut pulp. Then infuse the strained liquid with the bay leaf in the refrigerator for 24 hours. Stir in the sugar. Keep in the refrigerator.

ICE CAKES

Infuse the orange blossoms in 250 g water at 175°F (80°C) for 1 hour; then strain and let the infused water cool.

Attach a ½-inch (1.5 cm) diameter, 3½-inch (9 cm) long PVC tube to a wine cork; press the end against the cork so it fastens perfectly. Next, insert a ¾-inch (2 cm) diameter, 2¾-inch (7 cm) long bronze tube over the PVC tube, applying gentle pressure on the cork in order to prevent it from breaking. Repeat to make a total of 6 tubular molds. Set the molds on a completely flat surface, fill the space between both tubes with orange blossom water up to the rim of the bronze tube, and freeze at –4°F (–20°C) for 10 minutes.

Remove the frozen water from inside the mold by rubbing the bronze with the PVC on the inside with your hands for a few seconds; store in the freezer. With the help of a 2½-inch (6 cm) round cookie cutter, group 6 of these cuchuflís vertically, each one touching each other, to form a symmetrical round tubular structure. Then return to the freezer. Repeat the process 4 times.

PICA LEMON FOAM

Fill a shallow dish with cold water and submerge the gelatin sheet in it. Set aside.

In a pan, mix together the lemon juice, 200 g spinach water, and sugar. Bring to 120°F (50°C) while stirring to dissolve the sugar; add the hydrated gelatin sheets. Fill a siphon with the mixture and load it two times with N_2O cartridges. Set aside at 39°F (4°C).

WALNUT COOKIES

Blend in a food processor 20 g of the reserved walnut pulp at 194°F (90°C) for 10 minutes at maximum speed. Let it cool at room temperature and mix it with the flour and 100 g water.

Preheat a flat panini griddle on both sides, so the plates are smooth and can be in full contact with each other. Pour 1 full tablespoonful of the mixture onto the grill, close it and press on it with a cloth, softly pressing in a uniform manner for 1 minute until the cookie is light, airy, and dry. Remove the cookie, cut it with a 2½-inch (6 cm) round cookie cutter, and store in an airtight container. Repeat to make 4 cookies.

PRE-SPRING FLOWER DISTILLATE

Distillate the plum tree flowers and the almond tree flowers separately in a rotary evaporator.

PRE-SPRING FLOWER VINAIGRETTE

Mix the almond yogurt whey with the almond flower distillate and the plum flower distillate.

TO SERVE

Rub and carefully remove the ice cakes from the flat surface. Make sure they are level on both ends of the tubes, in order to have an even estructure for the ice cake.

Pour 10 g of very cold water into each of 4 bowls. Set an ice cake in each bowl and freeze until 1 single piece is formed. Remove from the freezer, shake the siphon containing the pica lemon foam mixture, and fill the tubes three-quarters full. Arrange a walnut cookie on top of each ice cake and cover the surface completely with quisco parasites, using the almond yogurt as adhesive. Finish with 9 plum tree flowers, arranged in an irregular manner over the cookie. When serving, pour 1 tablespoon of the walnut milk and 1 tablespoon of the flower vinaigrette into the bowl. Serve immediately.

→ 124

Black Flower

Serves 4

For the black carrot:
4 medium carrots
1 kg seawater

To serve:
2 moist cotton wool bundle
120 golden poppies
2 thinly sliced rounds of black carrots
4 thin ½-inch (13 cm)–long tree twigs

BLACK CARROT

Immerse the carrots in the seawater in a bowl. Place the bowl inside a vacuum machine and vacuum 6 times. Remove and dry the carrots; wrap each one in plastic film and then in aluminum foil. Let the carrots cure at 130°F (55°C) and 66% humidity for 2 months.

TO SERVE

Moisten the cotton wool and place in 2 bowls so it reaches halfway to the rim. Cut the stems of the golden poppies and insert them in the cotton.

Use a 3-inch (8 cm) cookie cutter to cut the black carrot rounds into half-moons. Dehydrate at 120°F (48°C) for 2 minutes. Take the ends of the half-moon and join them by overlapping one end over the other to give the appearance of a flower. Insert the flowers onto each thin twig, to be used as a skewer. Insert 2 black flower skewers per bowl and serve immediately.

Quintay Mushroom Dessert

Serves 4

For the salted walnuts:
50 g sea salt
500 g walnuts

For the mushroom ice cream:
6 g unflavored gelatin sheets
1.5 kg whole (full-fat) milk
90 g glucose powder
450 g heavy (double) cream
150 g mushroom powder
12 g ice-cream stabilizer
150 g powdered milk
150 g sugar
180 g dextrose powder

For the walnut praline:
500 g walnuts
250 g canola (rapeseed) oil
7 g fine sea salt

For the chilenito rounds:
1 egg
15 g egg yolk
62.5 g all-purpose (plain) flour, sifted
7.5 g pisco
3.7 g solid vegetable shortening

For the pine toffee:
500 g heavy (double) cream
80 g pine twigs
50 g pine nuts
310 g glucose
400 g sugar
50 g powdered sugar

For the caramelized milk:
1 kg whole (full-fat) milk
For the manjar:
1 kg whole (full-fat) milk
300 g sugar

To serve:
2 g roasted flour
4 pine toffees
300 g fresh pine twigs

SALTED WALNUTS

Combine 1 kg water with the salt and soak the walnuts in the brine for 24 hours. Strain and toast the walnuts at 215°F (100°C/Gas Mark 4) for 30 minutes. Let cool to room temperature.

MUSHROOM ICE CREAM

Fill a shallow dish with cold water and submerge the gelatin sheets in it. Set aside.

In a bowl, blend the milk, glucose, and cream with the mushroom powder. Infuse at 175°F (80°C) for 1 hour. Then strain the infusion and reduce the temperature to 120°F (50°C) in an ice bath.

In a separate bowl mix together the stabilizer, powdered milk, sugar, and dextrose. Add the mixture to the cooled infusion mixture. Stir with a whisk until it reaches 185°F (85°C). Remove from the heat and cool in an ice bath. When the mixture reaches 120°F (50°C), add the hydrated gelatin and stir. Store the mixture at 39°F (4°C) until the next day.

Just before serving, process the mixture in an ice-cream machine at top speed right until it is creamy but firm. Place the ice cream in a cylindrical container and store at 25°F (–4°C).

WALNUT PRALINE

Blend in a food processor the walnuts with the canola oil and salt at top speed. Freeze in a beaker until frozen, then process in a Pacojet and store at 39°F (4°C) until ready to serve.

CHILENITO ROUNDS

Preheat the oven to 425°F (220°C/Gas Mark 7). In a bowl, mix the egg, egg yolks, and flour. In a small pan over low heat, combine the pisco and the shortening, and warm until the shortening has melted. Add the flour-egg mixture to the shortening-pisco mixture, and mix until a homogeneous, thin, and not very elastic dough forms. Roll the dough out between 2 silicone mats until paper thin and almost translucent. Using a 2½-inch (6 cm) cookie cutter, cut out 4 rounds; remove and discard the excess dough. Using a fork, prick each round in 4 places, leaving a space between the marks. Put the dough rounds on a baking sheet and bake for 6 minutes or until lightly browned. Remove and let cool on a wire rack.

PINE TOFFEE

In a bowl, infuse the cream with the pine twigs and nuts for 2 hours. Strain, reserving the cream.

In a pan, combine the glucose, sugar, and 80 g water. Heat it to 370°F (186°C) then cool it and incorporate the pine cream at 237°F (114°C). Stir slowly until you have a homogeneous mixture, and then reduce it by 20%. Transfer the toffee mixture to a bowl and let cool to room temperature. Form the cooled toffee into 6-g cylinders and roll them in the powdered sugar. Set them aside, while still in the sugar.

CARAMELIZED MILK

Preheat a nonstick skillet over high heat.

Add the milk in 20-g portions and cook until it is dry and caramelized. Remove the caramelized milk skin with a silicone spatula. After all the milk has been caramelized, Blend in a food processor at maximum power to create a very fine powder. Store the powder in an airtight container.

MANJAR

Stir the milk and sugar in a pan over low heat without stopping for 1½ hours, until it forms a dense but fluid paste of caramelized milk. When you take the manjar off the heat, keep stirring until the temperature drops to 120°F (50°C). Allow the manjar to reach room temperature, then store it at 41°F (5°C).

TO SERVE

Place the pine twigs evenly on the left side of each dish and put the pine toffees between the pine twig, starting symmetrically from the middle, to scent the dessert.

On the other half, spread the manjar and add pieces of salted walnuts. Using a fine-mesh strainer (sieve), sprinkle caramelized milk and roasted flour over the right half of the dish. Pipe walnut praline on the center of the dish, and then add a scoop of the mushroom ice cream.

Dip a spoon in cold water forming a quenelle with the ice cream and place a chilenito round on top of the ice cream.

→ 138

Chilean Espino Coulant

Serves 4

For the kirinka:
200 g kirinka seeds

For the kirinka boiled carrots:
4 carrots approximately 9 cm long
50 g quicklime
1 kg sugar
300 g unsweetened cocoa powder

For the Chilean espino coulant:
120 g heavy (double) cream
80 g whole (full-fat) milk
14 g kirinka coffee
1 egg yolk
200 g chocolate (80% cacao)
4 small children's balloons

To serve:
10 Chilean espino seed pods
4 espino twigs

KIRINKA

Preheat the oven to 425°F (220°C/Gas Mark 7).

Bake the kirinka seeds for 25 minutes, until evenly toasted. Let them cool, then grind in a coffee grinder to form a fine powder.

KIRINKA BOILED CARROTS

Peel the carrots. Fill a pan with 1 kg water, and pour the quicklime into it. *Please note that you cannot do this in the reverse order as it may cause an explosion.* Add the carrots and let them stand for 3 hours, stirring every 30 minutes.

Drain and rinse the carrots thoroughly with running water to remove all traces of quicklime. Dry them thoroughly. Combine 2 kg water with the carrots, sugar, cocoa, and 100 g of the kirinka in a pot and cook over low heat, stirring every once in a while, until the mixture has reduced by 50%, resulting in a dense and aromatic dark brown syrup. Remove the carrots and let them drain on a rack at room temperature for 10 minutes.

To finish the preparation, preheat the oven to 175°F (80°C/Gas Mark ¼).

Put the carrots on a baking sheet and dehydrate them for 40 minutes, until they have a wooden, rough appearance and a resistant outer layer; the center should be as smooth as a puree.

CHILEAN ESPINO COULANT

In a pan, heat the cream, milk, and kirinka coffee to 140°F (60°C). Remove the pan from the heat. Add the egg yolk and whisk, then strain into a bowl.

Melt the chocolate in a bain-marie and stir in the strained milk mixture. Let the mixture cool. Then use a food syringe to fill each balloon with 1 oz (30 cc) of the mixture. Tie the balloons closed with a tight knot. Let them stand in a bain-marie at 115°F (45°C) for at least 1 hour.

TO SERVE

Open the pods and spread the raw espino seeds on each plate. On an espino twig, stick the kirinka boiled carrots. Remove the coulant from the bain-marie and immerse it in liquid nitrogen for 30 seconds. Using a sharp paring knife, quickly make an incision forming a superficial cross on each balloon; then immerse it in water at 105°F (40°C) so the balloon peels off the coulant. Immerse it again in liquid nitrogen for 8 seconds and serve immediately.

→ 195

Cheese and Mushrooms Alfajor

Serves 4

For the alfajor rounds:
1 egg yolk
180 g all-purpose (plain) flour
30 g Autumn Mushroom Powder
(see Basic Recipes → 273)
150 g unsalted organic butter,
at room temperature
50 g powdered sugar

For the filling:
1 g unflavored gelatin sheet
100 g Chanco cheese
100 g manjar

For the alfajor preparation:
50 g bitter chocolate (80% cacao)

To serve:
4 cups kirinka coffee
20 g 100% unsweetened cocoa powder

ALFAJOR ROUNDS

In a bowl, mix the egg yolk, flour, mushroom powder, butter, and powdered sugar to form a dough. Set it aside covered in the refrigerator for 1 hour.

Roll the dough out to 1/5-inch (0.5 cm) thickness. Cut out 8 rounds with a ¾-inch (2 cm) cookie cutter. Let the dough rounds cool in the refrigerator for 20 minutes.

Preheat the oven to 425°F (220°C/Gas Mark 7) and bake the rounds for 7 minutes.

FILLING

Fill a shallow dish with cold water and submerge the gelatin sheet in it. Set aside.

Cut the cheese into small chunks. In a pot, heat the manjar to 140°F (60°C). Add the cheese and the hydrated gelatin sheet, stir, and transfer to a pastry (piping) bag.

ALFAJOR PREPARATION

Melt ¾ of the chocolate in a bain-marie until the temperature reaches 113°F (45°C). Remove from the bain-marie, lowering the temperature to 81°F (27°C), then add the remaining ¼ of the chocolate. Return it to the bain-marie until it reaches 90°F (32°C). (This process is called tempering the chocolate.)

Place the alfajor rounds on a wire rack, and pipe 5 g of the filling onto the center of each round. Cover the filling with another alfajor round.

Pour the chocolate over the alfajor and wait for it to solidify at room temperature. Then put the rounds into an airtight container and refrigerate.

TO SERVE

Place a cup of kirinka coffee on a stone plate. Wet the chocolate-coated alfajor under cold running water, and roll it in the cocoa. Place the alfajor at one side of the kirinka coffee.

ARAUCANÍA

→ 190

Quinoa Chilota and Pewén Cookies

Serves 4

For the fermented pewén nuts:
200 g pewén nuts
4 g Cáhuil fleur de sel

For the pewén emulsion:
50 g organic unsalted butter
300 g whole (full-fat) milk

For the quinoa chilota cookies:
100 g quinoa from Chiloé

To serve:
4 meli fruits
2 planters with moss and
a small araucaria tree

FERMENTED PEWÉN NUTS

Bring a large pot of water to a boil, and boil the pewén over high heat for 1 hour. Cover and set aside for 30 minutes. Then skin the nuts one at a time and vacuum-pack them with the fleur de sel. Store in a cool place to ferment for at least 5 months.

PEWÉN EMULSION

Blend in a food processor the fermented pewén nuts, butter, and 150 g of the milk at 175°F (80°C). Add the rest of the milk and stir to achieve a firm texture.

QUINOA CHILOTA COOKIES

Put the quinoa in a strainer (sieve) and rinse it under cold running water, stirring it vigorously, to remove the excess of saponin. Bring a large pot of water to a boil, add the quinoa, and cook for 40 minutes, stirring every now and then. Strain, then blend in a food processor immediately while still warm (the temperature will help to achieve a smooth and consistent mix). Let cool completely, then fill a plastic pastry (piping) bag with the quinoa. Preheat the oven to 425°F (220°C/Gas Mark 7). Pipe the quinoa onto a silicone baking mat, forming 4 circles of 1 cm of thickness each. Bake 20 minutes until they expand to form cookies of irregular shapes and sizes, in a range of approximately 3 cm. Let the cookies cool to a medium temperature, then hollow them out with a spoon to make a long, uniform, thin cookie layer. Fill with the pewén emulsion.

TO SERVE

Fill each quinoa cookie with a meli fruit and pipe the rest of the pewén emulsion inside it. Arrange the 4 cookies over a moss base with a small araucaria tree and serve at room temperature.

→ 122

Piures and Mandarin Skin Bonbons

Serves 4

For the piure skins:
4 piures

For the mandarin skin:
1.25 kg Chilean mandarin
5 g organic unsalted butter
10 g sugar
2 g fine sea salt

To serve:
2 g Cáhuil fleur de sel

PIURE SKINS

Make a small incision in each piure and turn them over. Remove all the guts to clean them out, leaving only the reddish part. Then thin them further by scraping the remaining meat softly with a paring knife, until only the fine exterior skin of the piure remains.

MANDARIN SKIN

Peel the mandarins. Bring 10 kg of cold water to a boil; then add the mandarin skin and cook for 5 minutes. Strain and repeat the process 10 times, using fresh water each time.

Immediately combine the mandarin skins with the butter, sugar, and salt and blend in a food processor at 195°F (90°C) for 10 minutes. Put the puree in a 16-inch (40 cm) skillet (frying pan) and simmer for 40 minutes, stirring continuously to evaporate the water. Remove from the heat, let cool, and put inside a pastry (piping) bag.

TO SERVE

Fill the piure skins with the mandarin puree and close them well. Arrange them on the plates and sprinkle with the fleur de sel.

Curanto and Witch Potato Milcao

Serves 4

For the curanto:
1 stick tepú wood
50 g chicken drumsticks
100 g Chilean mussels
100 g Chilean machas
20 g pork ribs
10 g olive oil
20 g longaniza sausage
100 g dry white wine
1 g seaweed merkén, crushed
½ garlic clove from Chiloé,
lightly crushed
112 ml rainwater from Patagonia

For the clarified broth:
1.5 g powdered agar agar

For the witch potato milcao:
100 g witch potato
7 g fine sea salt
25 g chuño,
dehydrated potato flakes
1 kg canola (rapeseed) oil

To serve:
4 earth-filled buckets
espino twigs
moss

CURANTO

Light the tepú wood in a deep metal pan. Place it over a gas burner until it starts to expel yellow smoke. Arrange the chicken legs, Chilean mussels, Chilean machas, and pork ribs in a perforated metal pan. Fit the perforated pan over the one containing the burning wood and cover with aluminum foil. Smoke for 7 minutes.

Preheat three skillets (frying pans) over medium-high heat. Add the olive oil, and caramelíze the chicken, the longaniza sausage, and the pork in separate pans, until they have an even golden color.

Put the chicken, longaniza sausage, mussels, machas, and pork ribs in a vacuum-pack bag. Add the white wine, seaweed merkén, garlic, and rainwater. Vacuum-pack, and cook for 48 hours at 175°F (80°C). Strain, and press the meat through a very fine-mesh strainer into a bowl. Strain once more through a fine cloth.

CLARIFIED BROTH

Bring 300 g of the curanto broth to a gentle boil in a pan and dissolve the agar agar in it, stirring with a ballon whisk for 5 minutes. In a separate pan, heat 700 g of the curanto broth to 175°F (80°C). Add the smaller amount to the larger one and stir well. Pour into a baking pan, let cool to room temperature, and freeze.

Remove the frozen broth from the pan. Spread a cloth over a perforated pan and set that pan on top of another pan. Put the frozen broth on top of the cloth; this is to let the broth drip through the cloth, leaving any impurities and agar agar in the cloth. Set the arrangement in the refrigerator to drain at 39°F (4°C) overnight.

WITCH POTATO MILCAO

Bring 1 kg water to a boil in a pan, and cook the witch potato for 15 minutes.

Mash the potato by hand using a fork, adding 5 g of the salt and the chuño. Work until the mixture forms a paste that does not stick to the hands. Shape the mixture into four 15-g buns and smash them until they are 1½ inches (4 cm) in diameter and ⅓ inch (1 cm) thick. Let the dough stand covered at room temperature for 1 hour.

Heat the oil in a skillet to 350°F (180°C). Add the potato cakes and fry for 5 minutes. Let them cool slightly on paper towels, then sprinkle with the remaining salt.

TO SERVE

Insert a glass container in each bucket so that its rim is level with the earth. Then arrange espino twigs around the container and cover the earth with moss. Just before serving, mist the buckets with water and set the twigs alight until they are lightly smoking. Place the milcao on one side of the twigs, and pour the curanto broth into the glass container.

→ 101

Mushrooms from Early Autumn

Serves 4

For the smoked peumo leaves:
30 g peumo leaves
200 g apple cider vinegar
5 g olive oil

For the radish leaves:
100 g radish leaves
200 g apple cider vinegar

For the dried enoki:
100 g enoki mushrooms

For the red pine mushroom ashes:
100 g red pine mushrooms
5 g fine sea salt

For the gargal mushroom extract:
400 g gargal mushrooms

For the mushroom brittle:
100 g rice
12 g Autumn Mushroom Powder (see Basic Recipes)
20 g dried mushrooms (*Suillus luteus*)
150 g sunflower oil
1 g fine sea salt

For the caramelized loyo:
1 loyo mushroom weighing at least 400 g
20 g olive oil

To serve:
1 g fine sea salt
16 white goosefoot weed leaves
12 red autumn white goosefoot weed leaves
12 molle pepper sprouts
8 fiddleheads

SMOKED PEUMO LEAVES

Vacuum-pack the peumo leaves with the vinegar. Let them stand for 2 weeks.

Prepare espino coals. Blanch the leaves in boiling water for about 1 minute, then dry them and brush with olive oil. Cook over soft embers 1 minute per side. Set to the side and let cool at room temperature. Store when they are cold.

RADISH LEAVES

Cut the radish leaves with a small leaf-shaped cookie cutter, making sure that the central leaf vein is centered in the cookie cutter. Vacuum-pack the leaves with the vinegar, and let stand for 24 hours.

Remove the leaves and the vinegar from the bag and arrange them in a bowl. Vacuum in a vacuum-sealing machine 6 times, until the leaves are translucent. Preheat the oven to 212°F (100°C/Gas Mark ¼). Arrange the radish leaves between 2 silicone baking mats being careful that they are perfectly flattened. Bake for 40 minutes. Remove from the oven, let the leaves cool down just slightly, and detach them from the surface with an angled spatula (keeping the baking surface at a high temperature which will aid in removing the leaves without breaking). Store them when they're dry.

DRIED ENOKI

Fray the enoki stems along their full length. Spread out the filaments on a tray and dehydrate at 140°F (55°C) for 8 hours. Then store on a paper towel inside an airtight container.

RED PINE MUSHROOM ASHES

Preheat the oven to 400°F (200°C/Gas Mark 6).

Cut the red pine mushrooms into very thin slices and bake for 15 minutes. Let them cool to room temperature. Then finish by holding them, one at a time, over the flame of a gas burner for 2 seconds. Let them cool completely; then grind in a coffee grinder.

Add the salt and store in an airtight container.

GARGAL MUSHROOM EXTRACT

Let the gargal mushrooms stand in the refrigerator overnight at 39°F (4°C). Then pass the mushrooms through a low-speed extruder. Finally, strain through cheesecloth (muslin) into a bowl. Store in the refrigerator for a maximum of 4 days.

MUSHROOM BRITTLE

Cook the rice in a large pan of boiling water for about 1 hour until the grains dissolve or are completely overcooked. Drain, then combine with the mushroom powder and the dried mushrooms in a food processor. Grind to a smooth paste. Roll out the paste on a nonstick surface and dehydrate at 115°F (45°C) for 12 hours. Then cut the brittle into ¾-inch (2 cm) squares.

Heat the oil to 400°F (200°C) in a deep fryer. Deep fry the mushroom brittle pieces in small batches for 20 seconds. Remove the brittle from the oil and let cool slightly. Then fry again for another 3 or 4 seconds, so the pieces expand to look like a pork rind. Set them aside on paper towels and season with the salt.

CARAMELIZED LOYOS

Preheat 4 small nonstick skillets (frying pans) over high heat so each piece of loyo can be cooked individually.

Using a cookie cutter, slice the loyo horizontally into 4 pieces that are 3 inches (8 cm) in diameter and ½ inch (1.5 cm) thick. Divide the olive oil among the skillets and cook a loyo slice in each pan until caramelízed on both sides. Avoid cooking them for too long on each side so they don't lose too much water.

TO SERVE

Preheat 4 rectangular plates.

Arrange a piece of loyo, directly from its skillet, in the center of each plate; sprinkle with the salt. Then add the mushroom brittle and intersperse the leaves of radish, peumo, white and red goosefoot weed, molle pepper sprouts, fiddleheads, and dried enoki, until the piece of loyo is completely covered. Sprinkle the red pine mushroom ashes on top. Pour the gargal mushroom extract into a hollow in the plate or in a small bowl and place it to one side on the plate and serve immediately.

Shoe Mussel Chupe

Serves 4

For the cheese carrot infusion:
40 g cheese carrots (see page 227)
2 avocado leaves

For the corn smuts mixture:
70 g payar beans
50 g clarified butter
30 g corn smuts
0.5 g Cáhuil fleur de sel

For the chupe base:
100 g white loaf bread
150 g whole (full-fat) milk
50 g white onion
2.5 g pajaritos
3 g fine sea salt

For the smoked shoe mussels:
1 piece tepú wood
2 shoe mussels

To serve:
2 g Cáhuil fleur de sel

CHEESE CARROT INFUSION

Pour 500 g water into a pan, add the cheese carrots, and heat to 185°F (85°C). Then turn off the heat and let it infuse for 24 hours.

Remove the central vein of the avocado leaf and infuse the leaves in cold water for 2 hours. Strain.

CORN SMUTS MIXTURE

Let the payar beans soak in lukewarm water overnight. Then cook them in 1 kg water in a pressure cooker for 1½ hours.

Preheat a skillet (frying pan), add the clarified butter, and lightly caramelíze the corn smuts on both sides. Blend the payar beans with the caramelízed corn smuts in a food processor at 175°F (80°C) for 15 minutes. Add the fleur de sel to create a smooth and homogenous paste.

CHUPE BASE

Tear the bread into small pieces and soak in the milk for 40 minutes.

Preheat a skillet.

Cut the white onion into small dice and cook it directly in the dry skillet over high heat so it gets slightly burned. Combine the onion, milk-soaked bread, 100 g cheese carrot infusion, and the pajaritos in a pan. Simmer and reduce slowly until the pajaritos melt and become as elastic as melted cheese. Let the base cool. Season with fine sea salt.

SHOE MUSSELS

Light the tepú wood in a deep metal pan. Place it directly over the gas burner until it starts to expel yellow smoke. Place the whole shoe mussels in a perforated metal pan, fit it on top of the deep metal pan, and cover with aluminum foil to form a smoker. Smoke for 10 minutes or until the mussels have opened slightly. Remove and finish opening the shells (they should be barely cooked). Cool them to 39°F (4°C) and store at the same temperature.

TO SERVE

Preheat the oven to 350°F (180°C/Gas Mark 4). Cut the smoked shoe mussels into 4 pieces of equal size.

Prepare four 4½-inch (11 cm)-wide bowls. Fill each bowl with 60 g of the chupe base and put one piece of shoe mussel in the upper part of the chupe; add the salt. Cover with the corn smuts mixture and spread it out, forming a layer over the mussel approximately ⅓ inch (1 cm) thick. Bake for 10 minutes, until the surface begins to crackle. Let stand for a few minutes, then serve.

→ 90

Wilted Spring Leaves with Murra Seasoning, Nalca, and Charcoal-Grilled Jibia

Serves 4

For the early plum tree leaves:
40 plum tree leaves
1 kg apple cider vinegar

For the murra fruit seasoning:
15 g mote koji
100 g olive oil
100 g murra fruit extract
20 g flowers miso

For the jibia:
120 g jibia

For the nalcas:
80 g nalcas
40 g lemon juice
10 g olive oil

To serve:
5 g olive oil
12 rue leaves
zest of 1 unripe Chilean mandarin, grated
1 g Cáhuil fleur de sel

PLUM TREE EARLY LEAVES

Vacuum-pack the plum tree leaves with the vinegar. Let stand in a dark place at room temperature for at least 2 months.

MURRA FRUIT SEASONING

Grind the mote koji to a fine powder in a stone mortar. In a bowl, combine the mote koji, olive oil, murra fruit extract, and flowers miso. Mix with a whisk to form a stable emulsion. Store in the refrigerator.

JIBIA

Cut the jibia into ⅓ x ¾-inch (1 cm x 2 cm) rectangles, approximately 10 g each. Set the jibia aside, uncovered, in the refrigerator at 39°F (4°C) for 12 hours so that it becomes slightly aged.

NALCAS

Peel the nalca stems, and cut into thin rounds. In a bowl, marinate the nalca in the lemon juice and olive oil for 24 hours.

TO SERVE

Brush 80 g murra fruit seasoning on a plate, preferably a white one. Set it aside in the refrigerator.

Build an espino coal fire to red-hot embers and let it burn down. Put the jibia in a perforated metal pan and cover with aluminum foil. Set the pan 12 inches (30 centimeters) above the embers, pour the olive oil on the embers, and smoke for 1 minute. Remove, and grill the jibia on both sides to achieve a uniform caramelization. Season each piece à la minute with a rue leaf, the mandarin zest, and fleur de sel.

Arrange 40 g nalca and the jibia on the plate following the direction of the murra seasoning brush marks. Cover each plum tree leaf with a brush of murra fruit seasoning. Let the leaves stand for at least 5 minutes before covering the nalca and jibia with the leaves, using a mixture of different sized leaves.

→ 203

Pantrucas Cooked in Meat Broth with Morels

Serves 4

For the pantrucas:
150 g whole wheat flour
100 g pewén flour
20 g pork lard
250 g warm water
5 g fine sea salt

For the morels:
50 g Chilean morels

To serve:
1 kg Brown Beef Stock (see Basic Recipes → 273)
10 g Mushroom Oil (see Basic Recipes → 273)
20 molle pepper sprouts

PANTRUCAS

Mix the wheat and pewén flours in a bowl, blending thoroughly, and form the mixture into a volcano shape. Add the lard, warm water, and salt. Knead until it forms a firm but soft dough. Sprinkle the surface of the dough with flour, cover the bowl with plastic wrap (clingfilm), and let stand at room temperature for 30 minutes.

Roll the dough out and extend on a floured surface to ⅓-inch (1 mm) thickness, and use a 1-inch (3 cm) cookie cutter to cut out 64 rounds. Wrap them in plastic wrap and refrigerate.

MORELS

Cut the morels into 1/10-inch (5 mm)–thick slices. Refrigerate.

TO SERVE

Warm 4 plates.

Heat the brown beef stock in a pan, and cook the pantrucas for 5 minutes in the stock.

Preheat a skillet (frying pan) and sauté the morels over high heat heat for 2 minutes.

Arrange 16 pantrucas in a circle on each plate, letting them overlap and place the sauted morels over them. Add the mushroom oil. Put 5 molle pepper sprouts on each plate. Serve immediately.

→ 209

Wild Boar in a Clay Oven with Nettle Meringue

Serves 4

For the wild boar loin:
4 kg Chilean espino coal
7 kg lenga wood
800 g wild boar loin (with fat)
300 g hazelnut butter

For the wild boar glaze:
200 g Brown Beef Stock (see Basic Recipes → 273)
200 g wild boar cooking juices

For the salted nettle meringue:
100 g nettles
200 g boiling water
1 g xanthan gum
40 g egg whites
5 g fresh yeast

For the cotton candy:
100 g organic sugar
10 g toasted wheat

To serve:
5 g Cáhuil fleur de sel
50 g black Chiloé garlic
0.5 g fine sea salt
1 g toasted Chilean hazelnuts
12 wild garlic flowers

WILD BOAR LOIN

Light the espino coal and lenga wood in a clay oven and burn for 2 hours, until it is filled with red-hot embers. Keep in mind that the internal temperature of a clay oven with 7 kg of wood reaches up to 485°F (250°C), and there is a constant circulation of smoke.

Place the wild boar loin in a perforated metal tray and place it on the clay oven, so the smoke penetrates over the surface.

Brush the meat with the hazelnut butter every minute, so it hydrates the meat while inside the oven, and cook it until the fat is completely caramelized, approximately 5 minutes. The interior of the wild boar loin should still be raw.

Cut the meat into 1-inch (3 cm)–thick pieces, each weighing about 80 g. Let cool and store covered in the refrigerator.

WILD BOAR GLAZE

Mix the brown beef stock with the wild boar cooking juices in a pan, and reduce over low heat for 1 hour. Store in an airtight container in the refrigerator.

NETTLE MERINGUE

Scald the nettles in a pan of boiling water for 15 seconds, then cool in an ice bath. Drain, then blend in a food processor for 5 minutes at 140°F (60°C), until it has a uniform and smooth texture. Pass the nettles through a strainer (sieve) and store it in the refrigerator.

Dissolve the xanthan gum with the egg whites in a bowl over a medium hot water bath. Beat the egg whites until soft peaks form and stir in the yeast and 20 g of the nettles. Store in an airtight container in the refrigerator.

FOR THE COTTON CANDY

Grind the sugar and toasted wheat in a spice blender until it forms a fine powder. Turn on the cotton candy machine and make 4 cotton buns. Store in an airtight container at room temperature.

TO SERVE

Preheat 4 stone plates.

Put the meat back in the clay oven, coat the raw surface with the hazelnut butter, and roast for 30 seconds. Season with the fleur de sel and let the meat rest for 30 seconds before serving.

Heat the glaze in a pan, place a piece of wild boar in the center of each plate and cover it with the glaze. Thinly slice the black garlic and put 3 slices on top of the meat. Use a pastry (piping) bag to surround the meat with the nettle meringue, and brown the meringue lightly with a blowtorch, then season with fine sea salt. Put the cotton candy on top. Grate the toasted Chilean hazelnuts over the cotton candy, and season by scattering petals of wild garlic flowers on the side.

→ 144

Witch Potato Baked in a Long Rescoldo

Serves 4

For the witch potato:
5 kg Chilean espino coal
200 g witch potatoes

For the kolof root and pajaritos cream:
200 g Kolof Root Broth (→ 273)
200 g Pajaritos Cream (→ 274)

For the alfalfa oil:
200 g alfalfa, leaves removed
100 g canola (rapeseed) oil

For the lovage oil:
200 g lovage
100 g canola (rapeseed) oil

To serve:
20 g horseradish
100 g yellow oxalis flowers
2 g jasmine essence
2 g Cáhuil fleur de sel
16 violet flowers

WITCH POTATO

Build an espino coal fire with red-hot embers and let it burn down until it has burned completely. Pile up the ashes, which should still have a very gentle heat, and insert the witch potatoes inside the ashes. Let them stay there until the following day.

KOLOF ROOT AND PAJARITOS CREAM

In a pan, reduce the kolof root broth by 50%. Then mix it with the pajaritos cream, stirring well. Store in the refrigerator.

ALFALFA OIL

Blend the alfalfa with the canola oil in a food processor at 150°F (65°C) for 15 minutes. Strain it through a fine cloth and reserve the oil.

LOVAGE OIL

Blend the lovage with the canola oil in a food processor at 150°F (65°C) for 15 minutes. Strain it through a fine cloth and reserve the oil.

TO SERVE

Warm 4 plates.

Remove the witch potatoes from the rescoldo and brush the skin off each potato to remove the excess ash. Pour 10 g of the alfalfa oil on one side of each plate and 10 g of the lovage oil on the other side. Spread 50 g of the kolof root and pajarito cream all over the plate; grate the horseradish on another side and cover with yellow oxalis flowers. Using your hands, tear the potatoes in half; season them with the jasmine essence and the fleur de sel. Arrange them in a scattered fashion over the plate, keeping them at the same temperature as when they were removed from the rescoldo. Place 2 violet flowers on top of each witch potato.

→ 192

Muchay and Koji Cake

Serves 4

For the muchay:
1 kg mote wheat
100 g sugar
5 g fresh yeast
50 g mote koji

For the koji cake:
100 g koji
100 g mote koji, partially fermented and solidified
5 g sunflower oil

MUCHAY

Bring 3 kg water to a boil in a pot, and cook the mote wheat in it for 30 minutes. Strain, reserving the mote wheat. Set aside the strained broth and let it cool to room temperature. Immediately grind the mote wheat in a mortar while it is still hot. Add the sugar, yeast, mote koji, and the cooled strained broth. Let stand for at least 24 hours in the refrigerator. Then strain and cool again.

KOJI CAKE

Grind all the koji in a coffee grinder until it forms a fine and homogenous powder.

Heat the sunflower oil in a skillet (frying pan). During the process of fermentation, the mote koji will have solidified into a cake-like structure, and can be easily split with the hands. Break off four 25 g pieces of mote koji, and place in the skillet. Caramelize them on both sides.

Sprinkle koji on the surface of each piece once cooked.

TO SERVE

Pour 60 g of the cold muchay in each of 4 clay drinking vessels, arrange a koji cake on one side, and serve to be eaten with the hands.

→ 217

Jibia and Apple

Serves 4

For the jibia:
200 g jibia
100 g kolof dried under the sun

For the lemon apples:
200 g green apples
200 g lemon juice

For the cold pulmay:
30 g white onion
20 g Chilean green chile
20 g tepú wood
30 g flesh of Chilean mussels
30 g flesh of picorocos
10 g cilantro (coriander)
100 g lemon juice
30 g olive oil
20 g pisco

For the grilled parsley chlorophyll:
200 g canola (rapeseed) oil
100 g parsley stems

To serve:
44 mala hierba weed leaves

JIBIA

Age the jibia for 2 days in the refrigerator, covered in the dried kolof.

Remove the kolof with a cloth, taking away the sediment, and cut the jibia into ⅓ x 1-inch (1 × 3 cm) rectangles. Refrigerate until it is time to use it.

LEMON APPLES

Cut the apples into ⅓ x 1 × 1-inch (1 × 3 × 3 cm) triangles. Place them in a small bowl and add the lemon juice. Put the bowl in a vacuum machine and vacuum 5 times. set aside in the refrigerator until serving time.

COLD PULMAY

Roughly chop the white onion and green chile into quarters.

Light the piece of tepú wood and burn until it releases yellow smoke.

Place the tepú wood in a large pot and set it over direct heat; put the chopped chile and onion, together with the mussels and picorocos, in a strainer (sieve) and set it over the pot. Cover with aluminium foil and smoke over high heat for 10 minutes.

Blend the smoked ingredients in a food processor at top speed. Add the cilantro, lemon juice, olive oil, pisco, and 50 g water. Process at medium speed for 8 minutes. Then strain the contents and set them aside to cool in the refrigerator.

GRILLED PARSLEY CHLOROPHYLL

Sprinkle 20 g of the canola oil over the parsley. Place it in a perforated metal pan and set it over the tepú embers used for smoking the mussels. Cool to room temperature. Combine the smoked parsley with 180 g canola oil and blend in a food processor for 10 minutes at 150°F (65°C). Strain over a fine cloth. Store the strained liquid in the refrigerator.

TO SERVE

Chill 4 plates.

Arrange the cold jibia pieces, alternating with the apple pieces, on the plates. Scatter the mala hierba leaves over them, adding volume. Add some drops of grilled parsley chlorophyll and stir gently. Put the pulmay in the blast freezer for 1 minute so it is very cold but not frozen. Pour the pulmay onto the plates. Serve right away.

→ 153

Steamed Loyos

Serves 4

For the loyo oil:
1 kg loyos
5 g plus 5 kg canola (rapeseed) oil

For the roasted pewén and hazelnut paste:
500 g Chilean hazelnuts
10 g pewén miso
10 g morel miso

For the steamed loyo:
1 pieces loyo
0.5 g fine sea salt

To serve:
4 medium-sized yuyo leaves
12 molle pepper sprouts
12 yuyo flowers
4 yuyo buds
12 alfalfa leaves
12 wild carrot flowers
12 wild onion flowers
4 arugula (rocket) flowers
8 beach dill sprigs
1 g Cáhuil fleur de sel

LOYO OIL

Preheat the oven to 325°F (160°C/Gas Mark 3).

Cut the loyos into big irregular pieces and arrange them in a metal baking pan, leaving spaces between them. Sprinkle the 5 g canola oil over the pieces. Bake for 10 minutes, and then look to make sure that the loyos have been browned; leave them in the pan.

Fill the pan with the 5 kg canola oil and cover with aluminum foil. Let stand on top of the oven or in a warm place until the following day. Then strain and store the oil in a vacuum bag.

ROASTED PEWÉN AND HAZELNUT PASTE

Cook the hazelnuts in a large pot of boiling water for 15 minutes. Dry them and dehydrate at 140°F (60°C) for 1 hour. Let them cool to room temperature.

Preheat a nonstick skillet (frying pan).

Toast the hazelnuts until they turn a caramel color. Blend them together in a food processor with the pewén miso and the morel miso until it forms a rustic paste.

STEAMED LOYO

Bring a large pot of water to a boil, place a steamer rack in it, and reduce the heat to low. Cut the loyo lengthwise into ¾-inch (2 cm)–thick pieces and arrange them inside the steamer. Cook for 20 minutes. Then remove and add the fleur de sel.

TO SERVE

Warm 4 plates.

Brush the pieces of loyo and the yuyo leaves with 20 g loyo oil. Place 2 pieces and 1 leaf on the center of each plate. Spread 4 g of the roasted pewén and hazelnut paste on top. Then distribute the molle pepper sprouts, yuyo flowers, yuyo buds, alfalfa leaves, wild carrot flowers, wild onion flowers, arugula flowers, and beach dill sprigs over all. Add the fleur de sel and serve immediately.

→ 223

Pewén and Hazelnut Bites

Serves 4

For the fermented pewén:
200 g pewén nuts
4 g Cáhuil fleur de sel

For the maqui fruit cookies:
500 g semolina
10 g pewén flour from Araucanía
7 g fine sea salt
8 g fresh yeast

For the grated pewén:
5 pewén nuts
(they must be the first of the season since they are milkier).

For the pewén pâté:
50 g very unripe almonds
(from late spring, with more solid texture)
300 g whole (full-fat) milk
100 g organic salted butter

For the hazelnuts:
100 g Chilean hazelnuts

To serve:
6 sweet alyssum flowers

FERMENTED PEWÉN

Bring a large pot of water to a boil. Add the pewén nuts and cook over high heat for 1 hour; cover and let sit off the heat for 20 minutes.

Next, remove the skins one at a time and pack the nuts, along with the salt, in a vacuum bag. Store in a cool place to ferment for at least 5 months.

MAQUI FRUIT COOKIES

Preheat the oven to 425°F (220°C/Gas Mark 7).

In a bowl, mix the semolina with the pewén flour, salt, fresh yeast, and 250 g water, forming a paste. Allow to ferment for 15 minutes, then spread the paste by hand, with the help of semolina sprinkled like fine rain over the working surface. Cut into four 2¾ x 2-inch (7 × 5 cm) ovals and bake for 3 minutes; turn over the ovals and continue baking for 3 more minutes. Remove and let cool to room temperature.

GRATED PEWÉN

Grate the pewén nuts with a Microplane. Store between moistened sheets of paper.

PEWÉN PÂTÉ

Cut the unripe almonds into paper thin slices.

In a food processor, blend the milk and butter at 160°F (70°C) at high speed. With the machine on, add 200 g fermented pewén nuts, one at a time, grinding until it forms a dense but smooth paste. Let cool, then put in pastry (piping) bags.

HAZELNUTS

Fill a large pot with cold water, add the hazelnuts, and bring to the boiling point. Continue cooking for 30 minutes. Remove from the heat, drain the nuts, and allow them to cool until you can handle them. Remove the skin immediately and store the nuts in the refrigerator.

TO SERVE

Cut the hazelnuts in half. Pipe the pewén pâté onto half of the maqui fruit cookies; place the hazelnut halves on top. On the other half of the maqui fruit cookies, place the grated pewén and the sweet alyssum flowers. Arrange 2 cookies per plate, on 2 shareable plates.

→ 202

Topinambour and Changles from Oncol

Serves 4

For the topinambour puree:
1 kg topinambours
100 g organic unsalted butter
6 g fine sea salt

For the topinambour skins:
100 g topinambour skins
500 g canola (rapeseed) oil
3 g fine sea salt

For the topinambour and meat ravioli:
70 g whole wheat flour
30 g topinambour flour
1 egg
200 g Brown Beef Stock
(see Basic Recipes → 273)

For the changles:
20 g changles from Oncol
0.5 g Cáhuil fleur de sel

To serve:
4 topinambour flowers

TOPINAMBOUR PUREE

Fill a large pot with the 6 kg water and bring to a boil. Cook the topinambours in the boiling water for 10 minutes. Drain, then remove the skins with your hands, making sure you remove the entire peel. Set the skins aside. While above 165°F (75°C), immediately blend the tubers in a food processor for 10 minutes, until they form a smooth paste.

Put the puree in a pan and bring to a simmer. Add the butter and continue to reduce until it forms a dense puree. Season with salt. Cover and refrigerate.

TOPINAMBOUR SKINS

Dehydrate the topinambour skins at 185°F (85°C) for 12 hours. Then heat the canola oil to 400°F (200°C) in a pan, and fry the skins in the hot oil. Drain and set them aside on paper towels; sprinkle with the salt.

TOPINAMBOUR AND MEAT RAVIOLI

To make the pasta dough, in a bowl, mix together the wheat flour, topinambour flour, and egg. Form into a dough and pass it through a pasta roller until it is almost translucent.

To make the filling, heat the brown beef stock in a pan and reduce it by 50%. Pour it into a deep baking pan and let cool until it is ⅓ inch (1 cm) thick and gelled. Using a 1-inch (3 cm) round cookie cutter, cut out 4 disks of the gel.

Place the disks on half of the rolled pasta dough and cover with the remaining dough, making sure the dough adheres well. Select a round cookie cutter that is one size larger than the first one and cut out the ravioli.

CHANGLES

Just before serving, cook the changles on a griddle. Sprinkle with the fleur de sel.

TO SERVE

Bring a large pot of water to a boil and cook the ravioli briefly in order for the internal meat broth to melt.

Place the ravioli in the center of each plate. Surround it with a 3½-inch (9 cm) ring, and fill the ring with the topinambour puree, forming a perfect circle and fully covering the ravioli. Cover half the puree with the topinambour flower petals, concealing any open space, and the other half with the grilled changles, interspersed with the topinambour skins. Suggest that these be eaten by cutting the dish in the center, so the ravioli bursts.

→ 131

Shoe Mussels from Valdivia with Rock Green Sauce

Serves 4

For the rock green sauce:
50 g white onion
30 g cilantro (coriander)
2 g rock parsley
10 g beach asparagus
50 g lemon juice
5 g olive oil
1.5 g fine sea salt
5 g pelillo seaweed
1 piece early-season Chilean mandarin skin

For the ulte in kolof broth:
2 ulte stems
20 rock clovers
1 kg Kolof Root Broth (see Basic Recipes → 273)

For the shoe mussels au naturel:
4 shoe mussels

For the anchovy and pajaritos cream:
100 g Pajaritos Cream (see Basic Recipes → 274)
1 g anchovy garum
1 g mushroom garum

For the fermented lemon:
½ Black Fermented Lemon (see Basic Recipes → 273)

To serve:
36 pieces of sea stars
2 g seaweed merken
5 g katsobushi-style mackerel
44 pieces rock spinach
1.6 g Cáhuil fleur de sel

ROCK GREEN SAUCE

In a food processor grind the white onion, cilantro, rock parsley, and beach asparagus with the lemon juice. Strain and mix the strained liquid with the olive oil and salt. Infuse the pelillo seaweed and the grated mandarin skin in the sauce for 2 hours at room temperature. Keep in the refrigerator.

ULTE IN KOLOF BROTH

In a large pot of boiling water, lower the heat and cook the ulte, adding the rock clovers to acidify the water, in order to get a soft texture on the ulte, for 1 hour. In a separate pan, reduce the kolof broth by 50%. Remove the ulte and finish cooking it in the kolof broth reduction for 45 minutes. Cut it into 1 × ⅙-inch (3 × 0.5 cm) sticks.

SHOE MUSSELS AU NATUREL

Cut the anterior muscle of the shoe mussels, open the shells, and remove the mussels carefully with a spoon. Clean the guts and keep in the refrigerator until the moment of serving.

ANCHOVY AND PAJARITOS CREAM

Mix the pajaritos cream with the mushroom garum and anchovy garum. Pack in a small plastic pastry bag and keep in the refrigerator.

FERMENTED LEMON

Cut the lemon into sticks that are 1 inch long and ⅙ inch thick.

TO SERVE

Chill 4 plates.

Cut a piece of cardboard into 4 pieces that measure 6 × 7 inches (15 × 18 cm). Fold starting from the shorter end into ⅓-inch (1 cm) folds, like an accordion. Distribute 9 sea stars on each cardboard paper and sprinkle with the sea lettuce merkén.

Pipe 15 g of the anchovy and pajaritos cream on the left side of each plate, forming 11 dots in such a way that they can serve as support for the rock spinach. Arrange the ulte sticks and the fermented lemon sticks in an asymmetric way on the sides of the pajarito cream; pour the rock green sauce in between. Sprinkle the katsuobushi-style mackerel and lean the rock spinach in front of each pajarito cream dot and between the vegetable sticks, slightly directed towards the sides. Place the shoe mussel on the right side of the plate. Add the salt and cover the mussel with the cardboard paper, so each person may season it à la minute on their own.

→ 157

Fermented Pewén Chupe

Serves 4

For the fermented pewén:
200 g pewén nuts (must be very fresh and collected at the beginning of the season so they are milky)
4 g Cáhuil fleur de sel

For the fermented pewén chupe:
50 g organic unsalted butter
300 g whole (full-fat) milk
4 g pajaritos

For the grated pewén:
120 g pewén nuts

For the wild fruits:
5 male arrayanes
2 chupón fruits

To serve:
Four 4½-inch (12 cm) parchment paper squares
44 yuyo flowers

FERMENTED PEWÉN

Bring a large pot of water to a boil, add the pewén nuts, and cook over high heat for 1 hour; cover and then let sit off the heat for 45 minutes. Next, remove the skins one at a time and pack the nuts, along with the salt, in a vacuum bag. Store in a cool place to ferment for at least 5 months.

FERMENTED PEWÉN CHUPE

In a food processor, mix 100 g fermented pewén with the butter and 150 g of the milk, and blend at 175°F (80°C) to form a smooth and uniform mixture; then gradually add the remaining 150 g the milk until it has the characteristic thick chupe texture. In a pan, add the pajaritos and melt them, stirring continuously as you would with cheese, until it has the same elasticity as cheese.

GRATED PEWÉN

Peel the pewén nuts and grate them with a very fine grater. Store between moistened paper towels so they maintain their characteristic moisture.

WILD FRUITS

Cut the arrayanes in half and remove the seeds. Remove the skin of the fruit and cut the chupones in half. Just before serving, cut the pieces vertically into ⅓-inch (1 cm) chunks, retaining the seeds.

TO SERVE

Divide the chupe into individual portions over parchment paper, and heat in the oven at 350°F (180°C/Gas Mark 4) for 1 minute. When ready to serve, torch the surface and flip it down as if it were a tarte tatin. Evenly sprinkle the grated pewén, the flowers, the chupones, and the arrayanes on top. The dish should be very hot, to allow the raw pewén to release its aroma.

→ 213

Veal from Parral Cooked in its Own Milk

Serves 4

For the veal:
400 g 3-week-old free-range veal short ribs
1 tepú wood stick

For the glaze:
10 kg veal bones with some meat attached
10 g olive oil
500 g white onion, coarsely chopped
15 kg whole (full-fat) milk

For the grilled milk skins:
200 g whole (full-fat) milk

To serve:
3 g Cáhuil fleur de sel
28 alfalfa leaves, soaking in 1 g olive oil
4 espino twigs
4 drops forest extract

VEAL

Remove the excess fat from the meat and place the ribs in a perforated metal pan. Burn the tepú wood until it starts to release yellow smoke profusely. Move the burning piece of wood to a deep metal pan, fit the perforated pan on top, and cover with aluminum foil. Set over a direct fire. Smoke for 7 minutes. Remove and vacuum-pack the ribs. Cook with a sous vide machine at 160°F (70°C) for 40 hours.

GLAZE

Preheat the oven to 425°F (220°C/Gas Mark 7).

Put the bones in a baking pan and roast for 40 minutes, until they are caramelized. Meanwhile, heat the oil in a large pot, add the onion, and caramelize it. Add the bones and the milk; bring to a very low heat and cook for 8 hours, avoiding excess boiling.

Strain through a very fine-mesh strainer (sieve) and discard the bones and onion. Then strain again, this time through cheesecloth (muslin), to remove any impurities. Let the broth set a side in the refrigerator for 1 day.

Skim the grease from the surface of the broth and bring it to a very low heat in a pan. Reduce by 50%. Set aside in the refrigerator.

GRILLED MILK SKINS

Sprinkle 20 grams of the milk over a hot flat grill and let dry until caramelized, just before the burning point (*bien cuit*). With the aid of a flat spatula and using a zigzag movement, gently and quickly remove the milk skins. Repeat to make 8 grilled milk skins. Let cool to room temperature.

TO SERVE

Preheat a skillet (frying pan) over low heat.

Cut the veal into 4 equal portions. Arrange the meat in the top area of the skillet, and add the glaze. Holding the skillet at a slant, glaze the meat continuously, using a spoon. Note that the glaze must not cool down under any circumstance; otherwise the emulsion might lose its characteristics. Once the glaze is reduced by 50%, remove the meat from the heat and arrange a portion in the center of each plate. Sprinkle the fleur de sel, and cover the meat with the grilled milk skins. Add 7 alfalfa leaves to each plate. Place an espino twig at one side and add a drop of forest extract to each twig. Serve immediately.

→ 188

Raw Beef, Mother of Kombucha, and Nalca Candy

Serves 4

For the nalca candy:
1 kg nalca stems
500 g canola (rapeseed) oil
500 g Kombucha (see Basic Recipes → 273)

For the raw beef crudo:
100 g beef fillet
5 g pewén miso
10 g olive oil

To serve:
8 g kombucha mother

NALCA CANDY

Peel the nalca stems. Thinly slice the stems into 5-inch (13 cm) strips. In a bowl, let the nalca sheets soak in the canola oil for 24 hours in the refrigerator. Put the nalca and oil in a vacuum machine and vacuum 10 times; then let it stand for 24 hours in the refrigerator.

Drain off the excess oil. In a pan, cook the nalca in the kombucha until the liquid has reduced by 50%. Remove from the pan and let it cool at room temperature.

Preheat the oven to 325°F (160°C/Gas Mark 3). Put 4 nalca sheets between 2 non-stick surfaces and add weight over them. Cook with convection for 30 minutes. Lower the temperature to 250°F (130°C/Gas Mark ½) and bake for 20 more minutes. Allow to cool. Cut 4 nalca sheets in the shape of a leaf, 4 inches long and 2 inches wide (10 cm x 5 cm). Dehydrate at 140°F (60°C) for 12 hours, forming a concavity from the stem to the upper part of the leaf. Store in an airtight container at room temperature.

RAW BEEF CRUDO

Pass the meat through a meat grinder. In a bowl, mix the meat, pewén miso, and olive oil. Refrigerate.

TO SERVE

Place a piece of leather on a rectangular plate. Spread the raw beef in 25 g servings on each plate, alternating with the mother kombucha and forming a symmetrical rectangle between the spaces left by the meat. Serve the nalca candy at one side, leaning on a rock base, which can be used to spread the raw beef crudo.

| 168

Version 1
Tres Leches and White Strawberries from Purén

Serves 4

For the Chacabuco goat milk ice cream:
1 g unflavored gelatin sheet
250 g goat milk
3 g glucose powder
125 g heavy (double) cream
1 g ice-cream stabilizer
60 g powdered milk
62.5 g sugar
15 g dextrose powder

For the pajaritos cream:
500 g organic heavy (double) cream
100 g pajaritos yogurt

For the beet sponge cake:
2 eggs
30 g sugar
20 g raw beet (beetroot) puree
12.5 g plain beet (beetroot) juice
50 g all-purpose (plain) flour

For the seasoned beet (beetroot) juice:
2 beets (beetroots)
10 g lemon juice
1 g fine sea salt
25 g olive oil

For the donkey milk snow:
25 g white strawberries
250 g donkey milk
50 g Purén white strawberry juice

For the alfalfa chlorophyll:
200 g alfalfa stripped of its leaves
100 g sunflower oil

For the elderflower glaze:
2 g unflavored gelatin sheet
100 cc elderflower concentrate
0.6 g powdered agar agar
11 g miroir glaze
4 carved irregular twigs
5 g elderflower soaking in 100 g white strawberry vinegar

For the Purén white strawberries:
8 Purén white strawberries

For the murra fruit nappe:
100 g miroir glaze
1.5 g maqui fruit extract
12 g murra fruit extract

GOAT MILK ICE CREAM

Fill a shallow dish with cold water and submerge the gelatin sheet in it. Set aside.

Combine the goat milk, glucose, and cream in a pan, and heat to 120°F (50°C). Mix the stabilizer, powdered milk, sugar, and dextrose together in a bowl. Slowly add the dry ingredients to the milk mixture, using a whisk, heating until the mixture reaches 183°F (84°C). Cool, constantly whipping in an ice bath, to 115°F (45°C). Then add the hydrated gelatin sheet and stir until it dissolves homogenously. Let stand at 39°F (4°C) for at least 12 hours.

Pour the mixture into an ice-cream machine and process at maximum speed. Pour the ice cream into 1½-inch (4 cm) round silicone baking molds and bring the temperature down in a blast chiller for 10 minutes, to –22°F (–30 C).

PAJARITOS CREAM

Mix the cream and the pajaritos yogurt in a yogurt maker. Process at 105°F (40°C) with 60% humidity for 7 hours. Remove and stir vigorously.

BEET SPONGE CAKE

Preheat the oven to 350°F (180°C/Gas Mark 4).

In a mixer, beat the eggs and sugar until foamy. Add the beet puree and juice. With the mixer on medium speed, use a strainer (sieve) to sprinkle the flour into the mixture.

Bake in a baking pan at medium convection. Remove from the oven and let cool at room temperature for 1 hour. Remove the cake from the pan and cut 4 portions with a 1½-inch (4 cm) round cookie cutter.

BEET JUICE

Using an extruder, squeeze 2 beets to obtain 70 g juice. Mix the lemon and beet juices together, then add the salt and olive oil (the latter should be slightly spread out on the surface, forming small drops).

DONKEY MILK SNOW

Mash the white strawberries with 50 g water in a bowl, and then strain, reserving the juice. Freeze the donkey milk together with the white strawberry juice in a baking pan at –22°F (–30°C) for 20 minutes. Mash. (A bit of liquid nitrogen may be added to avoid losing the temperature until the mixture has the texture of a very fine granité.) Set aside at –4°F (–20°C).

ALFALFA CHLOROPHYLL

Mash the alfalfa at 150°F (65°C) in a food processor for 12 minutes. Strain through a fine cloth set in a coneshaped funnel, and set the liquid aside.

ELDERFLOWER GLAZE

Fill a shallow dish with cold water and submerge the gelatin sheet in it. Set aside.

Mix the elderflower concentrate with the agar agar and the glaze in a pot. Bring to a boil and cook for 8 minutes. Then let it cool to 115°F (45°C) and add the hydrated gelatin; mix well to dissolve it. Use a brush to spread the mixture over the twigs; chill the glazed twigs in the refrigerator for 5 minutes; and then repeat the process until there are 5 layers of elderflower glaze. Attach the elderflowers to the branches, covering them entirely.

PURÉN WHITE STRAWBERRIES

Cut the white strawberries in half.

MURRA FRUIT NAPPE

In a bowl, mix the miroir glaze with the maqui and murra extracts, stirring until completely mixed.

TO SERVE

Set the sponge cakes on a wire rack. Remove the goat ice cream from the molds, place 1 over each sponge cake and cover with the nappe. Set in the center of each plate.

Use a pastry (piping) bag to decorate the ice cream with the parajitos cream, then add the alfalfa chlorophyll on top. Add the donkey milk snow and place 4 white strawberries halves on it. To complete the dessert, arrange the elderflower skewer on the dish and add the seasoned beet juice just before serving.

→ 166

Version 2
Tres Leches and Three Wild Fruits

Serves 4

For the Chacabuco donkey milk ice cream:
1 g unflavored gelatin sheet
250 g donkey milk
125 g donkey cream
3 g glucose powder
1 g ice-cream stabilizer
62.5 g sugar
15 g dextrose powder

For the pajaritos cream:
500 g organic heavy (double) cream
100 g pajaritos yogurt

For the beet sponge cake:
2 eggs
30 g sugar
20 g beet (beetroot) pulp
12.5 g plain beet (beetroot) juice
50 g all-purpose (plain) flour

For the seasoned beet juice:
2 beets (beetroots)
10 g lemon juice
25 g olive oil
1 g fine sea salt

For the almond milk snow:
500 g almonds
250 g donkey milk
50 g Purén white strawberry juice

For the alfalfa chlorophyll:
200 g alfalfa stripped of its leaves
100 g sunflower oil

For the orange-blossom glaze:
2 g unflavored gelatin sheet
100 g orange-blossom concentrate
0.6 g powdered agar agar
11 g miroir glaze
4 carved, irregular twigs
4 marigold flowers

For the murra fruit nappe:
100 g miroir glaze
1.5 g maqui fruit extract
12 g murra fruit extract

For the three wild fruits:
72 black murtilla fruits, freshly harvested in Patagonia
20 maqui fruits
8 sea strawberries

CHACABUCO DONKEY MILK ICE CREAM

Fill a shallow dish with cold water and submerge the gelatin sheet in it. Set aside.

Combine the donkey milk, cream, and glucose in a pan, and heat to 120°F (50° C).

Mix the stabilizer, sugar, and dextrose in a bowl. Slowly add the dry ingredients to the milk mixture, using a whisk, heating the mixture to 185°F (85°C).

Cool, constantly whipping in an ice bath, to 115°F (45°C). Then add the hydrated gelatin sheet and stir until it dissolves homogenously. Let stand at 39°F (4°C) for at least 12 hours.

Process the mixture in an ice-cream machine at maximum speed. Distribute it among half-sphere-shaped silicone molds, 1½ inches (4 cm) in diameter, and cool the temperature down in a blast chiller for 10 minutes, to –22°F (–30 C).

PAJARITOS CREAM

Mix the cream and the pajaritos yogurt in a yogurt maker. Process at 105°F (40°C) with 60% humidity for 7 hours. Remove and stir vigorously.

BEET SPONGE CAKE

Preheat the oven to 350°F (180°C/Gas Mark 4).

In a mixer, beat the eggs and sugar until foamy. Then add the beet pulp and juice. Reduce to half speed to add the flour in a shower, using a sifter (sieve). Bake in a baking pan for 18 minutes with convection set to medium. Remove from the oven and cool at room temperature. Then unmold the cake and cut it into 4 portions with a 1½-inch (4 cm) round cookie cutter.

SEASONED BEET JUICE

Using an extruder, squeeze 2 beets to obtain 70 g juice. Mix the lemon and beet juices together, then add the salt and olive oil (the latter should be slightly spread out on the surface, forming small drops).

ALMOND MILK SNOW

Bring a pan of water to a boil, dip the almonds in the water, and remove the skins. Soak the skinned almonds in water overnight; then drain, and blend at maximum power. Strain the mixture through cheesecloth (muslin) and mix the strained milk with the white strawberry juice.

Freeze the almond milk in a deep baking pan at –22°F (–30°C) for 20 minutes. Blend in a food processor. (A little liquid nitrogen may be added to avoid melting the mixture, until it acquires the texture of a very fine granité.) Store at -20°C.

ALFALFA CHLOROPHYLL

Blend in a food processor the alfalfa at 150°F (65°C) for 12 minutes. Strain it through a cheesecloth set in a cone-shaped funnel, and set the liquid aside.

ORANGE-BLOSSOM GLAZE

Fill a shallow dish with cold water and submerge the gelatin sheet in it. Set aside.

Mix the orange-blossom concentrate with the agar agar and the glaze in a pan. Bring to a boil and cook for 8 minutes. Let it cool to 115°F (45°C), and add the hydrated gelatin; mix well to dissolve.

Spread the mixture on the twigs with a brush, refrigerate for 5 minutes, and then repeat the process. Alternate until you have 5 layers of the orange-blossom concentrate nappe. Stick the marigold petals on the twigs so the skewer can't be seen.

MURRA FRUIT NAPPE

In a bowl, mix the miroir glaze with the maqui and murra extracts, stirring until completely mixed.

THREE WILD FRUITS

Remove the outer skin of the black murtilla berries, maqui fruits, and sea strawberries right before serving.

TO SERVE

Set the sponge cakes on a rack and unmold the donkey milk ice cream over them. Coat the ice cream immediately with the murra fruit nappe. Place in the middle of each plate.

Pipe the pajaritos cream over the top, and add the alfalfa chlorophyll, maqui fruits, and sea strawberries. Pour the almond milk granité quickly over the fruit, and place 18 black murtilla berries on top of it. To finish, place the orange-blossom skewer on each dish, and add the beet juice mixture when serving.

→ 169

Version 3
A Year Around the Peumo

Serves 4

For the peumo leaves:
100 g new peumo leaves, harvested in spring
200 g Peumo Vinegar (see Basic Recipes → 274)

For the peumo umeboshi:
1.5 kg green peumos harvested in February
375 g fine sea salt

For the green peumos confit:
1 kg green peumos, harvested by the end of summer (March)
100 g sugar
1 g Cáhuil fleur de sel

For the peumo sponge cake:
2 eggs
30 g sugar
50 g all-purpose (plain) flour, sifted

For the peumo ice cream:
6 g unflavored gelatin sheets
12 g ice-cream stabilizer
180 g dextrose powder
150 g powdered milk
150 g sugar
1.5 kg Chacabuco goat milk
90 g glucose powder
450 g heavy (double) cream
50 g peumo
50 g Kombucha mother of peumo flower buds

For the nappe:
100 g miroir glaze
1.5 g maqui fruit extract
12 g murra fruit extract
5 g Chiloé quinoa miso

For the milk snow infused with peumo leaves:
200 g whole (full-fat) milk
50 g pre-spring peumo leaves (August)

For the peumo puree:
500 g autumn peumo (May)
100 g organic unsalted butter
2 g fine sea salt

For the peumo fruit:
16 fresh peumos, harvested in August

To serve:
4 peumo branches, frozen

PEUMO LEAVES

Vacuum-pack the leaves with the peumo vinegar and set aside for 1 year.

UMEBOSHI

Arrange a handful of peumos at the bottom of a glass jar and add a fine layer of the salt. Continue making the layers until the jar is full. Once the jar is full, put pressure on the surface by using a cloth with a weight. Keep the peumos in the jar for 20 days.

Pour off and reserve the liquid from inside the jar; set the liquid aside. Dehydrate the peumos under the sun for 3 days. Then put them back into the jar and add the reserved liquid. Leave standing for 25 days before using.

GREEN PEUMO CONFIT

Wash and dry the peumos and vacuum-pack them together with the sugar. Cook in a sous vide machine at 185°F (85°C) for 12 hours. Remove, then press with your hands to grind the peumos to a puree. Strain through a fine strainer (sieve), pressing on the peumos with a rubber spatula; discard the pits. Add the fleur de sel and refrigerate the confit.

PEUMO SPONGE CAKE

Preheat the oven to 350°F (180°C/Gas Mark 4).

In a mixer, whisk the eggs until frothy; add the sugar and 15 g peumo confit. Reduce the mixer to medium speed, and add the flour, sprinkling it like rain. Bake in a baking pan for 18 minutes at medium convection. Remove from the oven and let it cool at room temperature. Remove the cake from the mold and cut it into 4 rounds with a 1½-inch (4 cm) round cookie cutter.

PEUMO ICE CREAM

Fill a shallow dish with cold water and submerge the gelatin sheets in it. Set aside.

In a bowl, mix the stabilizer, dextrose, powdered milk, and sugar; set aside. In a pan, combine the goat milk, glucose, cream, and peumo; heat to 175°F (80°C) and let it infuse for 1 hour.

Strain the goat milk mixture, and add 100 g peumo confit. Blend the mixture in a food processor and bring the temperature down to 120°F (50°C). Stir in the bowl of dry ingredients and raise the temperature to 183°F (84°C), stirring constantly. Cool in an ice bath; when it reaches 120°F (50°C), add the hydrated gelatin sheets and stir until dissolved. Leave the mixture standing at 39°F (4°C) for at least 12 hours.

Cut the kombucha mother in very small dice. Process the ice cream mixture in an ice-cream machine at full speed; halfway in the ice-cream process, add the kombucha mother and keep whipping the ice cream. Distribute the ice cream among 4 half-sphere-shaped silicone molds, 1½ inches (4 cm) in diameter, and cool in a blast chiller for 10 minutes at –22°F (–30°C).

NAPPE

Mix the miroir glaze with the maqui extract, murra extract, and quinoa miso. Stir and store in the refrigerator.

MILK SNOW INFUSED WITH PEUMO LEAVES

Infuse the milk with the peumo leaves at 185°F (85°C) for 3 hours. Strain and freeze the milk in a deep baking pan at –22°F (–30°C) for 20 minutes. Grind, then add liquid nitrogen to avoid the preparation losing temperature until it acquires the texture of a fine granité. Set aside at –4°F (–20°C).

PEUMO PUREE

Cut the peumos in half and remove the pits. Blend in a food processor with the butter and salt at 175°F (80°C) for 20 minutes to obtain a smooth puree.

PEUMO FRUIT

Cut the peumos in half, remove the pits, and put the halves together again, adhering them with their own pulp. Store in the refrigerator.

TO SERVE

Chill 4 plates.

Unmold the ice cream over the sponge cake, and nappe the ice cream immediately with the murra fruit nappe. Arrange in the center of a dish.

At one side of the ice cream, pour a small spoonful of peumo puree. Slice the peumo umeboshi into paper thin slices and cover the peumo puree with them. Pour the snow and then the peumo fruit, over the top. Arrange a frozen skewer on the left side, attaching 4 peumo leaves to the skewer, and serve at once.

Meat Dessert

Serves 4

For the veal:
100 g veal short ribs from Parral
1 tepú wood twig

For the glaze:
150 g Brown Beef Stock
(see Basic Recipes → 273)
20 g semisweet (dark) chocolate

For the burnt and spiced white chocolate:
150 g white chocolate
1 g freshly ground cumin
1 g freshly ground molle pepper
0.5 g freshly ground star anise
1 g freshly black pepper
1 g freshly ground cardamom
8 g freshly grated Chilean mandarin zest

For the meat toffee:
100 g Brown Beef Stock (see Basic Recipes)
50 g lactose powder
10 g glucose
50 g powdered sugar

To serve:
2 g olive oil
0.5 g Cáhuil fleur de sel
1 g rock clovers
1 green Chilean mandarin

VEAL

Place the veal in a perforated metal pan. Burn the tepú wood until it starts to release yellow smoke profusely. Move the burning piece of wood to a deep metal pan, fit the perforated pan on top, and cover with aluminum foil. Set over a direct fire and smoke for 7 minutes. Remove and vacuum-pack the meat. Cook in the sous vide machine at 160°F (70°C) for 30 hours.

GLAZE

In a pan, warm the beef stock over medium heat. Add the chocolate and mix well. Keep warm at low temperature.

BURNT AND SPICED WHITE CHOCOLATE

Preheat the oven to 375°F (190°C/Gas Mark 5) with maximum convection.

Put the white chocolate onto a nonstick surface and bake for 25 minutes, stirring every 5 minutes with a spatula, particularly in the middle of the chocolate. Remove from the heat and allow to cool to room temperature.

In a coffee grinder, grind the cumin, molle pepper, star anise, black pepper, and cardamom. Stir the spices into the white chocolate mixture. Next, add the freshly grated mandarin zest. Mix well and store at 41°F (5°C).

MEAT TOFFEE

In a pan, combine the beef stock and the lactose and simmer until reduced by 90%. Add the glucose and stir continuously while cooling down to room temperature. Once cold, add the powdered sugar and store in an airtight container in the refrigerator.

TO SERVE

Cut the meat into 4 portions.

Preheat a skillet over medium heat.

Add the olive oil and place the pieces of meat on the upper part of the pan. Glaze continuously. As the glaze begins to thicken, reduce to low heat and continue cooking until the glaze forms a thin and shiny layer.

Place the meat in the center of each plate; cover it with the burnt and spiced white chocolate, leaving a glimpse of the meat visible. Add the fleur de sel. Remove the leaves from the rock clovers and scatter them over the meat; finish with the meat toffee. Grate the green mandarin zest onto the preparation. Serve immediately, keeping the meat warm while each plate is cold.

→ 170

Overly Fermented Bread Ice Cream with Green Pebre

Serves 4

For the fresh bread ice cream:
1 marraqueta bread
156 g whole (full-fat) milk
2 g glucose powder
63 g heavy (double) cream
1 g ice-cream stabilizer
30 g powdered milk
10 g sugar
7.5 g dextrose powder

For the koji ice cream:
2 g unflavored gelatin sheet
5 g koji
156 g whole (full-fat) milk
63 g organic heavy (double) cream
2 g glucose
1 g ice-cream stabilizer
30 g powdered milk
12 g sugar
7.5 g dextrose powder

For the bread:
160 g all-purpose (plain) flour
95 g whole (full-fat) milk
5 g fresh yeast
1 g fine sea salt

For the green tomato pebre:
10 green tomatoes
3 lemons from Pica
80 g sugar
0.5 g fine sea salt

For the tomato tea:
5 green tomatoes
50 g lemon verbena leaves
200 g liquid nitrogen
100 g canola (rapeseed) oil

To serve:
1 ají amarillo chile, finely diced
16 green tomato seeds
32 chupones
16 lemon geranium leaves

FRESH BREAD ICE CREAM

Preheat the oven to 400°F (200°C/Gas Mark 6).

Bake the marraqueta bread until it browns evenly, so the bread´s flavor will be more intense. Combine the marraqueta and milk in a pan; let the bread steep, crushing it into pieces so the milk will absorb the flavor.

Add the glucose and cream to the steeped milk in the pan, and stir constantly over medium low heat until it reaches 120°F (50°C). In a bowl, stir together the stabilizer, powdered milk, sugar, and dextrose; add the mixture to the milk mixture. Whisk until it reaches 185°F (85°C). Remove from the heat, cool in an ice bath, and store the ice cream mixture at 39°F (4°C) until the next day.

Right before serving, process the mixture in an ice-cream machine at top speed and remove as soon as the ice cream is creamy but firm. Put the ice cream in a pastry (piping) bag with a metal nozzle and store it at 28°F (–2°C).

KOJI ICE CREAM

Fill a shallow dish with cold water and submerge the gelatin sheet in it. Set aside.

Blend the koji with the milk, cream, and glucose in a food processor at top speed. Steep at 175°F (80°C) for 15 minutes. Strain, and place the strained mixture in an ice bath to cool to 120°F (50°C). In a bowl, mix together the stabilizer, powdered milk, sugar, and dextrose; add this to the milk mixture and stir with a beater in a pan over medium heat until the mixture reaches 175°F (80°C). Remove from the heat, and place in an ice bath again. When the mixture reaches 120°F (50°C), add the hydrated gelatin sheet and stir. Store the mixture at 39°F (4°C) until the next day.

Right before serving, process the mixture in an ice-cream machine at top speed, and remove it as soon as the ice cream is creamy but firm. Put the ice cream in a pastry bag with a metal nozzle and store it at 28°F (–2°C).

BREAD

In a bowl, mix the flour, milk, fresh yeast, and salt to make a dough; knead vigorously for 10 minutes, and let it leaven for 4 hours.

Preheat the oven to 475°F (245°C/Gas Mark 9).

Roll the dough out gradually until it is 0.4 inch (1 cm) thick. Cut the dough with a 4-inch (10 cm) round cookie cutter; then cut the rounds in half to form half-moons. Place the pieces on a preheated baking sheet and bake for 4 minutes, until the dough inflates evenly. Let the breads cool.

GREEN TOMATO PEBRE

Open the green tomatoes with a cut along the sides to the base, and remove the seeds completely with a spoon, keeping the round shape. Reserve the seeds. Cut the walls of the tomato in a fine dice.

Grate the skin of each pica lemon over a mortar. Add the juice of the lemons, the sugar, and the salt. Mash together until you have a smooth, slightly liquid paste. In a bowl, mix together the diced tomato and mashed lemons.

Right before serving, cut the verbena leaves into very small pieces and add them to the tomato mixture.

TOMATO TEA

Crush the green tomatoes, place them in a strainer (sieve) lined with a cheesecloth (muslin), and strain overnight to obtain a transparent liquid.

Freeze the lemon verbena leaves and the canola oil in the liquid nitrogen. Blend in a food processor the frozen verbena and oil quickly, then strain. Add the strained green tomato liquid and stir gently.

TO SERVE

Place some of the pebre on each plate, forming a half-moon that is the same size as the bread, add the finely diced ají amarillo, and distribute the reserved green tomato seeds and the chupones showing their seeds. Add the lemon geranium leaves at random.

In the middle of the bottom of each bread, make a hole with a paring knife so you can insert the metal nozzle of the pastry bag in it.

Fill the bread quickly with each flavor of ice cream, using half of the space inside the bread for each flavor. Put it on the side of the pebre. When you serve the dish, pour 2 teaspoonfuls of the green tomato tea over the pebre.

→ 140

Valdivian Salad with Cenizo, Queule, and Chilean Alive Huepos

Serves 4

For the queule umeboshi tapenade:
100 g queule umeboshi
100 g anchovies
50 g parsley
50 g toasted walnuts
30 g olive oil

For the dry cenizo leaves:
20 cenizo leaves
500 g apple vinegar

To serve:
52 fresh cenizo leaves
8 huepo

QUEULE UMEBOSHI TAPENADE

Remove the queule umeboshi skin and set aside at room temperature. Blend the queule umeboshi, anchovies, parsley, toasted walnuts, and olive oil until smooth. Place in an airtight container, cover, and refrigerate.

DRY CENIZO LEAVES

Preheat the oven to 167°F (75°C/Gas Mark ¼). Place the cenizo leaves and apple vinegar in a bowl and place it in a vacuum sealer machine. Use the vacuum 6 times and store in the refrigerator. Put the cenizo leaves between two non-stick surfaces. Bake for 30 minutes until the leaves are translucent. Store in an airtight container at room temperature.

TO SERVE

Use a pastry (piping) bag to spread dabs of the tapenade in the center of each plate forming a rough circular shape, with ¾ inch (2 cm) gaps between them. Each plate must have 18 dabs of tapenade ⅓ inch (1 cm) high. Arrange the fresh cenizo leaves on top of these dabs and alternate with 5 dry cenizo leaves.

Cut the central muscle of the huepo and quickly open the shell. Make a diagonal cut where the tongue starts. Continue to cut in this way in ½ inch (1.5 cm) pieces just like cutting thick sashimi. Place 4 still-moving pieces between the leaves. Serve immediately.

PATAGONIA

→ 214

Flowers Grissini

Serves 4

For the grissini:
50 g all-purpose (plain) flour
1 g fresh yeast
3 g squid ink
2 g Chilean pejerrey (silverside) garum

For the artichoke puree:
4 artichokes
20 g olive oil
1 Oversalted Fermented Lemon (see Basic Recipes → 273)
4 topinambour flowers

For the green crumbs:
2 kg Chilean espino coal
20 g canola (rapeseed) oil
150 g parsley stems
200 g Dry Marraqueta Crumbles (see Basic Recipes → 273)

To serve:
4 bunches of decorative leaves
12 yuyo flowers
8 sweet alyssum flowers
8 alfalfa flowers
12 society garlic petals
8 yarrow leaves
4 sea star flowers
8 wood sorrel flowers
8 molle pepper buds
4 drops jasmine essence

GRISSINI

Preheat the oven to 375°F (190°C/Gas Mark 5).

In a bowl, mix the flour, yeast, squid ink, silverside garum, and 60 g water. Form a paste and let it leaven at 85°F (30°C) for 30 minutes.

Roll out the dough until it is 1/5 inch (0.5 cm) thick, and cut it into 4 3/4 x 1/5-inch (12 × 0.5 cm) sticks. Place them on a nonstick surface, trying to keep a space of 1/3 inch (1 cm) between them. Bake for 8 minutes. Remove and let them cool to room temperature.

ARTICHOKE PUREE

Bring 2 kg water to a boil in a pressure cooker. Add the artichokes and pressure-cook for 20 minutes. Allow the artichokes to cool to room temperature, then remove and reserve the edible parts from the leaves and the hearts. Juice the fermented lemon to extract 20 g juice, and blend in a food processor with the olive oil and topinambour flower petals at top speed at 150°F (65°C) for 15 minutes. Freeze the puree in a Pacojet container, then process it to a smooth and uniform puree. Store in the refrigerator.

GREEN CRUMBS

Build an espino coal fire with red-hot embers and let it burn down. Spread the canola oil over the parsley stems; place them on a perforated metal pan, and heat it over the espino embers until the parsley is slightly grilled. Blend the dry marraqueta crumbles in a food processor at top speed for 1 minute to make a fine powder. Increase the temperature to 150°F (65°C) and add the grilled parsley. Continue blending at medium speed and gradually increase the speed for 3 minutes. Dehydrate at 115°F (45°C) for 30 minutes. Cool the crumbs and store in the refrigerator.

TO SERVE

Immerse the grissini, one at a time, into the artichoke puree until three-quarters of each are covered, taking care not to break them; then roll them on the green crumbs, covering the artichoke puree completely.

Arrange the grissini on a stone recipient with two perforations in the top. Fill each holder with a bouquet of decorative leaves, so they are firm but are easy to remove. Randomly attach the yuyo flowers, alyssum, alfalfa, garlic petals, yarrow leaves, sea star, wood sorrel flowers, and molle pepper buds; season with a drop of jasmine essence on the tip of each grissini. Serve right away, using one stone for two people.

→ 210

Ice Cuchuflí Stuffed with Calbuco Black-Bordered Oysters

Serves 4

For the ice cuchuflí:
50 g seawater

To serve:
4 Calbuco black-bordered oysters
2 g beach asparagus
2 g rock onions
2 g rock clover stems
Frozen volcanic stones

ICE CUCHUFLÍ

Insert a ½-inch (1.5 cm)–diameter, 3½-inch (9 cm)–long PVC tube into a wine cork. It is important that you press against the tip so it fits perfectly. Then slide a ¾-inch (2 cm)-diameter, 2¾-inch (7 cm)-long bronze tube over the PVC tube. Apply pressure gently to prevent the cork from breaking. Set 4 of these tube molds on a completely flat surface, fill them with the seawater to the edge of the bronze tubes, and freeze at –4°F (–20°C) for 10 minutes.

Remove from the freezer and remove the inner ice tubes, rubbing the bronze for a few seconds. Store in the freezer.

TO SERVE

Cut the Calbuco black-bordered oysters in half and put them, raw, inside the ice cuchuflí; continue with the beach asparagus, rock onions, and rock clover stems. Arrange the ice cuchuflí on a dish, placing it next to frozen volcanic stones.

→ 183

Guanaco Crudo and Arrayán

Serves 4

For the crudo:
150 g guanaco meat

1 g sea salt
½ Roasted Sea Carrots
(see Basic Recipes → 274), ground
10 g olive oil

For the maqui crackers:
142 g semolina
2 g fresh yeast
2 g fine sea salt
5 g maqui extract

For the maqui gel:
1.3 g powdered agar agar
0.7 g xanthan gum
7.3 g maqui extract,
plus extra for thinning

For the maqui tartara sauce:
80 g Pajaritos Cream
(see Basic Recipes → 274)
20 g maqui extract
3 g capers
4 g prepared mustard
25 g Mayonnaise
(see Basic Recipes → 273)

To serve:
10 g lemon juice
1 g maqui extract
8 female arrayanes
25 onion flowers
5 g powdered maqui extract

CRUDO

Age the meat at 37°F (3°C) for 15 days.

When you are ready to use the meat, remove the excess fat and grind the meat with a hand meat grinder. Season with the sea salt and ground roasted sea carrots; add the olive oil. Store at 39°F (4°C) until ready to serve.

MAQUI CRACKERS

Preheat the oven to 425°F (220°C/Gas Mark 7).

In a bowl, mix together the semolina, yeast, salt, maqui extract, and 70 g water; knead vigorously. Let the dough sit at warm room temperature for 30 minutes to ferment.

Roll the dough out until it is 1/5 inch (1 mm) thick. Use a 2 × 3-inch (5 × 8 cm) oval cookie cutter to cut out 4 pieces. Bake the crackers with 0% moisture for 5 minutes. Remove from the oven and cool to room temperature.

MAQUI GEL

In a pan, mix 60 g water with the agar agar, xanthan gum, and maqui extract; dissolve while cold and whisk by hand. Then heat to the boiling point, and when mixture reaches a boil, stir and cook for 8 minutes. Cool at room temperature until solid. Crush with a little more maqui to create a semi-fluid gel that can be put in a pastry (piping) bag. Put the mixture into a small pastry bag and store at 39°F (4°C).

MAQUI TARTARA SAUCE

In a bowl, blend the pajaritos cream, maqui extract, capers, mustard, and mayonnaise together. Put the mixture through a fine strainer in order to get a shiny, smooth tartara sauce. Place the sauce in a small plastic pastry bag.

TO SERVE

Just before serving, season the meat with the lemon juice as if it were ceviche. Spread the crudo evenly over the maqui crackers. Add 2 drops of maqui extract on top of the meat.

Pipe the tartara sauce and maqui gel on the meat, forming small balls the size of arrayanes. Then add arrayanes in between the sauce and the gel, without leaving any empty spaces. Add the onion flowers on top. Sprinkle the powdered maqui extract on one half of the plate, keeping it from moving over onto the other side, and place the maqui tartara right in the middle of the plate. Serve cold immediately.

→ 83

Version 1 The Hunt of the Deer

Serves 4

For the Chilean espino
coal-grilled vegetables:
3 kg Chilean espino coal
1 loyo
150 g pajaritos yogurt whey
1 beet (beetroot)

For the beet sauce:
1 beet (beetroot)
1 g maqui fruit extract
4 g murra fruit extract

For the sea bread:
70 g whole (full-fat) milk
250 g fresh yeast
20 g sugar
30 g Cáhuil fleur de sel
1.2 kg all-purpose (plain) flour
1.2 kg whole wheat flour
75 g cilantro (coriander) seeds
15 g merkén
150 g rock spinach leaves
150 g cilantro (coriander) leaves
150 g parsley sprigs
100 g squid ink

For the chocolate antlers:
5 g Brown Beef Stock
(see Basic Recipes → 273)
40 g semisweet (dark) chocolate
10 g unsweetened dark cocoa powder
1 g Cáhuil fleur de sel
0.5 g ground pink peppercorns

For the venison:
60 g venison sirloin
1 tepú wood twig

To serve:
20 yarrow leaves

CHILEAN ESPINO COAL-GRILLED VEGETABLES

Build a Chilean espino coal fire with red-hot embers. Hang the loyo 70 cm above the embers for 5 hours, brushing it with the pajarito yogurt whey to prevent it from dehydrating. Remove and set aside.

Wait until the embers burn down into ashes and then immerse the beet in them; leave until the following day. Then rinse off the beet and cut it into 1/5-inch (1 mm) slices.

BEET SAUCE

Using an extruder, squeeze the beet to obtain juice. Mix it with the maqui and murra fruit extracts. Store at 41°F (5°C) for 24 hours before serving.

SEA BREAD

In a large bowl, mix the milk with the yeast and sugar to form a leaven. Let it ferment for 30 minutes. Then stir the mixture and add 800 g water, the fleur de sel, and the all-purpose flour and whole wheat flour. Knead vigorously.

Blend the cilantro seeds, merkén, rock spinach leaves, cilantro leaves, parsley, squid ink, and 200 g water in a food processor, and add the mixture to the dough. Continue kneading until it forms an elastic and homogenous mixture. Let the final dough ferment, covered with plastic wrap (clingfilm), for 45 minutes at 85°F (30°C).

Preheat the oven to 350° F (180°C/Gas Mark 4).

Form the dough into a large loaf and bake with 90% humidity for 20 minutes. Then raise the temperature to 425°F (220°C), and bake without moisture for 10 minutes. Let the bread cool down fully. Break the bread into small pieces, and dehydrate at 175°F (80°C) for 3 hours. Let it cool to room temperature, and grind at maximum power to create crumbs.

CHOCOLATE ANTLERS

Mix the beef stock with the dark chocolate in a heatproof bowl; melt in a bain-marie. Pour the mixture into 4 molds with the shape of venison horns. Immerse the molds in abundant ice water for 4 minutes; then carefully remove the chocolate horns from the molds. Set them aside in a container containing a mixture of the cocoa, fleur de sel, and pink peppercorns.

VENISON

Cut the venison meat into 4 rectangular pieces of 15 g each. Light the tepú wood twig in a deep metal pan; as soon as it starts smoking, place the pan on a direct fire. When it starts emitting yellow smoke, arrange the pieces of venison on a perforated metal pan, cover it with aluminum foil, and set it on the other pan. Smoke the meat for 2 minutes. Remove and store at 39°F (4°C).

TO SERVE

Cook the pieces of venison on the grill until golden brown. Slice the coal-grilled loyo and beet with a mandolin. Place a loyo slice on one side of the plate; arrange a beet slice on top of the loyo. Spoon the beet sauce in the center of the plate, and beat it so that it splatters to the sides. Sprinkle with the sea bread crumbs, scatter the yarrow on top, and set the chocolate antlers in place right before serving.

→ 84

Version 2 The Hunt of the Deer (dessert version)

Serves 4

For the venison:
60 g venison sirloin
1 tepú wood twig
15 g olive oil
1 g Cáhuil fleur de sel

For the chocolate antlers:
5 g Brown Beef Stock (see Basic Recipes → 273)
40 g semisweet (dark) chocolate
10 g unsweetened dark cocoa powder
1 g Cáhuil fleur de sel
0.5 g ground pink peppercorns

For the beet sauce:
1 beet (beetroot)
1 g maqui fruit extract
4 g murra fruit extract

For the blood emulsion:
100 g venison blood
10 g clarified butter, melted
20 g red murtilla
1 g fine sea salt

For the maqui fruit powder:
100 g maqui fruit

To serve:
80 murtillas
1 g roasted maqui fruit powder
16 yarrow leaves

VENISON

Cut the venison meat into 4 rectangular pieces of 15 g each.

Light the tepú wood twig in a deep metal pan. As soon as it starts smoking, place the pan on a direct fire. When it starts emitting yellow smoke, arrange the pieces of venison on a perforated metal pan, cover it with aluminum foil, and set it on top of the deep metal pan containing the tepú wood. Smoke the meat for only 1 minute.

Remove the meat, brush it with olive oil, and cook on the grill until golden brown. Remove from the griddle and sprinkle the fleur de sel on top of the venison pieces.

CHOCOLATE ANTLERS

Mix the beef stock with the dark chocolate in a heatproof bowl; melt in a bain-marie. Pour the mixture into 4 molds the shape of stag horns. Immerse the molds in abundant ice water for 4 minutes; then carefully remove the chocolate horns from the molds. Set them aside in a container containing a mixture of the cocoa, fleur de sel, and pink peppercorns.

BEET SAUCE

Using an extruder, extract the juice from the raw beet; mix it with the maqui fruit and murra fruit extracts. Store at 41°F (5°C) for 24 hours before serving.

BLOOD EMULSION

Blend the venison blood in a food processor on medium speed at 160°F (70°C) for 10 minutes, gradually adding the butter in a thin stream. Add the fresh murtillas and the salt; grind until it forms a smooth and homogenous paste. Cool to room temperature and store the emulsion in a plastic pastry bag at 39°F (4°C).

MAQUI FRUIT POWDER

Dehydrate the maqui fruit at 175°F (80°C) for 3 hours. Then blend in a food processor at maximum power until it forms a very fine powder. Finally, roast slightly on a dry skillet (frying pan). Store in an airtight container.

TO SERVE

Place the venison pieces on one side of each plate. Pipe the blood emulsion around the meat and stick the murtillas on top of it, without leaving any visible spots of emulsion. Place 15 g of the beet sauce in the center of the plate, and beat it so it splatters to the sides. Sprinkle with the roasted maqui fruit powder, and place the yarrow leaves in a random manner. Right before serving, set the chocolate antlers in place, leaning slightly onto the venison meat.

Grilled Guanaco Skirt Steak

Serves 4

For the compost flakes:
100 g trimmed crusts of bread

2 g cilantro (coriander) seeds
30 g parsley sprigs
2 g merkén
1 g fine sea salt
40 g squid ink

For the spinach and alfalfa puree:
10 g spinach
5 g alfalfa
1 g lemon verbena stems
10 g wood sorrel
20 g parsley

For the burnt butter emulsion:
500 g organic unsalted butter
50 g guanaco blood

For the skirt steak:
1 kg tepú wood
100 g guanaco skirt steak
3 g fine sea salt

To serve:
1 g Cáhuil fleur de sel
0.5 g koji merkén

COMPOST FLAKES

Preheat the oven to 250°F (120°C/Gas Mark ¼) for 10 minutes.

Combine the crusts of bread with the cilantro seeds, parsley, merkén, salt, and squid ink in the food processor. Add 100 g water and blend, forming a thick paste. Spread it over a nonstick surface with a rubber spatula, making a thin layer. Cover it with another nonstick surface and bake for 20 minutes. Remove and allow to cool to room temperature. Then break it with your hands into small irregular flakes and store in an airtight container.

SPINACH AND ALFALFA PUREE

Blend the spinach, alfalfa, lemon verbena, wood sorrel, and parsley together in a food processor at medium speed until the mixture forms a slightly rustic puree, preserving the texture of the stems.

BURNT BUTTER EMULSION

Melt the butter in a small pan over high heat. When it starts to brown, reduce the heat to low and cook until it is a caramel color. Remove it from the heat and let it cool to room temperature. Strain the butter through a coffee filter to remove the sediment.

In a pan, warm the guanaco blood to 90°F (32°C). Stirring continuously, pour the blood in a thin stream into the burnt butter and continue to stir until it forms an emulsion.

SKIRT STEAK

Prepare red-hot embers with the tepú wood, letting it cool until the upper layer is barely warm. Cut the guanaco skirt steak, removing the muscle layer from the surface in order to allow for cooking one single piece per person over the embers. Cook the skirt steak over the embers, brushing it with the burnt butter to prevent it from drying out. Turn it over and repeat the process. Remove from the embers and season with salt.

TO SERVE

Sprinkle some of the fleur de sel onto a cutting board. Remove the guanaco skirt steak from the embers and place it on the cutting board. Cut it into 16 pieces and sprinkle with the remaining the fleur de sel.

Place 4 pieces of skirt steak on each plate, slightly separated from one another. Cover each piece completely with the flakes, add 3 drops of the spinach and alfalfa puree, and then add more flakes to cover the puree. Sprinkle the koji merkén randomly and serve immediately.

→ 204

Guanaco and Murtillas

Serves 4

For the sun-dried murtillas:
24 murtillas

For the black quince and meat sauce:
500 g Brown Beef Stock (→ 273)
½ black quince
4 g powdered agar agar

For the yeast soufflé:
1 g xanthan gum
40 g egg whites
5 g fresh yeast
10 g whole (full-fat) milk
0.5 g fine sea salt

For the melí-infused butter:
300 g clarified butter
1 melí twig

For the guanaco:
1 lenga wood twig
2 melí twig leaves
200 g guanaco sirloin
1 kg Chilean espino coal
1 g Cáhuil fleur de sel

To serve:
32 fresh murtillas
4 thin espino twigs

SUN-DRIED MURTILLAS

Dry the murtillas in the sun for one week, turning them over on a daily basis. Store in an airtight container.

BLACK QUINCE AND MEAT SAUCE

In a pan, heat the beef stock with the black quince. Let it infuse for 30 minutes off the heat. Blend in a food processor at 195°F (90°C) for 15 minutes; then strain, and add the agar agar. Boil for 5 minutes so the agar agar can dissolve completely. Pour into a N_2O siphon and load it twice. Before serving, heat the siphon to 140°F (60°C) for at least 1 hour.

YEAST SOUFFLÉ

Preheat the oven to 160°F (70°C/Gas Mark ¼).

Dissolve the xanthan gum in the egg whites and beat them until stiff. In a separate bowl, dissolve the yeast in the milk. Add the milk and salt to the whipped egg whites. Spread the meringue over a nonstick surface to make a layer that is ⅓ inch (1 cm) thick, and bake for 4 hours. Remove and let the soufflé sit on the nonstick surface and cool at room temperature.

Use a metal 2¾ x 2-inch (7 × 5 cm) oval cookie cutter to cut out 4 pieces. Store in an airtight container.

MELÍ-INFUSED BUTTER

Vacuum-pack the clarified butter with the melí twig. Infuse at 175°F (80°C) for 5 hours. Open the bag and strain the butter.

GUANACO

Heat the lenga twigs and melí leaves in a clay oven until smoking. Put the guanaco sirloin in the clay oven and smoke it for 10 minutes. Keep at room temperature. Cut into pieces of 50 g and reserve in the refrigerator.

Prepare an espino coal fire, build up a red-hot ember, and then spread the embers out in order to achieve a soft and disperse heat.

Arrange the pieces of guanaco sirloin on a grill over the embers; brush the surface of the guanaco with the melí-infused butter every 2 minutes as the meat is cooking, to prevent it from drying out; turn the meat over and repeat. Make sure that it is cooked until medium rare. Add the fleur de sel and let the meat stand for 1 minute before serving.

TO SERVE

Preheat 4 plates.

Fasten 8 fresh murtillas on the thorns of each espino twig, using the twig as a skewer.

Arrange the meat in the center of each plate. Spread the meat sauce over it with the siphon, and cover the sauce with the yeast soufflé. Then add the murtilla skewer on top. Finish with a little more quince and meat sauce on the right side of the plate. Add the sun-dried murtillas.

→120

Mille-feuille of Vine Leaves, Wild Apples, and Magellan Lamb Cooked à l'Inverse

Serves 4

For the mille-feuille:
10 g canola (rapeseed) oil
20 tender grape leaves
1 g fine sea salt

For the kombucha:
250 g kombucha juice
2.7 g powdered agar agar
50 g kombucha mother
1 g xanthan gum

For the wild fruits:
80 wild pink apples

For the mojo:
1 white onion
10 g olive oil
1 garlic clove
0.1 g dry oregano
0.1 g merkén
10 g Cáhuil fleur de sel
500 g apple cider vinegar

For the Magellan lamb:
12 kg Chilean espino coal
1 Magellan lamb (about 9 kg)

To serve:
50 g Pajaritos Cream
(see Basic Recipes → 274)
8 molle pepper sprouts
8 small lemon balm leaves
8 wood sorrel leaves
8 lemon geranium leaves
2 g Cáhuil fleur de sel

MILLE-FEUILLE

Heat a nonstick skillet over medium heat, add the canola oil. Add the grape leaves 2 at a time and press them evenly in the pan, using a folded paper towel to avoid getting burned. Check the caramelization every now and then; the idea is to achieve a bright golden color. At the same time, the leaf must dehydrate almost completely. Set the leaves aside between paper towels sprinkled with fine sea salt.

KOMBUCHA

Pour the kombucha juice into a pan, add the agar agar, and bring to a boil; cook for 8 minutes. Let the mixture cool to room temperature. Once it gells, blend it in a food processor, adding the kombucha mother and xanthan gum. Pour the mixture into a small bowl, put it in a vacuum machine, and vacuum to remove any excess bubbles. Fill small pastry (piping) bags with the kombucha.

WILD FRUITS

Cut 4 wild apples in half and set the others aside.

MOJO

Cut the onion in strips. Heat the olive oil in a skillet over high heat, and caramelize the onion. Then add the garlic and cook until slightly browned. Add the oregano, merkén, fleur de sel, and vinegar. Remove and blend in a food processor at top speed.

MAGELLAN LAMB

Build an espino coal fire with red-hot embers. Tie all the lamb limbs to a metal cross with wire, including three points at the neck, thorax, and pelvis. Place the lamb, slanted at an angle of 22.5 degrees, over a base of very thin espino embers, and roast for 4 hours. It is important that the embers are red-hot. Also, it is important to maintain low and constant heat during the 4 hours. Continually hydrate the inside part of the animal, which is in direct contact with the heat, with mojo.

Move the lamb away from the fire and reposition it at a 45-degree angle, and then return to the fire, cooking for 4 hours. Follow the same procedure: reposition the lamb to a 67-degree angle to cook for 1 hour and then to a 90-degree angle to cook for 1 hour, until it has cooked for approximately 10 hours in total. Each time you reposition the lamb, make sure the embers are red-hot.

When the lamb reaches the 90-degree angle, its back should still be raw. Feed red-hot embers into the fire to increase the temperature to a very strong heat and turn the lamb around so its back faces the fire. Cook for another 2 hours. Hydrate the back by spreading the animal's own fat during cooking to prevent excess dehydration. Also add mojo all over the back of the animal. Once 1 hour has elapsed, start cutting the lamb in symmetrical deep cuts, starting from the hind limbs towards the thorax and begin serving while the rest of the lamb continues to cook.

TO SERVE

Pipe the kombucha and the pajarito cream over the grape leaves and scatter the pepper, lemon balm, sorrel, and lemon geranium leaves over it. Then stack 1 grape leaf on top of the other to complete 4 stacks of 4 leaves each. Cut 4 apples in half, and space them on the surface to stabilize the upper leaf. Add the final leaf, and then put the remaining herbs and 16 wild pink apples on top, using the kombucha and pajaritos cream to hold them in place. Place the mille-feuille on a napkin folded in thirds.

Chop the lamb and add fleur de sel on the lower side. Serve immediately at one side of the napkin on a warm dish.

→193

Snowy Quinoa Koji Milk and Wild White Apples

Serves 4

For the cheese apples:
4 Valdivia apples

4 g mold spores (*Penicillium candidum*)

For the elderflower meringue:
250 g sugar
25 g elderflower vinegar
2 egg whites

For the quinoa koji milk:
200 g Chiloé quinoa koji
1 g fine sea salt
10 g sugar

To serve:
6 wild white apples
4 cheese apples

CHEESE APPLES

Use a 1¾-inch (4.5 cm) mandolin to cut slices from the apple; use a round cookie cutter to remove the skin from the slices. Make 6 vertical incisions and 6 horizontal incisions, each about 1/50 inch (0.7 mm) on the upper part of the apple; making sure that each incision reaches to the middle of the apple. Bring a pan of water to a boil and scald the apples for 2 minutes, letting the cuts open like a flower. Then cool them in an ice bath, drain, and set on a smooth surface.

Sprinkle the mold spores over the apples and gently rub in. Set aside to ferment at 55°F (13°C) and 65% humidity for 48 hours. Then store at 39°F (4°C) until ready to serve.

ELDERFLOWER MERINGUE

Combine the sugar, 50 g water, and the elderflower vinegar in a pan and begin to heat over high heat. When the sugar syrup reaches 230°F (110°C), whip the egg whites in a bowl,. When the sugar syrup reaches 243°F (117.5°C), add it slowly to the whites and continue whipping until they form peaks. Let the meringue cool to room temperature. Set aside half of the meringue in the refrigerator. Spread the other half on a nonstick surface and dehydrate at 160°F (70°C) for 5 hours. Store in an airtight container.

QUINOA KOJI MILK

Combine the quinoa koji and 800 g water in a bowl, and set aside for 12 hours. Then blend the mixture in a food processor and strain it through cheesecloth (muslin). Stir the salt and sugar into the strained milk, and store it in the refrigerator.

TO SERVE

Thinly slice the white wild apples.

Place an inoculated apple on one side of each bowl and put the elderflower meringue on the other side; cover it with the dehydrated meringue. Arrange 12 wild white apple slices randomly over the inoculated apple. Pour the quinoa koji milk over all, then serve.

Maqui Cake

Serves 4

For the maqui juice:
4 tender maqui leaves
50 g maqui fruit extract
50 g sugar
3 g fine sea salt

For the maqui pajaritos yogurt:
100 g pajaritos yogurt
20 g maqui fruit extract

For the Chiloé sheep milk ice cream:
2 g unflavored gelatin sheet
1 g ice-cream stabilizer
[illegible] g powdered milk
62.5 g sugar
15 g dextrose powder
250 g Chiloé sheep milk
3 g glucose powder
125 g heavy (double) cream

For the maqui sponge cake:
2 eggs
30 g sugar
20 g maqui pulp
20 g maqui fruit extract
50 g whole wheat flour

For the maqui glaze:
100 g miroir glazing
20 g maqui fruit extract

For the maquis:
25 g fresh maqui berries
5 g olive oil
1 g Cáhuil fleur de sel

MAQUI JUICE

In a container, infuse the tender maqui leaves in 50 g water at 175°F (80°C), covered, for 2 hours. Then strain and chill the leaves. Vacuum-pack the leaves, adding the maqui extract, sugar, and salt. Store in a chamber with controlled temperature at 105°F (40°C) for 2 days. The result will be similar to a sparkling wine.

MAQUI PAJARITOS YOGURT

Strain the pajaritos yogurt through a cheesecloth (muslin) overnight, until it has the consistency of Greek yogurt. Then mix it with the maqui extract. (Only 15 g of maqui pajaritos yogurt will be used in this dish, but it is not possible to prepare a smaller amount.)

CHILOÉ SHEEP MILK ICE CREAM

Fill a shallow dish with cold water and submerge the gelatin sheet in it. Set aside.

In a pan, mix together the stabilizer, powdered milk, sugar, and dextrose. Pour the sheep milk into another pan, add the glucose and cream, and heat it to 150°F (65°C); then add the milk mixture to the dry mixture. Slowly raise the temperature to 185°F (85°C), stirring continuously with a whisk. Then cool the mixture to 115°F (45°C) in an ice bath; add the hydrated gelatin and stir. Once the temperature is down to 50°F (10°C), add 5 g maqui juice. Process the mixture in an ice-cream machine at top speed. Remove it carefully and fill four 1½-inch (4 cm) half-sphere-shaped silicone molds. Blast-chill at –22°F (–30°C) for 15 minutes. Remove the ice cream from the molds and store the 25 g portions, separated from each other, at –4°F (–20°C).

MAQUI SPONGE CAKE

Preheat the oven to 350°F (180°C/Gas Mark 4). Whip the eggs and sugar together until frothy, and then add the maqui pulp and extract. Use a sifter (sieve) to sprinkle in the flour, and mix it in. Bake in a baking pan for 18 minutes with medium convection. Remove from the oven and chill. Then remove the cake from the pan and divide it into 4 portions with a 1½-inch (4 cm) round cookie cutter.

MAQUI GLAZE

Blend the miroir glaze and the maqui extract in a bowl and stir until completely blended.

MAQUIS

In a bowl, stir the fruit with the olive oil, and add the salt.

TO SERVE

Put the sponge cake rounds on a rack set over a rimmed pan. Place the ice cream half-spheres on top of the maqui sponge cake rounds, and pour the maqui glaze over the ice cream with a spoon, letting it completely cover the ice cream. Set in the center of each plate. Spoon the maqui pajaritos yogurt around the ice cream, and arrange the maqui fruit over the yogurt, leaving no free space between pieces of fruit. Serve immediately.

Glacial Coldness

Serves 4

For the cold meringue:
2.5 g menthol crystals
250 g egg whites
250 g sugar

For the lemon base:
190 g condensed milk
200 g evaporated milk
3 g unflavored gelatin sheets
90 g lemon juice

To serve:
1 g powdered unsweetened cocoa powder
100 g liquid nitrogen

COLD MERINGUE

Preheat the oven to 175°F (80°C/Gas Mark ¼).

Grind the menthol in a mortar. In a bowl, beat the egg whites until stiff, and gradually add the sugar; add the menthol right before it becomes a shiny and firm meringue.

Place the meringue in a plastic pastry (piping) bag fitted with a ⅓-inch (1 cm) flat metal nozzle. Pipe 4 circles forming a mound onto a nonstick surface and bake for 3 hours. Remove from the heat, let cool to room temperature, and store in an airtight container.

LEMON BASE

Chill the condensed milk and evaporated milk separately at 39°F (4°C) for 4 hours.

Hydrate the gelatin sheets in cold water and set aside. Then dissolve the gelatin in the lemon juice in a small bowl and set aside. Pour the chilled evaporated milk into a bowl and whisk it for 15 minutes with a mixer at top speed. Then reduce the speed to half power and incorporate the chilled condensed milk in a slow stream; add the hydrated gelatin sheet with the lemon juice in the same manner. Store the resulting foam in a plastic pastry (piping) bag and leave it to cool at 39°F (4°C) for 1 hour.

TO SERVE

Pipe the lemon base onto the center of each plate and sprinkle the cocoa powder over of it.

Cool the meringues directly in the liquid nitrogen for 30 seconds. Remove them one at a time and lean a meringue onto the foam on each plate. Serve immediately.

BASIC RECIPES

AUTUMN MUSHROOM POWDER

Makes 75 g

100 g pine mushrooms

Dry the pine mushrooms in a dehydrator at 175°F (80°C) for 12 hours. Grind in a coffee grinder to form a fine powder. Sift through a fine sieve, and store in an airtight container at room temperature.

BLACK FERMENTED LEMONS

Makes 3.5 kg

5 kg lemons

Put the lemons on a sunny rooftop and leave them for 2 months, until they look dry and black. Store in an airtight container at room temperature for maximum 4 months.

BROWN BEEF STOCK

Makes 2.5 kg

4 kg beef bones

Preheat the oven to 400°F (200°C/Gas Mark 6).

Roast the bones until golden. Place the roasted bones in a large stockpot and add enough cold water to cover. Bring to a boil over high heat and skim the foam and fat from the surface. Reduce the heat to low and simmer for about 7 hours. Strain the stock through a fine-mesh strainer (sieve) and discard the bones. Keep in the refrigerator for 1 week, or 4 months if it is frozen.

DRY MARRAQUETA CRUMBLES

Makes 400 g

500 g marraqueta bread

Preheat the oven to 250°F (120°C/Gas Mark ½).

Crumble the marraqueta bread. Dry it in the oven for 20 minutes with full convection. Remove and cool to room temperature. Store in an airtight container at room temperature for maximum 1 month.

KIRINKA

Makes 1.5 kg

2 kg espino seedpods

Preheat a skillet (frying pan) over medium-high heat. Toast the espino pods for 15 minutes or until they turn a deep black color. Let cool, and then grind until they form a fine powder. Vacuum-pack. Store at room temperature.

KOLOF ROOT BROTH

Makes 2.5 kg

3 kg kolof roots

Bring 3 kg water to a boil in a large pot over medium heat, add the roots, and boil uncovered for 10 hours. After the broth has been reduced, cover the pot and leave the roots inside to steep overnight. The next day, repeat the process: Strain the broth and set it aside. Fill the pot with another 3 kg water, add the roots, and cook over medium heat for 10 hours until you get a shiny, dark broth. (You can use the same roots to repeat the process. You will get a second broth with different qualities from the first, but it will be very high quality.) Strain and store the broth separately. First and second batch broths can be used interchangeably.

KOMBUCHA

Makes 1 kg

5 g rose of the year

100 g sugar

50 g kombucha mother

In a pan, combine 1 kg water with the rose of the year and the sugar. Heat to 175°F (80°C). Cool to 98°F (37°C) in an ice bath, and then add the kombucha mother. Store at room temperature in a container that allows a circulation of air for the kombucha mother to breath. After a week, reserve the liquid and use the kombucha mother for a new batch.

MAYONNAISE

Makes 550 g

1 egg yolk

500 g canola (rapeseed) oil

2 g fine sea salt

Put the egg yolk in a bowl and slowly add the oil in a fine stream, whisking constantly until the mayonnaise has a smooth texture. Season with the salt. Keep in the refrigerator a maximum of 3 days.

MUSHROOM KOMBUCHA

Makes 1 kg

5 g mushroom

100 g sugar

50 g kombucha mother

In a pan, heat 1 kg water with the mushroom and sugar to 175°F (80°C). Cool to 98°F (37°C) in an ice bath, and then add the mother kombucha. Store at room temperature in a container that allows a circulation of air for the kombucha mother to breath. After a week, reserve the liquid and use the kombucha mother for a new batch.

MUSHROOM OIL

Makes 1.8 kg

1 kg pine mushrooms (*Suillus luteus*)

2 kg canola (rapeseed) oil

Preheat the oven to 425°F (220°C/Gas Mark 7).

Roast the mushrooms in a baking pan for 15 minutes or until they are a deep golden brown. Let cool; then add the oil and cover with plastic wrap (clingfilm). Set aside for 24 hours. Strain, then store the oil in a dark place at room temperature for 6 months.

OVERSALTED FERMENTED LEMONS

Makes 5.5 kg

5 kg lemons

625 g fine sea salt

Cut an X in the upper part of each lemon. Add 8% of each lemon's weight in salt to that lemon. Vacuum-pack. Let the lemons ferment for at least 2 months at room temperature.

NOISETTE BUTTER

Makes 300 g

500 g unsalted butter

Melt the butter in a pan over low heat for 2 to 3 hours, stirring occasionally. When the butter has become dark brown, remove it from the heat and let stand until the burnt solids settle at the bottom of the pan, approximately 1 hour. Then gently pour the brown butter into a container, leaving the burnt solids behind. Store in the refrigerator for 1 week.

PAJARITOS CREAM

Makes 1.2 kg

1 kg organic heavy (double) cream

200 g pajaritos yogurt

Mix the cream and the pajaritos yogurt in a yogurt maker. Process at 104°F (40°C), with 60% moisture, for 7 hours. Then remove and stir vigorously.

PEUMO VINEGAR

Makes 4 kg

5 kg peumo

50 g vinegar mother

Peel the peumos and discard the skin. Extract all the juice of the fruit and reserve the juice. Freeze the remaining pulp; then thaw it over a fine cloth set over a bowl; you will get a clarified juice of peumo. Combine the 2 juices and the vinegar mother in a container with enough headroom to allow the breathing of the vinegar. Store in a dark place at room temperature for up to 3 months.

ROASTED KOLOF

Makes 35 g

50 g kolof

Preheat the oven to 350°F (180°C/Gas Mark 4). Roast the kolof for 3 hours. Let cool to room temperature and then store in an airtight container at room temperature for up to 3 months.

ROASTED SEA CARROTS

Makes 35 g

50 g sea carrots

Preheat the oven to 350°F (180°C/Gas Mark 4). Roast the sea carrots for 3 hours. Let cool to room temperature and then store in an airtight container at room temperature for up to 3 months.

SMOKED LUCHE

Makes 600 g

1 kg Chilean espino coals

1 kg luche

Work the coals until they are red hot and smoking. Place them in a clay oven and let it cool to 95°F (35°C). Put the luche in a metal pan, and let it stand for about 2 weeks inside the oven. Remove and store in an airtight container at room temperature for up to 4 months.

Cristián Sierra
SOUS CHEF

Francisco Castillo
SOUS CHEF

Francisco Pedemonte
CHEF DE PARTIE

Flor Camorlinga
CHEF DE PARTIE

Matías Garay
SOUS CHEF

Gibrán Alcantar
CHEF DE PARTIE

Vinicius Pichuante
SOUS CHEF

Jonathan Campos
CHEF DE PARTIE

Rodolfo Rodríguez
CHEF DE PARTIE

Hernán Sarabia
CHEF DE CUISINE

Ximena Araya
HUMAN RESOURCES

Diego Durán
INGREDIENTS

Javier Viera
CHEF DE PARTIE

Héctor Vergara
INGREDIENTS

Mario Eyzaguirre
MAITRE D'

Eliazar Medina
WAITER

Wilson Vásquez
ASSISTANT SOMMELIER

Diego Villagrán
WAITER

Dragan Celic
HEAD SOMMELIER

Fernando Monzón
WAITER

Bertony Simeus
DISHWASHER

Max Delice
DISHWASHER

INDEX

All herbs are fresh, unless otherwise specified.

All cream is 36–40% fat heavy whipping cream unless otherwise specified.

All milk is full-fat (whole) at 3% fat, homogenized and lightly pasteurized, unless otherwise specified.

Bread crumbs are always dried, unless otherwise specified.

Cooking times are for guidance only, as individual ovens vary. If using a fan (convection) oven, follow the manufacturer's instructions concerning oven temperatures.

Exercise a high level of caution when following recipes involving any potentially hazardous activity, including the use of high temperatures, open flames, slaked lime, and when deep-frying. In particular, when deep-frying, add food carefully to avoid splashing, wear long sleeves, and never leave the pan unattended.

Some recipes include raw or very lightly cooked eggs, meat, or fish, and fermented products. These should be avoided by the elderly, infants, pregnant women, convalescents, and anyone with an impaired immune system.

Exercise caution when making fermented products, ensuring all equipment is spotlessly clean, and seek expert advice if in any doubt.

When no quantity is specified, for example of oils, salts, and herbs used for finishing dishes or for deep-frying, quantities are discretionary and flexible.

All herbs, shoots, flowers, and leaves should be picked fresh from a clean source. Exercise caution when foraging for ingredients; any foraged ingredients should only be eaten if an expert has deemed them safe to eat.

All spoon and cup measurements are level, unless otherwise stated.
1 teaspoon = 5 ml
1 tablespoon = 15 ml

Australian standard tablespoons are 20 ml, so Australian readers are advised to use 3 teaspoons in place of 1 tablespoon when measuring small quantities.

Phaidon Press Limited
Regent's Wharf
All Saints Street
London N1 9PA

Phaidon Press Inc.
65 Bleecker Street
New York, NY 10012

phaidon.com

First published 2017
© 2017 Phaidon Press Limited

ISBN 978 0 7148 7397 8

A CIP catalogue record for this book is available from the British Library and the Library of Congress.

All rights reserved.
No part of this publication may be reproduced, stored in a retrieval system, or transmitted, in any form or by any means, electronic, mechanical, photocopying, recording, or otherwise, without the written permission of Phaidon Press Limited.

COMMISSIONING EDITOR
Emily Takoudes

PROJECT EDITORS
Olga Massov, Ellen Christie

PRODUCTION CONTROLLER
Sarah Kramer

PHOTOGRAPHY
Cristóbal Palma
Claudio Vera: 42–3, 62–3, 78–9

DESIGN
Studio Joost Grootens/
Joost Grootens, Silke Koeck, Chen Jhen

Printed in China

Phaidon would like to thank Francisco Castillo, Ellen Christie, Joost Grootens, Chen Jhen, Silke Koeck, Cristóbal Labbé, Cecilia Molinari, João Mota, Kathie Ness, and Kate Slate.